The rise and fall of mass marketing

**Comparative and International Business Series:
Modern Histories**
Edited by Geoffrey Jones and Mira Wilkins

Banks as Multinationals
Edited by Geoffrey Jones

Industrial Training and Technological Innovation
Edited by Howard F. Gospel

The rise and fall of mass marketing

Edited by
Richard S. Tedlow and Geoffrey Jones

London and New York

First published 1993
by Routledge
11 New Fetter Lane, London EC4P 4EE

Simultaneously published in the USA and Canada
by Routledge
29 West 35th Street, New York, NY 10001

© 1993 Richard S. Tedlow and Geoffrey Jones

Typeset in Linotron Times by J&L Composition Ltd,
Filey, North Yorkshire
Printed and bound in Great Britain by
Biddles Ltd, Guildford and King's Lynn

All rights reserved. No part of this book may be reprinted or
reproduced or utilized in any form or by any electronic,
mechanical or other means, now known or hereafter
invented, including photocopying and recording, or in any
information storage or retrieval system, without permission
in writing from the publishers.

British Library Cataloguing-in-Publication Data
A catalogue record for this book is available from the British Library.

ISBN 0–415–07573–4

Library of Congress Cataloging in Publication Data
has been applied for.

ISBN 0–415–07573–4

Contents

List of figures vii
List of tables ix
List of contributors xi
Preface xiii

1 **Introduction** 1
  Richard S. Tedlow and Geoffrey Jones

2 **The fourth phase of marketing: Marketing history and the business world today** 8
  Richard S. Tedlow

3 **Mass marketing motor cars in Britain before 1950: The missing dimension** 36
  Roy Church

4 **The rise and fall of mass marketing? Food retailing in Great Britain since 1960** 58
  Leigh Sparks

5 **Marketing and business history, in theory and practice** 93
  T.A.B. Corley

6 **The marketing of Scotch whisky: An historical perspective** 116
  Nicholas Morgan and Michael Moss

7 **A machine on every desk: The development of the mass market in computers** 132
  Geoffrey Tweedale

8 **Marketing in British banking, 1945–80** 150
  Margaret Ackrill

9 **International wheat marketing in the post-war period: An Australian perspective on the era of discriminating buyers** 162
Greg Whitwell

10 **An economic theory of marketing** 183
Mark Casson

11 **Conceptualizing an adaptable marketing system: The end of mass marketing** 205
Ken'ichi Yasumuro

Index 236

Figures

4.1	Retail sales in UK, 1957–91	61
4.2	Household composition (UK), 1961–89	64
4.3	Age structure of the UK population, 1961–91	65
4.4	Kwik Save Group plc: number of stores, 1963–91	71
4.5	Kwik Save Group plc: sales floorspace, 1965–91	71
4.6	Kwik Save Group plc: net margin, 1961–91	72
4.7	Kwik Save Group plc: pre-tax profit, 1961–91	73
4.8	Retail prices in UK, 1956–90	79
4.9	Food price inflation in UK, 1957–90	79
11.1	Japanese real per capita GNP, 1880–1980	209
11.2	Trends in Japan's real GNP growth rate, 1965–89	209
11.3	Flow chart of Sharp's refrigerator factory in 1979	219
11.4	Elevation of Sharp's refrigerator factory	220
11.5	Concept of the new factory system: washing machines, 1983	221
11.6	Simplification of design: washing machines	223
11.7	Computer network for marketing and production: washing machines	224

Tables

2.1	The three phases of American marketing history	19
2.2	Brands in the American carbonated soft drink market in 1990	28
4.1	General comparisons of retailing in Britain, 1961–88	67
4.2	Comparisons of food retailing in Britain, 1980, 1988	67
4.3	Market shares of leading UK food retail companies	68
4.4	The Kwik Save Charter	73
10.1	Four key aspects of marketing	184
11.1	Strategic integration of marketing and production through total planning procedure in the Sharp Corporation (1990)	226
11.2	The results of free-flow line in the Konishiroku Photography Industrial Company (Konika) in 1979	228
11.3	The average export–sales ratio of the top 200 Japanese manufacturing firms	233

Contributors

Margaret Ackrill has taught economic history for colleges of Oxford and Cambridge Universities, and is now a research fellow in the department of economic history of the London School of Economics. She has written on manufacturing industry and management, and is currently working on modern British banking history.

Mark Casson is professor of economics and head of the department of economics at the University of Reading. His recent publications include *Enterprise and Competitiveness* (1990) and *Economics of Business Culture* (1991).

Roy Church is professor of economic history at the University of East Anglia. He was formerly editor of the *Economic History Review*, and is author of *Herbert Austin: the British Car Industry to 1941* (1979), *The Rise and Decline of the British Motor Industry* (1992), and of a series of articles dealing with various aspects of the motor industry.

T.A.B. Corley has recently retired from the department of economics at the University of Reading. He has published extensively in the field of business history, most notably on the growth of multinational enterprises. His history of Huntley & Palmers was followed by a two-volume history of the Burmah Oil Company.

Geoffrey Jones is professor of business history in the economics department of the University of Reading. He is the author or editor of fifteen books and numerous articles on the history of international business and other topics, including *The State and the Emergence of the British Oil Industry* (1981); (ed. with P. Hertner) *Multinationals: Theory and History* (1986); *Banking and Empire in Iran* (1986); (ed.) *Banks as Multinationals* (1990), and (ed. with Harm Schröter) *The Rise of Multinationals in Continental Europe* (1993). Professor Jones is co-editor of the journal *Business History*, and is currently president of the Association of Business Historians.

Nicholas Morgan is archivist with United Distillers, the spirits company of Guinness plc, where he is involved with the marketing of spirits brands. Formerly a lecturer in Scottish history at Glasgow University, he has published widely on business and urban history.

Michael Moss, the archivist of the University of Glasgow since 1974, is responsible for the largest dedicated collection of business records in the world. He is the author of several books on the history of business enterprise, including with John Hume, *The Making of Scotch Whisky – A History of the Scotch Whisky Distilling Industry*, 1981.

Leigh Sparks is professor of retail studies at the Institute for Retail Studies and head of the department of marketing at the University of Stirling, Scotland. He has been researching retail and distribution topics for thirteen years and has published widely on his research results through both journal articles and book chapters. Leigh obtained his PhD from the University of Wales for work on employment aspects of food superstores. His first degree is in geography from Cambridge University. He is co-editor of the *International Review of Retail, Distribution and Consumer Research*, which is published by Routledge.

Richard S. Tedlow is professor of business administration and director of research at the Harvard Business School. His publications include *New and Improved: The Story of Mass Marketing in America*, published in 1990 by Harper/Collins in the USA and by Heinemann Professional Publishing in the UK.

Geoff Tweedale ran the National Archive for the History of Computing at Manchester University, 1987–91. He is presently a Leverhulme Research Fellow in the history department, Sheffield University.

Greg Whitwell is senior lecturer in economic history at the University of Melbourne. He is the author of *The Treasury Line* (1986), *Making the Market: The Rise of Consumer Society* (1989), and (with Diane Sydenham) *A Shared Harvest: The Australian Wheat Industry, 1939–89* (1991).

Ken'ichi Yasumuro is professor of international business at Kobe University of Commerce, and visiting professor at the department of economics, University of Reading. He has written a number of books in Japanese including *International Business Behaviour* (1982) and (with Yoshihara Hideki and Hayashi Kichiro) *Globalization of Japanese Business*.

Preface

The idea for this book grew out of a conference held at the University of Reading, UK, in May 1991. The participants, drawn from marketing, business history, economics and other disciplines, and from four continents, sought to explore the history of marketing, and its implications for the present day.

The conference took as its starting point the recent book, *New and Improved*, written by one of the editors, Richard S. Tedlow. A central concern was to consider how far the development of mass marketing in the United States, as presented by Tedlow, illustrates, either by similarity or by difference, the history of marketing in other nations. A second theme was to explore how the history of marketing could elucidate the future of marketing. All the chapters in this book began their lives at this conference, but they have all been rewritten, subsequently, and some bear little resemblance to their first forms.

International conferences are expensive and we would like to thank the sponsors of the meeting which gave rise to this book. Particular thanks are due to the Nuffield Foundation and the Economics Department at the University of Reading.

Richard S. Tedlow
Geoffrey Jones
Boston and Reading

1 Introduction

Richard S. Tedlow and Geoffrey Jones

I

Almost every book, indeed every article, on the history of marketing offers an attempted definition of the term. The reader of this volume will find many of the contributions herein doing just that. As Margaret Ackrill observes in Chapter 8, 'There is no agreement on a definition of marketing. A shelf-full of textbooks on the subject produces a shelf-full of differences' (p. 150).

Ackrill is correct. When one discusses marketing, is one discussing advertising, brand building, warehousing, transportation, pricing, consumer research, or a combination of the above? It is this very lack of consensus which forces authors to define the term.

These attempts at definition are so difficult because when one looks at different industries and different countries – not to mention different historical eras – the marketing tasks and challenges seem so different. Could the marketing of religious relics in the European Middle Ages (see Casson in Chapter 10) have anything in common with the marketing of washing machines in Japan in the 1980s (see Yasumuro in Chapter 11). Could the marketing of biscuits have anything in common with the marketing of sulphuric acid? Generalizations have been called odious. Are they not also particularly misleading with regard to this subject?

We are going to resist yet another definition of marketing here, hoping, to use another of Ackrill's phrases, that 'readers will be enlightened about its meaning as they proceed'. But we would like to offer a comment on why there are so many differences in definition.

True, marketing is different in different settings. But so is production. If the marketing of biscuits and sulphuric acid have little in common, neither (or at least one would hope) does their production. Production, in other words, varies at least as much across industries and probably even more across time than does marketing. Yet it would be rather unexpected to see an article on the history of biscuit-making begin with 'By production, I mean . . .'. It would be surprising to see an article on biscuit-marketing without it.

Why the difference? Tony Corley goes a long way toward offering an explanation in Chapter 5. To be brief, business history has taken from economic history a point of view that economic history has taken from economics. 'Economics', as the American economist Lloyd Reynolds has written, 'has always been concerned with supply, that is, with production' (Reynolds 1988: 300). If, as Corley says, one creates a model of a world in which 'products [are] essentially sold once they are produced' – an assumption lying at the heart of numberless economic models – 'then marketing skills can be dismissed as trivial if not economically wasteful'. For much of modern academic theorizing about the economy, marketing is not *needed*. Because it is not needed, it is not understood. Because there is no general understanding of it, each author begins at square one, a definition.

We want this volume to make a contribution to the small but growing number of studies which comprehend that without marketing there is no business. It is as simple as that. As Theodore Levitt has observed, 'A product is something people buy. If they don't buy it, it's not a product. . . . It's a museum piece' (Levitt 1974: ix). Nothing illustrates this more clearly than the fate of the Ferranti computer, to which Geoffrey Tweedale alludes in Chapter 7.

Alfred Chandler has demonstrated with convincing documentation that the heart of the now rapidly waning hegemony of the American business economy was the marriage of mass production to mass distribution (Chandler 1977: 285–376). Our book is about the history of the latter-named partner in this couple.

II

This volume is, in some respects, an exercise in comparative business history. It begins with the history of mass marketing in the United States, and then tries to discover the comparisons and contrasts with other nations. Our primary concern was comparison with the United Kingdom, which is why six of the following ten chapters give considerable attention to that country's experience, explored against the backdrop of developments in America. However, there are also chapters on Japan and Australia. Britain, as the first industrial nation, holds a special fascination for economic historians, but the story of that country's economic decline in the twentieth century has recently attracted new interest from writers seeking parallels with the poor economic performance of the United States in the contemporary period (Elbaum and Lazonick 1986). Curiously, the development of marketing within British business has been very little studied, the subject most often appearing in the context of an inconclusive debate about whether the British were 'bad' at it, and if so whether this compounded their competitiveness problems. A volume edited by Davenport-Hines (1986) represented one of the few studies to take the subject seriously. Most of its contributors took a critical view of British marketing performance over the long term. A subsequent study by Tony Corley (1987) reviewed aspects of consumer marketing in Britain, and stressed the urgent need for more rigorous research before firm conclusions could be reached. This book is, in part, an answer to his call.

In Chapter 2 Richard Tedlow presents his overview of the history of American mass marketing as a point of comparison with the experience of other countries, providing a 'benchmark' of sorts for later chapters. This chapter summarizes and expands the ideas put forward in *New and Improved* (Tedlow 1990). Tedlow argues that the history of consumer product marketing in the United States falls into three phases. These are fragmentation, lasting until around the 1880s; the era of unification, from the 1880s to the early 1950s, which saw the birth and flourishing of mass marketing; and a subsequent phase of segmentation, when segmented markets were 'virtually created by clever marketers'. Tedlow also detects the emergence of a fourth phase of marketing – micro-marketing, or hyper segmentation. Another glimpse of this future is offered in Chapter 11. Meanwhile, to his arguments about the history of American marketing and directions in which that history might lead, Tedlow adds a review of the criticisms that his approach has received from scholars in the United States.

Chapters 3 and 4 – by Roy Church on motor cars and Leigh Sparks on food retailing, respectively – transfer our attention to the United Kingdom. Although they deal with different industries and with different time periods, Church focusing on the first half of the present century and cars, and Sparks on the last thirty years and retailing, they both explicitly attempt to use the Tedlow framework rehearsed in Chapter 2 to sharpen understanding on the subjects in question. Church undertakes a comparative study of the evolution of motor car marketing in Britain and the United States. This comparison leads to the identification of an additional 'phase' missing from the original

Tedlow paradigm, concerned with design. In *New and Improved*, Tedlow offered a detailed case study of American retailing (both food and non-food). Sparks undertakes a direct comparison with the British experience, including an in-depth study of a leading British retailer, Kwik Save.

Chapters 5 and 6 both deal with products in which Britain has historically held a leading position. Branded, mass-marketed, non-ego-intensive items like pills (and later pharmaceuticals) and biscuits found a ready market in the world's first urban industrial society. Recently, Michael Porter has shown that even today British firms are strongly competitive in such products (Porter 1990: 484, 494). Corley's description of the nature of competition through marketing in which these firms engaged is set in the context of a wide-ranging assessment of the place of marketing in economics and business history, and an ambitious attempt to outline a new research agenda.

In Chapter 6, Morgan and Moss survey the history of what today is 'the United Kingdom's largest exporter earner' – a startling thought to those contemplating Britain's industrial history. In their study of the marketing of Scotch whisky, Morgan and Moss show that the description of marketing history Tedlow offers in Chapter 2 has its limits. The story of Scotch whisky does not conform to the phases Tedlow outlines for American marketing. In some respects Scotch marketing was remarkably advanced, with, for example, sophisticated market segmentation strategies being pursued in 'phase 2' of the Tedlow scheme. Scotch whisky, the authors argue, was a complex product, and it is not surprising 'that the history of its marketing should differ so much from a model formulated largely around the experience of Coca-Cola' (p. 130). It is up to the reader to decide the degree to which the story of Scotch whisky may illustrate more general differences between marketing history in the United States and in the United Kingdom.

Chapter 7 deals with a product which will prove to be as important to the twenty-first century as the automobile has been to the twentieth. In this study of the development of the mass market in computers, both in the United States and Britain, Tweedale shows clearly the critical importance of the broadest view of the full-service marketing function in establishing and maintaining competitive advantage and the resulting market leadership. Even the most visionary of its early votaries conceived of the computer as a special-purpose, big-ticket industrial good, the worldwide demand for which could be satisfied by just a handful of units. By 1987, 50,000 computers were being built and sold every day; and in the 1990s 'a machine on every desk' will probably be more a description than a prediction. Tweedale, too, has problems dividing the history of computing into Tedlow-type marketing phases, not least because they have never been a single product.

In Chapter 8, Ackrill takes a look at the history of the marketing of services. British banks were very slow to come to marketing. In fact, Ackrill believes that prior to 1945, they 'did no marketing whatever' (p. 150). With no frills and with a purposeful avoidance of the 'tides of fashion and fortune', banks strived to appear safe and respectable. They cherished their aloofness. All that changed with remarkable speed thanks both to internal developments and to foreign blandishments ('You have a friend at Chase Manhattan'). By the end of Ackrill's story, British banks were being forced to look less to their dignity and more to what appealed to their customers. In the meantime, much harm had been done, which was to prove hard to repair. The neglect of marketing was one factor in a dramatic loss of market share of deposits to both foreign banks and building societies. In the late 1950s Britain's clearing banks held over 85 per cent of bank assets in Britain. By 1978 their proportion had shrunk to less than 25 per cent.

With Chapter 9 this volume departs from both the United States and Europe for a new continent, and yet another new kind of product. The marketing of wheat is the story of competition not only between companies and between countries but also between hemispheres. To the uninitiated, wheat is merely an agricultural 'commodity'. But Whitwell's chapter helps us understand that there really is no such thing as a commodity. Dealing with the variety of wheat is an important theme of his chapter. The marketer strives to persuade the customer to commit to the variety the marketer can produce. This is a major and highly complex endeavour, and the stakes are high for all parties.

Chapter 10, written by Mark Casson, reveals an economist willing to take marketing seriously. He sets out in the book's penultimate chapter to use economics to assist the understanding of the evolution of marketing. This is a hard task. One problem, as Corley shows clearly in his chapter, is the past neglect of marketing by mainstream economists. The diffuse nature of marketing provides further handicaps for economists. Casson proposes an economic theory of marketing and, like Corley, draws attention to the important role that history can play in the further testing and refining of this theory. In a series of studies in the 1980s, economists and business historians based at the University of Reading, sought to construct a dialogue

6 *The rise and fall of mass marketing*

between 'theory' and 'history' to help understand that most dynamic of business institutions, the multinational enterprise (Casson 1983; Hertner and Jones 1986; Jones 1990). Casson's chapter, and others in this volume, makes the point that this approach can prove equally beneficial for our understanding of marketing.

In Chapter 11, Ken'ichi Yasumuro gives as clear an explanation as one is likely to find of why the era of mass marketing is coming to a close. Just as the peculiar conditions of the American market conditioned the rise of mass marketing, so the peculiar conditions of the Japanese market stimulated the emergence of its successor, adaptable marketing. In the 1950s and 1960s the Japanese market had been organized as a standardized, American-style mass market, but this had fitted awkwardly with consumer preferences, which preferred diversity. As Japanese incomes rose, the market for mass products was eroded. Under the pressure of the oil price rises of the early 1970s, Japanese manufacturers developed 'flexible' or 'lean' production, which enabled them to supply a diversity of products at costs often below those incurred by the mass producer.

Yasumuro illustrates with insight, and in illuminating detail, how advanced companies in Japan began to realize the age-old dream of having long production runs leading to scale economies in manufacture and yet at the same time sufficient variety at the point of sale to satisfy the consumer. That this goal could be achieved even in such complex, big ticket items as refrigerators and washing machines was remarkable testimony to Japanese business leadership. It is difficult to see how companies incapable of matching the achievement Yasumuro describes will be able to remain competitive in the future, though, as he emphasizes, adaptable marketing systems have their dangers when they lead to an uneconomic proliferation of products. Nevertheless the year 1991 ended with a poignant reminder of the advantages of adaptable marketing and flexible manufacturers over their mass producing and marketing rivals. The leaders of the Big Three American car companies travelled to Japan, accompanied by the President of the United States, to complain about the alleged 'unfair' barriers to their products on the Japanese market. The 'unfairness' apparently arose in part from the fact that the Japanese drove on the different side of the road from the Americans. American car companies had only ever attempted to export right-hand-drive cars to Japan, despite the fact that Japanese car firms had exported left-hand-drive vehicles to the United States for years.

III

The chapters by Tedlow and Yasumuro bracket this volume intellectually as well as physically. Tedlow talks about the history of marketing and asks what the future will be. Yasumuro answers that the future will bring better coordination between the two basic business functions – marketing and manufacturing. In between these essays, a wide variety of industries and eras are discussed. Each of these essays tells a story that enriches the literature of business history and informs the student of modern business as well. There is no single methodology of approach in this collection. The Tedlow phases of marketing are applied to non-American markets, and to a range of products, and sometimes found useful, and sometimes not. Corley seeks to move research away from development phases to explore common principles. We regard the diversity of approach within this volume as a strength rather than a weakness. This book is in part a dialogue between the authors, searching towards a greater understanding of marketing. It is a dialogue in which the reader, whether in academia or in business, is invited to join, and perhaps make the next contribution.

When one puts all of these chapters together, what is the message? The message can be summarized in two words: marketing matters. Neither in theory nor in practice can business be understood without a thorough comprehension of what marketing is and does.

REFERENCES

Casson, M. (ed.) (1983) *The Growth of International Business*, London: Allen & Unwin.
Chandler, Alfred D. (1977) *The Visible Hand*, Cambridge, Mass.: Harvard University Press.
Corley, T.A.B. (1987) 'Consumer marketing in Britain 1914–60', *Business History* XXIX (4).
Davenport-Hines, R.P.T. (ed.) (1986) *Markets and Bagmen*, Aldershot: Gower.
Elbaum, B. and Lazonick, W. (eds) (1986) *The Decline of the British Economy*, Oxford: Clarendon Press.
Hertner, P. and Jones, G. (eds) (1986) *Multinationals: Theory and History*, Aldershot: Gower.
Jones, G. (ed.) (1990) *Banks as Multinationals*, London: Routledge.
Levitt, Theodore (1974) *Marketing for Business Growth*, New York: McGraw-Hill.
Porter, Michael E. (1990) *The Competitive Advantage of Nations*, London: Macmillan.
Reynolds, Lloyd G. (1988) *Macroeconomics: Analysis and Policy*, Homewood, Illinois: Irwin.
Tedlow, R. (1990) *New and Improved: the Story of Mass Marketing in America*, Oxford: Heinemann.

2 The fourth phase of marketing
Marketing history and the business world today

Richard S. Tedlow

INTRODUCTION

In the United States in the mid-1980s, there was a new product introduction in the shampoo market. A brief look at this episode will illustrate vividly the potential usefulness of the history of marketing for achieving an understanding of the business world today.

Prior to Procter & Gamble's introduction of Pert Plus in 1985, the $1 billion United States shampoo market was highly segmented. Over 1,100 products competed, and none held a commanding share. According to the *Wall Street Journal*, when the Pert Plus combination shampoo and hair conditioner moved from Procter & Gamble's research laboratories to test market, 'top management responded with a yawn'. The product

> didn't even rate a new brand name. . . . Instead it was pumped into moribund Pert shampoo, then barely clinging to 2% of the United States shampoo market. 'Nobody paid a lot of attention to it,' [according to CEO] Edwin L. Artzt.
>
> ('How innovation' 1990)

The shampoo market was notorious for its fickle consumers. They flitted from one brand to another, and this apparently congenital absence of repeat-purchase behaviour negated the whole point of investment spending to build a brand ('How innovation' 1990). Pert itself was, according to the *Wall Street Journal*, 'perilously close to extinction in late 1985 when reformulated Pert Plus was halfheartedly test-marketed'. Artzt said that 'We weren't in the mood to put a lot of money into a 2% share brand.'

The 'half-heartedness' of the test marketing of Pert Plus is illustrated by the fact that Procter & Gamble invested little in advertising and promotion. Nevertheless, consumers took to the product almost instantaneously, doubling sales in half a year. 'We just damn near missed it,' said Artzt. As of this writing, estimates of Pert Plus market share range from 12 to 14.3 per cent.

Companies are constantly throwing products onto the market in the hopes that some will stick. According to one source, 12,153 new product introductions were attempted in American supermarkets in the first three-quarters of 1991 alone (Gorman Publishing 1991). A few succeed, but the overwhelming majority fail. There are millions of dollars spent each year to employ various tests short of a full-scale introduction to try to determine which will go one way and which another.

What was the *Wall Street Journal*'s explanation of the success of Pert Plus? This success was said to demonstrate 'one of the oldest marketing truisms: Consumers flock to true innovations, regardless of slick advertising or fancy packages' ('How innovation' 1990).

This explanation does not really explain very much. It seems to assert that if you build a better mousetrap, the world will beat a path to your door. It is unquestionably true that some products succeed without 'slick advertising or fancy packages'. The best example is illegal drugs (Schudson 1984: 32–6; Wilson and West 1981: 91–102). But most do not. They need to be aggressively marketed – which is why aggressive marketing techniques were developed in the first place.

Moreover, the journalist's explanation leaves unanswered the question of what constitutes a 'true innovation'. Does a combination shampoo-conditioner qualify? Such products had been around for about fifteen years prior to the introduction of Pert Plus, although they had not been of equivalent quality ('Time is right' 1991).

The experience of a different industry can also be used to highlight the problems with the assertion that true innovations automatically result in big sales. In the 1970s, the advent of the radial tyre resulted in a fundamental restructuring of the car tyre industry. The radial is unquestionably a better tyre than its predecessor. But it was not a true innovation in the 1970s. Goodrich had produced radials in the 1960s, but its lack of marketing muscle crippled consumer acceptance. This is a very good example of what really happens to 'true innovations' in the absence of 'slick advertising' and 'fancy packaging'. Michelin, the French manufacturer which is now the share leader in the tyre industry, had been mass producing radials since 1948. Even then, the basic idea was decades old. The first patent for radial tyres was issued in 1913 (Tedlow, forthcoming).

Were, therefore, radials a 'true innovation' in the 1970s? Yes and no. Technology casts a long shadow (a phrase borrowed from my Harvard Business School colleague, Richard Rosenbloom), but it will remain shadowy if unaccompanied by marketing imagination.

If the *Wall Street Journal* has, then, offered us a less-than-satisfying explanation for the success of Pert Plus, where else can we turn? There are, of course, no easy answers to the vital problem of why a few products succeed while most fail. But it is the thesis of this essay that a brief outline of the history of consumer product marketing in the United States will put the Pert Plus story in a context that will make it more understandable.

THE THREE PHASES OF MARKETING

Some aspects of marketing never change. Marketing always involves someone who has a need to be filled and someone else who claims to have just the thing to fill it. An exchange takes place. The buyer asks: Is what I am getting worth what I have to give for it? The seller asks the appropriate variant of the same question. This dynamic is as true today as it was in the early nineteenth century. It has been true since economic activity emerged from subsistence.

Marketing history is, however, characterized by change as much as it is by continuity. The changes which have taken place in the last century or so are unique. Some of them are irreversible.

For the sake of simplicity (and at the risk of oversimplification), I believe the history of consumer product marketing in the United States can be divided into three phases (Tedlow 1990: 4–8). It is difficult to date these phases with precision because different industries have their own unique histories. But speaking generally, I believe the first phase lasted from the founding of the United States up until the 1880s. The second phase lasted from the 1880s to the early 1950s. We are in the third phase right now, and there are indications of a metamorphosis into a fourth in the near future (Tedlow 1991).

Phase I: fragmentation

Prior to the 1880s, consumer product markets in the United States were divided into numerous geographic fragments. These fragments were usually dictated not by considerations of marketing strategy but rather by the brute facts of logistics. The United States had grown by 1880 to be a continental nation of three million square miles. Within its borders were almost all the extremes of topography and meteorology at nature's command. This meant that transporting goods in bulk from one region to another was prohibitively expensive. For a consumer product to achieve national distribution, it had to be characterized by a very favourable ratio of weight and bulk to value.

A good example is the fur industry, which was national, indeed international, in scope by the War of 1812. One of the most successful American firms in the first half of the nineteenth century was John Jacob Astor's American Fur Company. This company was the pedestal from which Astor constructed his immense fortune, the largest estate in the nation's history at the time of his death in 1848.

John Jacob Astor withdrew from the fur trade in the mid-1830s to devote his time to other ventures, especially real estate. Within a decade of his departure, the American Fur Company had declared bankruptcy. It is noteworthy that only a handful of consumer products now on the market in North America can date their birth to before 1880. It is said that Walter Baker's Chocolate was on one of the shelves of the store Abraham Lincoln tended in New Salem, Illinois in 1833. You can buy Walter Baker's Chocolate today. But the paucity of such examples stands in stark contrast to marketing's second phase (Tedlow 1990: 3–21; Chandler and Tedlow 1985: 55–82).

Phase II: unification

A fundamental change took place in consumer marketing in the United States in the 1880s. All of a sudden, numerous companies were founded which began to manufacture branded products to be marketed not merely locally or regionally, but all across the nation. And the brands these companies sold are still on the market a century later. Thus, for example, the American Tobacco Company was founded in 1881 (Tennant 1950); and Coca-Cola and Johnson & Johnson were both founded in 1886 (Foster 1986; Smith and Tedlow 1989, 1990). Procter & Gamble, it is true, opened its doors in 1837; but its career as an impact player in consumer product marketing can be more properly dated from 1879, the year Ivory Soap floated (Editors of *Advertising Age* 1988; Schisgall 1981).

Many other such firms were founded or achieved dominance during this period, including Diamond Match, Quaker Oats, Libby, McNeil & Libby, Campbell Soup, Pillsbury Flour, and Borden. George Eastman's hand-held Kodak camera came to market in 1887. The following year in Pittsburgh, Henry John Heinz established himself as one of the city's leading figures as he was completing his huge new cannery (Alberts 1973). Heinz had adopted a strategy of mass production and mass marketing that was to make his family's fortune and to make his name a household word down to the present day (Chandler 1977: 285–314; Tedlow 1990: 3–21).

What had happened to bring about this remarkable change? Two factors stand out. First, by the 1880s, the United States finally had in place a transportation and communication infrastructure which lowered the cost of mass marketing products by orders of magnitude. This infrastructure was the railroad and the telegraph.

The railroad was the most important innovation and grew into the most important industry in the United States in the nineteenth century. In 1840, there were about 3,300 miles of track in operation. By 1860, mileage had increased by more than a factor of nine. By 1890, there were 166,703 miles of railroad tracks in operation, over 40 per cent of which had been laid in the preceding decade (Tedlow 1990: 12–13). Without the railroad, national marketing would have been impossible.

The telegraph was also critical. It was the vehicle for the commercial information which business people demanded. It enabled them to direct a salesforce whose members worked thousands of miles from the home office. It helped them learn from that salesforce about market conditions in myriad localities. Thus a far-flung commercial enterprise could be intelligently managed from a central office.

In addition to the railroad and the telegraph, the other major innovation we must consider deals with manufacturing technology. A series of advances in machinery and manufacturing processes had, by the 1880s, made it possible to produce a standardized product in large volume and, just as importantly, in small packages. Continuous-process machinery was 'invented almost simultaneously for making cigarettes, matches, flour, breakfast cereals, soups and other canned products, and photographic film' (Chandler 1977: 289).

What could be packaged at the plant could be named at the plant. When the manufacturer could put his own name on millions of small packages thanks to this new machinery and distribute those packages nationally thanks to the railroad and telegraph, he could advertise nationally. The result was that he could transform the name of his product into a kind of supername – a brand (Tedlow 1990: 14).

This is why the 1880s marked the beginning of brand marketing and management. In the Phase I era of fragmentation, the consumer was separated from the manufacturer by a thick web of middlemen – brokers, jobbers, wholesalers, and the like. Phase I was an era of commodities – of crackers out of barrels, tea from chests, and flour out of sacks from the local grist mill. Marketing was still predominantly concerned with the problem of logistics (Tedlow 1990: 14–17). A product was shipped and packaged and then shipped and repacked into successively smaller units until the customer finally purchased it in a quantity appropriate to him or her.

In the age of packing and repacking, the packager, not surprisingly, was king. But in the new era of national mass marketing, it was the manufacturer with his big advertising budget who took over the role of channel commander in many product categories, especially standardized packaged products like Coca-Cola, Nabisco's Uneeda Biscuit, or Johnson's Baby Powder. The manufacturer also took command in the channels for big-ticket consumer durables such as sewing machines, which required demonstration, financing, and after-sales service.

In other consumer product lines, such as soft goods like apparel and textiles, it was often the large retailer who played the role of channel commander. Marshall Field, for example, was able to use the telegraph to place orders and the railroad to receive them with great speed. For certain of its soft goods, Field integrated all the way back to manufacturing, founding Fieldcrest Mills. Thus, Marshall Field and other large retailers became the brand for many of the products they sold (Twyman 1954).

Phase II products aimed not only at national distribution. They also sought to appeal to all conceivable consumers using a single brand or product form which could be regarded as standard. Coca-Cola is the perfect example (Tedlow 1990: 22–111). Consider the following text for a Coca-Cola advertisement published in 1905:

> Coca-Cola Is a Delightful, Palatable, Healthful Beverage. It Relieves Fatigue and Is Indispensible for Business and Professional Men Students, Wheelmen and Athletes Relieves Mental and Physical Exhaustion and, Is the Favorite Drink for Ladies When, Thirsty, Weary, Despondent.

There is nothing in this text which suggests a modern segmentation scheme. Executives were explicit in their belief that '[O]ur advertising must be an appeal to each class of people.' Thus, young or old, rich or poor, black or white, regardless of what section of the country you lived in, and regardless of what season of the year it was, if you had a 'thirsty throat' the folks at Coca-Cola wanted you to know they had just the drink for you (Tedlow 1990: 50).

Until 1955, when a king-size bottle was finally brought out, Coca-Cola was available in only two forms: at the soda fountain or in the famed 6½-ounce hobble-skirted bottle. If one walked into a typical American supermarket in 1955, one would most likely have seen three or four linear feet of these Coca-Cola bottles flanked perhaps by Pepsi as well as by branded ginger ale and perhaps root beer. The Coca-Cola would probably have occupied as much shelf space as all three other carbonated soft drinks combined.

Coca-Cola was changeless and ageless. The formula remained the same from year to year. There were no line extensions, and no other company could make use of the brand name for any other product. The Coca-Cola Company itself remained strictly focused on its product, advertising it incessantly and avoiding all temptation to diversify. The result was a remarkable profit machine powered by the most well-known brand name in the world.

Coca-Cola, in fact, became the international symbol of the American consumer culture, the quintessential democratic luxury. For a mere five cents or its equivalent in local currency, anyone, anywhere in the world, could sample this elixir and thus partake in some small way of the promise of American life. In the late 1950s, some nationalists around the world focused on Coca-Cola for this very reason as the sum and substance of what was wrong about what the United States was doing to their countries. The term 'Coca-colonization' came to represent the spirit of rebellion against not only American economic power, but against what was viewed as its cultural imperialism as well (Kael 1965: 150–5).

The contrast on many of the dimensions just denominated between Coca-Cola and Pepsi-Cola is quite striking. Coca-Cola, as mentioned above, was changeless. When the company tried to change the formula in April of 1985, there was an uproar so intense that it was forced to bring old Coke back. Pepsi-Cola, on the other hand, changed its formula in 1934 and again in 1950; and the world witnessed not even the merest murmur of unhappiness. Pepsi-Cola brought out its own king size in 1934, more than two decades before Coca-Cola did, and announced in a rather self-satisfied tone in its 1955 *Annual Report* that 'Big Red' was following its lead (p. 5). When Coca-Cola first decided to bring out a diet beverage, the company called it Tab. When Pepsi-Cola first brought out its diet beverage, it called it Diet Pepsi. Just as the formula was considered sacrosanct at Coca-Cola, so was the brand name, the leverage from which no product extension could be allowed to exploit. At Pepsi, obviously, there was no such reticence. The extremely successful diet

Coke was not introduced until 1982, when Coca-Cola, with a new CEO, was in the midst of a major transformation. A few years after that, Coca-Cola was licensing the use of its brand name on apparel, an arrangement which would have been unthinkable as recently as the late 1970s ('Coke plans' 1991). To cite yet another example of the contrast between these two products, Coca-colonization, as was just noted, became a well-known term in the 1950s. But no one ever spoke of 'Pepsi-colonization'.

The truth is that these two products, in many ways so similar, are also very different. The history of their competition will help us explain the transition in American consumer marketing from Phase II to Phase III.

Phase III: segmentation

Phase II marketing was made possible by revolutionary developments in transportation and communication and also by new production technologies. Most of these developments were exogenous to the firms which exploited them. For example, neither Johnson & Johnson nor Coca-Cola invented the railroad, but both realized that its existence facilitated a strategy of national mass marketing. James B Duke did not invent the Bonsack machine for mass producing cigarettes; Bonsack did. But Duke realized that it could change the tobacco industry, so he bought it (Chandler 1977: 249–50, 290–1).

Similarly, many key developments facilitating the change from Phase II unification to Phase III segmentation were external to the firm. Among the most important of these were radio advertising and television advertising. Equally important were broad changes in American culture which exercised a profound influence on the nature of consumer demand. As we shall see presently, the companies that benefited most from these developments did not cause them. They capitalized upon them.

Advertising by radio and especially by television brought the selling message of consumer products directly into the home with a drama and immediacy unprecedented in the history of marketing. Not even the barrier of literacy stood between the company and customer, as it does with much print advertising and packaging. Radio and television gave birth to the commercial jingle which was easy for consumers to keep in mind long after the commercial was over. Television was made to order for purposes of demonstration. It also enabled the advertiser to communicate a selling message through pictures and through the creation of an ambience that might be quite unconnected to the product claims of the advertising copy itself or even to the actual characteristics of the product.

The use of television for commercial advertising became permissible in North America long before it did in Europe or Japan. There were six commercial television stations in the United States in 1945 and 411 a decade later. Some of the most famous programmes regularly attracted very large audiences (Bureau of Labor Statistics 1965: 519; Barnouw 1966, 1968, 1970, 1978). Moreover, it soon became apparent that certain types of programmes attracted certain classes of viewers. All this meant that the opportunities for segmenting markets – that is, concentrating the selling appeal on one particular group of potential customers who might be defined by their age, income, and education (known as demographics) or by their lifestyle (known as psychographics) – were greatly enhanced (Buzzell and Lecocq 1977: 191–213).

In addition to this new technology which had been placed in the hands of marketers, the American consumer market after World War II was ripe for segmenting. Never before in American history had the 'generation gap' been so broad and so deep. Take the example of an American born in, say, 1947, as I was. My parents grew up during the Great Depression, which made a life-long impression on them. I grew up during the 1950s and 1960s. They grew up in poverty, while I had money in my pocket as an adolescent, not because I had earned it, but because times were good in the United States and my parents could give it to me. My parents lived through World War II; for me, it was something to experience through John Wayne movies. My parents grew up before the atomic bomb; I after it. My parents grew up before television. Like most Americans of my era, I watched about a thousand hours a year for the first two decades of my life.

When one puts all this together, the generation gap becomes more understandable. My parents' generation and my own had very different experiences of life and very different expectations from it. My generation – known as 'baby boomers' in the United States because of the population explosion in the late 1940s – were looking for badges of belonging which could serve both to link us to others in our age group and to differentiate us from our elders (Tedlow 1990: 7).

These badges could be of different types. In music, it was Elvis Presley reaching the nation with records and live performances first through radio, then television, then motion pictures. Not long after him the Beatles achieved the same level of adulation.

Entertainment could have effects on products which were quite unpredictable in this hothouse environment. A good example is the story of the Levi's 501, the basic blue jean that had for years been produced by Levi Strauss & Co., a San Francisco apparel manufacturer. Levi Strauss posted sales of $8 million in 1945. In fiscal 1990, its sales were $4.25 billion, making it the world's largest branded apparel manufacturer. What accounted for this remarkable growth?

In the mid-1950s, three motion pictures were made featuring rebellious but sympathetic teenage males who were alienated from their families, looking for fellowship from their young men comrades, and clumsily searching for love from the opposite sex. *The Wild One* starred Marlon Brando and *East of Eden* and *Rebel Without a Cause* starred the ill-fated James Dean. By chance the anti-hero protagonist in all three of these films wore Levi's 501s. These garments, which had previously been primarily identified as work clothing or western wear, now became known as the uniform of respectable rebellion. All this happened without Levi Strauss having to spend any advertising funds. There is a lot more to the story of Levi's growth from an $8 million to a $4.25 billion firm than these three films. But these films did not hurt (Tedlow 1991).

If there could be music for this new generation of privileged/alienated youth and clothing for them, too, could there not also be a soft drink targeted specifically at them? Marketers at Pepsi-Cola answered in the affirmative, and the 'Pepsi generation' was born – 'comin' at ya, goin' strong'.

One of the most successful marketing communications campaigns in history, the Pepsi generation succeeded in segmenting the carbonated soft drink market along both demographic and psychographic lines. During the 1930s and 1940s, Pepsi had appealed for business strictly on price. Its slogan, a classic radio jingle, was:

> Pepsi-Cola hits the spot.
> Twelve full ounces, that's a lot.
> Twice as much for a nickel, too.
> Pepsi-Cola is the drink for you.

As this jingle suggests, Pepsi asked for business on the grounds that it gave you more product for the same price as the competition. Its commercials were laced with an announcer repeating: 'Nickel, nickel, nickel'.

In the late 1940s, rising sugar prices forced Pepsi to raise its prices, or to lower the number of ounces it sold for a nickel. The business almost went bankrupt until a new CEO was able to reposition the product by attempting to associate it with a stylish, upper-middle-class lifestyle. It was only after Donald Kendall became CEO in the early 1960s, however, that the company attempted to target this new generation which seemed to be suffering such a gulf from its elders. This was the creation of the so-called Pepsi generation.

The basic idea was quite simple. Coca-Cola had always sold itself as the standard bearer of changeless, ageless Americana. 'We're tradition,' Coca-Cola said of its product. 'No, you're not,' Pepsi, in essence, replied. 'You're old.'

The Pepsi generation commercials were loud, brash, and aggressive. Needless to say, they never mentioned price. In fact, these commercials were not about the product at all. They were about the people whom the company wanted to portray as using it. For one spectacular television commercial called 'Surf football', Pepsi's advertising agency shipped a camera crew to the California beaches and shot thousands of feet of tape of young, beautiful, alluring, healthy-looking, adolescent women and men playing a pick-up game of touch football (American football, that is) at the water's edge. There was a jingle in the background and words being spoken, but the real message was in the picture of beautiful, insouciant youth. And the real message was 'Buy a Pepsi and you, too, can be like us.' If you, dear reader, ever see this advertisement, you will recognize that no one could ask for more.

A written description does not do justice to this advertisement nor to the series of those like it produced by Pepsi. The essence of the message was in the image presented to the public. The Pepsi generation would have been impossible without television.

If this demographic and psychographic segmentation had taken place only in this one industry, it would constitute merely a footnote, albeit an interesting one, to the history of marketing. However, in the post World War II era for the reasons enumerated above, the great American mass market began to split apart into innumerable product categories from low-ticket, impulse-purchase items like carbonated soft drinks all the way to expensive, ego-intensive consumer durables like automobiles. The mass market was also segmented at the retail level, with the decline of stores such as Sears and the A&P and the rise of specialty stores.

In the automobile industry, for example, there was a time when the American market was dominated not merely by one company, but by a specific model (Tedlow 1990: 112–81; Chandler and Tedlow 1985: 513–47). The Model T Ford accounted for 55.7 per cent of automobile sales in the United States in 1921. The Model T was the automotive equivalent of the 6½-ounce bottle of Coca-Cola in the soft drink industry. It was the standard, the one car with which everyone could feel comfortable and confident.

The automobile industry differs from soft drinks in that its segmentation began decades earlier. By the late 1920s, General Motors had successfully attacked the Model T's dominance by bringing out its famed product array characterized as the 'car for every purse and purpose'. As *Fortune* magazine described it, General Motors' product policy was 'Chevrolet for *hoi polloi* . . . Pontiac . . . for the poor but proud, Oldsmobile for the comfortable but discrete, Buick for the striving, Cadillac for the rich'. When combined with the annual model change, this segmentation scheme gave General Motors a grip on the American market which is only now loosening.

However, a look at how the automobile industry changed from 1925 to 1965 shows that General Motors' early segmentation was not yet fully articulated. It was based primarily on income and age – Chevrolet for the young and poor, Cadillac for the old and rich. But by the 1960s, one can see that automobile marketing had become far more segmented and on far more dimensions than was the case with GM's quintet of cars in the 1920s.

In the 1960s, one saw the marketing of over-engineered and over-powered cars aimed precisely at the children of the generation gap who were wearing their Levi's and listening to the Beatles sing 'I Wanna Hold Your Hand' as they sipped their Pepsi. The 1960s were the era of the 'pony' cars and the 'muscle' cars like the Pontiac GTO,

Table 2.1 The three phases of American marketing history

Phase	Characteristics	Approximate date
I: Fragmentation	• High margin • Low volume • Restricted market size due to high transportation costs and lack of timely information	To the 1880s
II: Unification	• High volume • Low margin • Incorporation of the whole nation in a mass market	1880s–1950s
III: Segmentation	• High volume • Value pricing • Demographic and psychographic segmentation	1950s–present

Source: Tedlow (1990: 8, 3–21)

the Ford Mustang, and the Plymouth Fury. Psychographic segmentation was being combined with demographics in the 1960s as it had not been in the 1920s.

Table 2.1 summarizes my view of the three phases of American marketing history. Please note that I draw a careful distinction between the market 'fragmentation' of Phase I and the market 'segmentation' of Phase III. Consumer markets were fragmented a century-and-a-quarter ago not out of managerial choice, but because of the logistical realities described above. But in recent years, markets have been segmented by aggressive executives searching to transform latent opportunities into profits. The Pepsi generation is the perfect example. This market segment did not naturally arise and march to Pepsi's corporate headquarters demanding a cola all its own. Rather, Pepsi's marketers sensed an opportunity presented by changing times and through great television advertising turned this potential into something kinetic. Unlike geographic market fragments of old, modern market segments are virtually created by clever marketers who figure out how to reconfigure and exploit latent consumer interests.

FROM PHASE I THROUGH PHASE II TO PHASE III: SIX PROPOSITIONS

This progression of American marketing through the phases just delineated is an attempt to describe what happened. But it leaves unanswered the how and the why. How and why was consumer marketing transformed from what it was a century-and-a-quarter ago to the altogether different reality we see today? To answer these questions, I would advance six propositions.

Six propositions explaining the historical changes in American mass marketing (Tedlow 1990: 18–19, 3–21):

1 The strategy of profit through volume was a breakthrough concept in the development of the mass market.
2 The drive and vision of individual business people played an essential role. People have mattered. Nothing was inevitable.
3 Mass production could not have existed without mass marketing. The entrepreneur organized the vertical system, and the manager ran the system and helped it evolve.
4 First-mover advantages have been real. They have led to high profits not despite, but because of low prices. These advantages have acted as barriers to the entry of new competition.

The fourth phase of marketing

5 New entrants into a market faced a basic choice. They could either copy the first-mover's strategy or try somehow to turn the market against the first mover by attempting a new strategy.
6 Change has been the law of business. Over the long term, those firms which have best managed internal and external change over time have been the winners.

It would tax the reader's patience to examine each of these propositions in detail, but let us try briefly to illustrate their explanatory usefulness.

1 Profit through volume

Ever since Asa Candler purchased Coca-Cola in 1891, his strategy was to mass market it all over the country. In earlier times, the owner of such a product might have tried to limit its outlets and keep its price high to achieve a high margin on the small number of purchases anticipated. Candler and his successor, Robert Woodruff, wanted to make money by selling as many Cokes to as many customers as possible. This meant keeping the price relatively low and making it up on volume.

The most successful implementation of the same strategy in the automobile industry was Henry Ford's Model T. Where others foresaw an industry characterized by short runs of expensive models, Ford wanted to put America on wheels by having huge runs of the same model and keeping margins and prices down.

2 Entrepreneurial vision

None of the changes discussed above happened automatically or inevitably. Someone had to believe that consumer package goods could be marketed nationally. Someone had to see the revolutionary opportunities presented by the railroad and telegraph. And someone had to take the risk by making the investments needed to turn vision into reality.

3 Vertical system

Much has been written about mass production, but without mass marketing it would have availed little for producer or consumer. The Coca-Cola Company built an elaborate network of bottlers, numbering 1,000 by 1930, to deliver the product to the end user. The independent bottler system was the key to Coca-Cola's achievement of national distribution through food stores as opposed to solely through soda fountains.

4 First-mover advantages

These are real, and when properly managed can last indefinitely. How much is Coca-Cola really worth today? Or Johnson's Baby Powder? Or Heinz Catsup? How much money have such products returned to their owners in profits over the past century? No one knows the answer to these questions, but surely the money involved is great.

5 Barriers to entry

The new entrant, anxious to share in the kind of returns a product like Coca-Cola has generated, is faced with one of two roads to follow. He can try to beat the first-mover at its own game, or he can try to change the rules. Speaking generally, changing the rules is usually a better bet. Pepsi-Cola first established itself as a player in its industry by offering more product for the same price as Coca-Cola. Eventually, it achieved something close to parity with its great rival by psychologically segmenting what had previously been thought of as a mass market.

6 Managing change

The history of marketing is the story of changes over time, many of which were set in motion by developments such as the railroads in the nineteenth century and television in the twentieth, which were not initiated by the companies which exploited them. Even Coca-Cola, the least changing of all American consumer goods, had to face tough new realities in the 1980s. The bottling network, without which it never could have achieved national distribution at the outset, became a cumbersome burden in the new mature world of global competition.

In the early 1980s, change came to Coca-Cola with a rush, caused by the ever-growing challenge of Pepsi. Both Coke and Pepsi became more vertically integrated. Coke brought out Cherry Coke and Diet Coke under the leadership of a new CEO, Cuban-born, Yale-educated Roberto C. Goizueta. Thus, Coca-Cola, for a century the most changeless and ageless of American companies, tried to position itself as the most agile. In the course of this transformation, the company lost its sense of limits. The result was the disastrous attempt to change the formula in mid-1985. But despite that dreadful experience, the company has remained committed to change as a way of life. In the words of its president, Donald R. Keough, in November of 1991: 'Our single and relentless focus has been internationalizing this business. To do so, we have become the most pragmatic company in the world. We want to do whatever works and we don't want any excuses.' The *New York Times* reported that 'flexibility' is a word Coca-Cola executives 'use constantly' ('For Coke' 1991).

The management of change had come even to the changeless company.

THE EVIDENCE

In the above, I have outlined the history of American consumer product marketing as I see it. I have also suggested how and why marketing practice developed as it did. I should take a moment to warn the unwary reader that not everyone who has studied the history of marketing sees its development as I do. Let me discuss two critiques of my book, *New and Improved*, to illustrate some of these differences, which are both methodological and substantive (Tedlow 1992).

The most noteworthy of the numerous observations about *New and Improved* appears in a book by Stanley C. Hollander (a pioneer historian of marketing) and Richard Germain entitled *'Was There a Pepsi Generation Before Pepsi Discovered It? Youth-based Segmentation in Marketing'* (1991). This book is important because it offers shrewd observations about both the methodology and the substance of marketing history. Let me address the methodological issues first.

Permit me to ask you, the reader of this chapter, to put yourself in the position that I faced late in 1984. It was then that I decided that I wanted to write a history of marketing. It seemed to me to be an important and interesting subject which had not attracted as much attention as it deserved. But what did it mean to write a history of marketing? What approach was best suited to capture the lessons this topic had to teach?

Referring specifically to the history of market segmentation, Hollander and Germain offer three choices. This subject could be approached through: (1) the measurement of all segmentation by all companies over an extended period of time; (2) case studies; or (3) the selection and historical examination of one particular form of segmentation. The first of these three options would doubtless be the most comprehensive. When I began thinking about *New and Improved*, I experimented along these lines. But I could not make this approach work. As Hollander and Germain themselves note, the first option 'would be both physically and economically impossible'. The second option – case studies – is the one I selected. The third option – writing the history of a particular market segment – is the one which Hollander and Germain pursue; and they do so with some notable success.

Let me now turn from these methodological observations to questions of substance. Hollander and Germain address specifically the issue of age segmentation during the period from 1880 to 1940. Their title asks: 'Was there a Pepsi generation before Pepsi discovered it?' Their answer is 'yes'. Their research 'supports the notion that youth marketing grew gradually during the late nineteenth century, and especially during the 1920s, and was a firmly established marketing practice by the beginning of World War II.' If this is so, a question is raised about my treatment of the Coca-Cola and Pepsi-Cola story in this essay. Was there really anything new about the Pepsi generation marketing segmentation campaign, or was it merely another attempt to do something which marketers had been trying to do for decades?

I acknowledge that youth marketing did indeed exist prior to the 1960s, as the Hollander and Germain paper well illustrates. Nevertheless, I persist in my belief that youth marketing in the 1960s was both quantitatively and qualitatively different from what had gone before. This I believe because of the nature of the 'generation gap' in the 1960s, as I have discussed above.

The most skilful marketers, like those at Pepsi, recognized this generational chasm and managed to identify their products with it. This was true even though – and this I find fascinating – there was nothing inherent in the core product that indicated it should be youthful in nature, just as there was nothing inherent in Coca-Cola that suggested it should be associated with traditional Americana. (In other words, these products are different from, for example, a college which by its very nature is going to try to make itself appealing to youth, i.e. people of college age.) By creating this identification of their product with this new generation, Pepsi marketers took the world as it was and made it more so (Bensman 1967: 68).

A not unrelated criticism of *New and Improved* deals with the issue of product proliferation more generally. In my opinion, the Phase II era of the mass market tended to be dominated by a brand of overwhelming power which served as a standard at which other brands tried to chip away, achieving only limited success in their efforts. Coca-Cola, as noted above, made a concerted effort to appeal to every segment of society.

I assert that this Phase II mass market era was succeeded by the present era of market segmentation. Thus, Pepsi-Cola attacked Coca-Cola by targeting a demographic and psychographic segment, what it labelled the 'Pepsi generation'.

However, in remarks on Susan Strasser's recent book entitled *Satisfaction Guaranteed: The Making of the American Mass Market* (1989), a reviewer noted that Strasser 'provides numerous examples of products ranging from Hunt Brothers' three grades of canned fruits and Arbuckle Brothers' different brands of coffee to Edison phonographs and Ingersoll watches that all were targeted at particular consumers along a broad price range' (Cohen 1990: 552). If these examples are accurate (and they are), can one really draw a sharp distinction between the Phase II era of the mass market and the Phase III era of market segmentation? Would it not be more accurate to say that Phase II merged imperceptibly into Phase III?

I persist in my belief that American consumer product marketing in 1970 was fundamentally different from 1920 and that the essence of that difference is captured by the Phase II and Phase III generalizations offered above. The basis for this belief is twofold.

First, the increase in the number of products offered to the consumer has been so sharp that what has resulted is a difference not only in degree but in kind. The number of stockkeeping units offered by the average retailer in 1920 was smaller by an order of magnitude than was the case in 1970. With this change has come a revolution in the shopping experience of the consumer and in the management of the operations not only of the retailer but of the whole vertical manufacturing/marketing system.

Second, the segmentation that took place after World War II was far more complex than anything that had preceded it. It is undeniably true that there had always been market segmentation based on price. For many years, firms would offer three lines – good, better, best, as they were known – of an essentially similar product. Business firms and individual entrepreneurs have from time immemorial tried to lure custom from one another on the basis of a lower price.

However, the segmentation of markets that has taken place since World War II has not relied solely on price. In fact, often market segmentation has not even relied on the characteristics of the product. We can use the example of the Pepsi generation once again to illustrate this observation. The Pepsi generation advertising campaign did not urge potential customers to buy the product because it was less expensive than Coca-Cola. That indeed had been precisely Pepsi's appeal in the 1930s and 1940s – the 'Twice as much for a nickel, too' campaign. Neither did Pepsi try to persuade customers to buy the product because it tasted better. And this was an approach Pepsi could have taken on a more massive basis than it did when taste tests which both it and Coca-Cola conducted in the 1970s indicated that more people actually did prefer the taste of Pepsi to the taste of Coca-Cola.

Instead of an appeal based on price ('Twice as much') or on product characteristics (the Pepsi challenge), the hallmark of Pepsi advertising not only since the Pepsi generation but since Alfred Steele came to the company in 1950 was that it focused on the customer. As is explained in *New and Improved*, Pepsi wanted to turn itself into a 'necktie' product. Neckties are sold not on the basis of price or product characteristics (for example, how many stitches per square inch the tie has) but rather by telling the customer what kind of person buys the kind of tie in question.

This genre of market segmentation – characterized by heavy advertising based on expensive market research and designed to create a community of customers out of thin air, as it were – would not have been possible without the drama and immediacy of television advertising. And it was not restricted to the carbonated soft drink market.

One statistic alone should illustrate this point. An American consulting firm has been reported as calculating that the 1982 Ford Thunderbird 'offered 69,120 possible option combinations'. If that is true, my guess is that there were more options offered that year on that car than were offered on all the automobiles combined that General Motors sold in 1928 (Cusamano 1985: 193).

The extent of segmentation in this era is also quite apparent when we return to the carbonated soft drink market as an example. Table 2.2 gives a list of carbonated soft drinks in the American market with any appreciable share in 1990. No such list could have been compiled in 1950, not to mention 1920. And this tremendous increase in product proliferation and market segmentation has led to a transformation in modern marketing that has been not only a matter of degree but a matter of kind. When, for example, Coca-Cola was marketing only a $6\frac{1}{2}$-ounce bottle of standard beverage and there was very little real competition, the company could operate quite effectively with a network of a thousand independent bottlers covering the United States. However, in this new world with well over a dozen major brands, with hard-hitting competition, and with a far more potent retail trade to sell through, Coca-Cola and Pepsi-Cola as well have both been forced, at enormous expense, to become more vertically integrated. Market segmentation has been a major factor in prompting both these firms to more nimble strategies which have demanded more centralized control of marketing.

Thus, I see an increase in variety as the most important factor differentiating Phase II from Phase III marketing. What is more I see this increase as causing major changes in the way the marketing function is managed. Phase III cannot be described as 'Phase II only more so'. It is almost as different from Phase II as Phase II is from Phase I.

Moreover, I see this increased market segmentation since World War II as having taken place on the retail as well as the manufacturing level of the vertical chain. There is not space here to provide an in-depth discussion, but as I discuss in *New and Improved*, Sears, Roebuck was the standard, mass marketer of general merchandise in the United States from the turn of the century to recent years. The same could be said of the A&P in food retailing. Both were great mass merchants – classic Phase II operations. Both have proven unable to flourish in a Phase III world of market segmentation of retail formats (Tedlow 1990: 182–343).

USING THE PAST TO UNDERSTAND THE FUTURE: TOWARD A FOURTH PHASE OF MARKETING

The business press today is full of articles about how new information technology is bringing about a profound change in marketing. What the railroads were to marketing in the last quarter of the last century and television has been in recent years, that and more will computer-collected and -analysed information become in the immediate future. Inventory, it has been said, is the price of the lack of information; and the information revolution is lowering that price in the factory, in the distribution system, and at the point of sale.

Information technology permits just-in-time systems which in turn facilitate the manufacture of a wide variety of products in short runs in situations where scale economies can still be captured. All through the distribution system, information allows this greater variety to be managed without overstocks or stock-outs and the end result is that the consumer has a greater variety of product from which to choose. The customer is thus more satisfied when he or she walks out of the store.

Table 2.2 Brands in the American carbonated soft drink market in 1990

Company and brand	1990 Million cases	% Market
Coca-Cola Co., total	3,194.5	40.4
Classic	1,532.5	19.4
diet Coke	723.6	9.1
Sprite	285.8	3.6
Caffeine-Free diet Coke	207.4	2.6
Coca-Cola	53.7	0.7
Cherry Coke	47.8	0.6
Minute Maid and Diet	57.4	0.7
Fanta	52.6	0.7
Diet Sprite	66.2	0.8
Diet Cherry Coke	16.4	0.2
Tab	13.2	0.2
Mello Yello	39.5	0.5
Caffeine-Free Coke	40.0	0.5
Mr. PiBB	22.3	0.3
Caffeine-Free Tab	0.5	<0.05
Others	35.6	0.4
Pepsi Co., total	2,520.0	31.8
Pepsi-Cola	1,370.0	17.3
Diet Pepsi	490.0	6.2
Mountain Dew	300.0	3.8
Diet Mountain Dew	40.0	0.5
Slice	75.0	0.9
Caffeine-Free Diet Pepsi	110.0	1.4
Caffeine-Free Pepsi	70.0	0.9
Pepsi Light	–	–
Others	9.0	0.1
Dr Pepper, total	460.4	5.8
Dr Pepper	382.2	4.8
Diet Dr Pepper	30.9	0.4
Caffeine-Free Diet Dr Pepper	30.9	0.4
Caffeine-Free Dr Pepper	1.1	<0.05
Welch's	41.8	0.5
Seven-Up, total	315.5	4.0
7-Up	229.9	2.9
Diet 7-Up	68.7	0.9
Cherry 7-Up	15.9	0.2
Like	0.5	<0.05
Others	0.5	<0.05
Cadbury Schweppes, total	250.1	3.2

Table 2.2 Continued

Company and brand	1990 Million cases	% Market
Canada Dry	96.0	1.2
Sunkist	56.0	0.7
Cott	–	–
No-Cal	–	–
Schweppes products	47.3	0.6
Crush	50.8	0.6
Royal Crown Cos., total	207.2	2.6
Royal Crown	107.0	1.4
Diet Rite Cola	54.0	0.7
RC 100 (regular & sugar-free)	–	–
Cherry RC	2.2	0.1
Diet Rite Flavors	2.2	<0.05
Nehi and others	34.0	0.4
Total (six companies)	6,947.7	87.8
Others	966.3	12.2
Grand total	7,914.0	100.0

Source: Standard and Poor's, *Industry Surveys: Food, Beverages, and Tobacco*, 27 June 1991.

The automobile industry well illustrates these trends. Nissan is presently introducing a new flexible manufacturing system the ultimate goal of which, according to Yoshitada Sekine, general manager of the engineering team that developed the system, will be to make it possible 'to produce any vehicle, at any time, at any production location, by anybody and in any volume required' ('Nissan's flexible' 1991). We are told that some day soon a customer will be able to order from the dealer precisely the automobile he or she wants and have it delivered to specification in a matter of days rather than months. In other words, the industry has changed completely from the days of the Model T, the strategy of which was strictly cost/price and based on rigid standardization.

'Micromarketing' is becoming one of the most oft-repeated terms in the marketing lexicon. It means hyper-segmentation, segmentation of the nth degree. Some marketers seem actually to have a vision of every customer constituting a segment of one. Forces pushing the world toward micromarketing are not solely on the supply side. It is, in other words, not solely caused by the development of the new information technology which has made it economically possible.

There is also a demand for micromarketing on the part of the buying public. To state the obvious, people want what they want, not something made for some mythical mass market. Consumers are becoming more demanding, and in their efforts to satisfy this trend, marketers are intensifying it. In other words, the more customized people want their products, the more marketers seek to customize them. The more that marketers make this effort, the greater is the perception on the customer's part that he or she can get exactly what is wanted. If that means caffeine-free diet Coke in a 12-ounce can, then that is what it shall be. The older $6\frac{1}{2}$-ounce standard package of standard Coca-Cola no longer satisfies.

With the demand there and the technology to satisfy it, the advent of micromarketing as a fourth phase in marketing's development should come as no surprise. This development fits a number of the themes we have just discussed. It is another example of a major change in marketing resulting from technical developments exogenous to the product marketers in question. It means greater choice for the consumer. It means that the marketer will take one step closer to every marketer's dream – to sell the potential customer precisely what he or she wants. That is so much easier than trying to convince the customer to buy what the factory has made. And once again, as with the railroad and the television, those firms that can adapt their product policy and their distribution systems to the new reality have the chance to capture first-mover advantages that may last for generations.

There is, however, another side to this micromarketing story which deserves our attention. When so many experts are looking in one direction (i.e. toward micromarketing) as they are at this writing, perhaps it would be interesting to look in the opposite direction to see what we can find. When we do so, we find at least two major forces which might inhibit micromarketing. These would include consumer confusion and saturation of the distribution channels.

With regard to the first of these – consumer confusion – consider the following passage from a 1985 article in the *New York Times*:

> There are nearly 300 long-distance telephone companies in the United States today, and 23 kinds of Nine Lives cat food. Revlon makes 157 shades of lipstick (41 of them pink) and Tower Video offers 5,000 video cassettes for sale or rent. The Love drugstore chain carries 41 varieties of hair mousse.
>
> ('Shopping' 1985)

This article was written a number of years ago; but the basic point it makes is, if anything, more valid today than it was then. The article asks whether there is 'such a thing as too much choice'. It also speaks of the 'new bewilderment' as confused consumers are confronted in the marketplace with scores of distinctions without differences.

The response of companies to such observations are reasonable and predictable. Speaking of its 157 shades of lipstick, a Revlon spokeswoman said: 'There is someone who wants each of them or they wouldn't be there. We don't make products to sit on the shelf' ('Shopping' 1985).

We will return to this observation in more detail presently; but for now let us give some thought to the final phrase: 'on the shelf'. Manufacturers may want to satisfy every consumer desire as precisely as possible, but they must reach these consumers through a distribution system which must operate within its own constraints. There is a finite amount of shelf space in the retail outlets of the United States and of the world. If one conceives of every woman in the United States wanting her own shade of lipstick and of a lipstick industry capable of producing that great a variety, there is still the problem of that shelf.

The distribution system has become the neck in the hourglass through which manufacturer must reach consumer. At some point, perhaps it will be when Revlon produces its 158th lipstick shade, the retailer will be forced to say 'enough'.

Indeed this is happening at this writing. The balance of power in American marketing in a number of product categories is now shifting to the retailers, because it is they who control the scarce resource. This is a resource they are selling in shelf allotment programmes. It is because of the scarcity of shelf space that manufacturers are having to devote a greater percentage of their brand management budget to trade promotion rather than to consumer promotion or to mass media advertising. And this is one reason why advertising agencies are suffering at this time ('What happened' 1991).

CONCLUSION

In light of the above observations, let us circle all the way back to the discussion of the shampoo business with which this essay began. It was there asserted that the *Wall Street Journal*'s explanation for the success of Pert Plus was less than fully satisfying and that perhaps a look at the history of American consumer product marketing might make it more understandable.

What Procter & Gamble did with Pert Plus was take a step back from the Phase III world of market segmentation to the Phase II world of mass marketing rather than take a step forward into the predicted Phase IV world of micromarketing. Instead of splitting one product into two – for example, bringing out diet Coke in addition to Coca-Cola – Procter & Gamble created one product where there were formerly two – that is, a combination shampoo/hair conditioner where once there had been separate shampoos and conditioners. The reason that the company did not at first believe the numbers Pert Plus was generating and recognize its own success – remember that CEO Artzt said, 'We just damn near missed it' – is that Pert Plus bucked a trend. The trend, as all the articles proclaim, is toward more variety. Pert Plus succeeded by doing the opposite of what everyone said, by diminishing variety.

Without access to P&G's research, we cannot say with confidence why Pert Plus succeeded. But some plausible guesses can be advanced. Shampoo is a low-ticket, non-ego-intensive, impulse purchase item for many consumers. That is why there is so much brand switching. Procter & Gamble, with Pert Plus, took some of the pain out of hair care. The customer now had to make only one decision rather than two. He or she had to buy only one package, thus saving time and perhaps equally important weight and space. This, after all, is an age in which a lot of people do a lot of travelling.

This is not the first time that a product has succeeded by doing the opposite of what everyone else was doing. In the 1950s and the 1960s, when American automobile manufacturers were producing 'muscle' and 'pony' cars in ever greater variety, Volkswagen achieved global success with its Beetle. The Beetle was a precise replica of the Model T Ford strategy – a simple, inexpensive, reliable appliance that performed the commodity function of transporting the owner from place to place. In a world of Mustangs and GTOs, the Beetle was an anomaly, certainly in the American market. This anomalous positioning was brilliantly transformed from a problem to an opportunity by the advertising of William Bernbach. The Volkswagen Beetle is as clear an example as one will find of a Phase II success in a Phase III world. It was the only model in the history of the automobile industry to outsell the Model T Ford.

On the other hand, as the stories of Sears and the A&P illustrate, bucking a trend can be disastrous. The firm must have a clear strategic vision and execute it skilfully, as did Volkswagen, rather than merely drift, as did these two big retailers.

In a word, then, what are the 'lessons of marketing history' for the business world today?

1 There have been identifiable changes in marketing practice, as outlined in this chapter.
2 These changes have often been made possible by developments exogenous to the particular industry which they impact and indeed to the marketing function itself.
3 An awful lot of money can be made by bucking trends at the strategic moment.

BIBLIOGRAPHY

Alberts, Robert C. (1973) *The Good Provider: H.J. Heinz and His 57 Varieties*, Boston: Houghton Mifflin.
'At INAME, "micro-marketing is the future"', *Adweek*, 15 January 1990.
Barnouw, Erik (1966) *A Tower in Babel: A History of Broadcasting in the United States to 1933*, New York: Oxford University Press.
—— (1968) *The Golden Web: A History of Broadcasting in the United States, 1933–1953*, New York: Oxford University Press.
—— (1970) *The Image Empire: A History of Broadcasting in the United States from 1953*, New York: Oxford University Press.
—— (1978) *The Sponsor: Notes on a Modern Potentate*, New York: Oxford University Press.
Bensman, Joseph (1967) *Dollars and Sense: Ideology, Ethics, and the Meaning of Work in Profit and Nonprofit Organizations*, New York: Macmillan.
Bureau of Labor Statistics, US Department of Commerce (1965) *Statistical Abstract of the United States, 1964*, Washington, D.C.: Government Printing Office.
Buzzell, Robert D. and Lecocq, Jean-Louis (1977) 'Polaroid France (S.A.)', in Steven H. Star, Nancy J. Davis, Christopher H. Lovelock and Benson P. Shapiro (eds) *Problems in Marketing* (5th edn), New York: McGraw-Hill, pp. 191–213.
Chandler, Alfred D., Jr. (1977) *The Visible Hand: The Managerial Revolution in American Business*, Cambridge, Mass.: Harvard University Press.
—— and Tedlow, Richard S. (1985) *The Coming of Managerial Capitalism: A Casebook on the History of American Economic Institutions*, Homewood, Ill.: Irwin.
Cohen, Lizabeth (1990) 'The mass in mass consumption', *Reviews in American History* 18(4) (December), 548–55.
'Coke plans retail store', *New York Times* 19 July 1991.
Cusamano, Michael A. (1985) *The Japanese Automobile Industry: Technology and Management at Nissan and Toyota*, Cambridge, Mass.: The Council on East Asian Studies at Harvard University and Harvard University Press.
Editors of *Advertising Age* (1988) *Procter & Gamble: The House That Ivory Built*, Lincolnwood, Ill.: WTC Business Books.

'Finding a niche with micro-marketing', *National Underwriter*, 20 August 1990, pp. 12, 35.
'For Coke, world is its oyster', *New York Times* 21 November 1991.
Foster, Lawrence G. (1986) *A Company That Cares: 100-Year Illustrated History of Johnson & Johnson*, New Brunswick, NJ: Johnson & Johnson.
'Frito's micro move', *Advertising Age*, 2 February 1990, p. 44.
Gorman Publishing Company (1991) *New Product News*, 7 October.
'Hair care market in the U.K.: two-in-ones rise', *European Cosmetics Markets*, September 1991.
'The hair care market: responding to niches, naturals and combos', *Drug and Cosmetic Industry*, April 1991.
Hapoienu, Spencer A. (1990) 'The rise of micromarketing', *The Journal of Business Strategy*, November/December, pp. 37–42.
Hollander, Stanley C. and Germain, Richard (1992) *Was there a Pepsi generation before Pepsi discovered it? Youth-based segmentation in marketing*, Lincolnwood, Ill.: NTC Business Books.
'How innovation at P&G restored luster to washed-up Pert and made it no. 1'. *Wall Street Journal*, 6 December 1990.
Hunt, Shelby D. and Burnett, John J. (1982) 'The macromarketing/micromarketing dichotomy: a taxonomical model', *Journal of Marketing*, 46 (Summer): 11–26.
'In search of micro niches', *Business Month*, July 1989, pp. 60–2.
Kael, Pauline (1965) Review of movie 'One, Two, Three', in *I Lost It At the Movies*, Boston: Little, Brown, pp. 150–5.
'Micromarketing for the branch network', *Bank Marketing*, June 1991, p. 26.
'Micro marketing into the niches: the eye of the stranger', *Marketing Communications*, March 1987, pp. 57–72.
'Micro marketing: must in the '90s', *Stores*, July 1990, pp. 50–1.
'Micro-marketing: no silver bullet, but an edge for sharpshooters', *Supermarket Business*, May 1991, pp. 51–2ff.
'Micromarketing offers macro-benefits', *Supermarket News*, June 24, 1991, p. 57.
'Micromarketing: a strategic advantage', *Discount Merchandiser*, May 1991, pp. 62ff.
'Micromarketing to deliver macro results', *Discount Store News*, 6 May 1991, p. 6.
'New hair care makes waves: two-in-ones add volume to shampoo sales', *Discount Store News*, 7 January 1991.
'Nissan's flexible "thinking" line for auto body assembly', *New York Times*, 25 August 1991.
'Partnerships facilitate micromarketing', *Discount Merchandiser*, August 1991, p. 28.
Pepsi-Cola Co. (1955) *Annual Report*.
'Reaching consumers in the 1990s: the rise of micromarketing', *Soap–Cosmetics–Chemicals Specialties*, May 1991, p. 42.
Schisgall, Oscar (1981) *Eyes on Tomorrow*, Garden City, NY: Doubleday.
Schudson, Michael (1984) *Advertising, The Uneasy Persuasion: Its Dubious Impact on American Society*, New York: Basic Books.
'Shampoo/conditioners catch on', *Chain Drug Review*, 28 January 1991.
'Shopping is getting a lot more complicated', *New York Times* 8 August 1985.

Smith, Wendy K. with Tedlow, Richard S. (1989) 'James Burke: a career in American business (A)', Boston: HBS Case Services no. 389–177.
—— (1990) 'James Burke: a career in American business (B)', Boston: HBS Case Services no. 390–030.
'Stalking the new consumer: as markets fracture, P&G and others sharpen "micro marketing"', *Business Week*, 28 August 1989, pp. 54–62.
Strasser, Susan (1989) *Satisfaction Guaranteed: The Making of the American Mass Market*, New York: Pantheon.
'Styling aids, all-in-one give hair care category a boost', *Drug Store News*, 20 August 1990.
Tedlow, Richard S. (1990) *New and Improved: The Story of Mass Marketing in America*, New York: Basic Books, Oxford: Heinemann.
—— (1991a) 'Levi Strauss & Co. and the AIDS crisis', Boston: HBS Case Services no. 391–198, rev. 9/5/91.
—— (1991b) 'Segmentation vs. the mass market', *WorldLink*, March/April 1991.
—— (1992) *New and Improved: The Story of Mass Marketing in America*, Japanese edition trans. by Fumio Kondo, Tokyo: Minerva Shobo.
—— (1993) 'Hitting the skids: tires and time horizons', in *Time Horizons in American Industry*, ed. Michael E. Porter.
Tennant, Richard B. (1950) *The American Cigarette Industry*, New Haven: Yale University Press.
'Three of Procter & Gamble's competitors will do good things for Vidal Sassoon Ultra Care and Head & Shoulders 2-in-1 formula', *Cosmetic Insiders' Report* 30 September 1991.
'Time is right for "combo" shampoos', *Supermarket News*, 7 January 1991.
'Two-in-ones soar', *Supermarket News*, 21 October 1991.
Twyman, Robert W. (1954) *History of Marshall Field & Co., 1852–1906*, Philadelphia: University of Pennsylvania Press.
'What happened to advertising: sure, recession hurts, but marketing trends are causing more lasting, structural change', *Business Week*, 23 September 1991, pp. 66ff.
'What micromarketing taught our reporter about his A&P', *Wall Street Journal*, 18 March 1991.
'Will three-in-one shampoos wash?', *Supermarket News*, 21 October 1991.
Wilson, Aubrey and West, Christopher (1981) 'The marketing of "Unmentionables"', *Harvard Business Review*, January–February 1981, pp. 91–102.
'Working in the new shampoos', *Supermarket News*, 21 October 1991.

3 Mass marketing motor cars in Britain before 1950
The missing dimension

Roy Church

One of the principal values of Professor Tedlow's analysis of mass marketing is that it attempts to conceptualize a sequential model against which national and international experiences may be compared. While the evidence he adduces derives from the history of firms, the phases which he identifies refer to market development in which external, economic and social environmental factors are as important as firm-specific strategies. He describes the evolution of marketing in the United States as having occurred in three phases. The first was characterized by market fragmentation: a multiplicity of product brands in virtually all markets in which manufacturers sought profitability through high prices and low volume sales. The second phase saw the emergence of a national market in which by about 1900 many national brands, produced and sold in high volumes at low prices, enabled a small group of companies, or a single aggressive company in some instances, to emerge from competition as dominant national market leaders. In the third phase a complex form of market fragmentation developed, differing from that of the pre-1900 period inasmuch that segmentation was not the outcome of imperfections in the market resulting from geographical and transport factors but was the effect of companies' marketing strategies intended to identify and develop market niches based on income, age, education and lifestyle (Tedlow 1990: 3–8).

An hypothesis of this kind inevitably faces difficulties if, as in this instance, little space is found to accommodate other quasi-theoretical approaches to marketing development. For example, textbooks have commonly drawn distinctions between different types of firms according to the dominance in corporate strategy of product, sales or marketing orientation. In firms dominated by the marketing concept the primary explicit focus of managers is to satisfy the needs of the customer, whereas it is the sellers' needs which preoccupy managers in firms in which the selling concept is dominant. The production concept which focuses managers' attention on achieving high production efficiency and wide distribution coverage is, in current marketing theory, the orientation least appropriate to the achievement of long-term, soundly based corporate success (Kotler 1988: 13–17).

While the organizational goals within some firms may differ, marketing theory implies that a progression from product, through selling, to marketing orientation is desirable. It also implies that the production concept has a longer history in guiding sellers, though there is also reference to firms altering the relative emphasis on these concepts in response to changing economic circumstances. Product orientation is justified either where demand far exceeds supply of a product which justifies concentrating effort on increasing production; or where the cost of a product is high, warranting the pursuit of productivity to secure lower price and an expanding market. These characteristics of a product-oriented company fit closely into Tedlow's Phase II. However, whereas in the history of a *product* the sequential development of a corporate philosophy to selling and later to marketing may seem plausible and helpful to the historian, the multi-product firm clearly creates a problem, especially if the range of products manufactured and sold is diverse. Insofar as products may be seen to possess lifecycles, an optimal corporate strategy needs to apply appropriate concepts according to particular competitive circumstances, products and markets. Likewise, the assertion that most firms practise the selling concept when they possess over-capacity also implies that there is a cyclical dimension to concept dominance.

The lack of specific historical perspective among authors of texts on marketing theory warns against uncritical borrowing of their concepts in the historian's attempt to discern patterns and explanations for marketing development. For example, Kotler condemned General Motors as a product-oriented company 'designing their product in the wrong way' (Kotler 1988: 15). Because GM failed to ask customers what they wanted and ignored market research GM has been accused of what Levitt called 'marketing myopia' (Levitt 1960: 50–1). Yet Kotler failed to place GM's corporate philosophy within the historical context of the 1920s and 1930s when that company at least attempted to anticipate consumer response, nor did he acknowledge GM's superior success in the market by comparison with Ford, whose lead was lost in large part because of Henry Ford's persistent preoccupation with the provision of cheap transport.

Whilst Ford perceived this to be the highest priority among potential car buyers, customers proved to be more willing to purchase a product possessing a variety of features, appearance and price. Tedlow's schema, in which mass marketing development is interpreted as a linear process, is vulnerable to the implicit acknowledgement in the literature that while companies may be characterized as being product-, sales- or marketing-oriented, any such description will probably not be valid at certain times, in certain circumstances and in relation to a company's entire activities.

A fundamental critique of marketing theory is beyond the scope of this chapter. There is no attempt here to question the validity of the Tedlow paradigm as applied generally to the United States, but rather to apply it to automobile industries of the United States and Britain, comparing the chronology and characteristics of marketing development until the 1950s. We ask to what extent, in definition and in timing, do the three phases described by Tedlow fit the British experience? To the extent that differences are revealed, how are they to be explained? and finally, are Tedlow's three phases adequate to describe sequential development in the mass marketing of motor cars? Such questions involve considerations of product development, credit, promotion, distribution, styling and design.

I

In Tedlow's schema Phase I is reckoned to have ended in the United States in 1908, with the appearance of the 'universalist' Model T Ford; the beginning of Phase III he locates in the early 1920s, when General Motors' strategy heralded an extended period of incremental rather than radical technological innovation, followed by a period of sustained non-price competition which lasted until the 1960s (Tedlow 1990: 112–81).

Designed as a 'universal' car and produced in high volume at low cost, the low price of the Model T tapped American mass consumption. Before 1908 the extent of motorization in the US differed little from that in western Europe (Bardou *et al.* 1982: 47). Henry Ford changed that at a stroke. The fact that Ford was not the first to experiment with low-cost production of sturdy low-priced vehicles – resembling horse-drawn buggies rather than carriages – points to the difference in the character of markets for motorized transport in the two continents. Whereas suitability for rough country usage over long distances influenced the trend of technical innovation towards the 'universal' car providing basic transport for American farmers, in

Europe hand-built individually constructed vehicles for a mainly urban clientele were more suited to potential British purchasers for driving on Britain's superior road surfaces.

The initiative in defining the market for motor cars in Britain was undertaken by a handful of mostly wealthy men, among them several aristocrats, who having imported motor cars from France proceeded to promote their qualities in Britain. Those who became importing agents adopted similar criteria in presenting the car as a luxury item for the pleasure of the rich at sport or play, while the profitability of the early car trade, based on high prices and short production runs, justified the persistence of this initial conceptualization of the market for motor cars in Europe (Church 1982: 1–12). In 1907 *The Economist* described the British motor car as a substitute for a carriage and pair, adding that the industry's growth depended on its ability to compete with the pony and trap (Plowden 1971: 39). Unlike Phase I in the American automobile industry, therefore, segmentation based on income and social distinction was a feature of the British market before Phase II characteristics came to dominate corporate strategies.

The phase of marketing most resembling that in Tedlow's model is Phase II, characterized by intense price competition. In Tedlow's schema the turning point was 1908 whereas in Britain it may be identified in 1920–1. A precursor to this was the establishment in 1909 of a Ford branch selling imported Model Ts in England (from 1911 imported in parts and assembled at the Manchester factory). Percival Perry, the English manager, formerly a motor agent selling Ford cars, henceforward received financial support for promotion, enabling him to begin to counter the T's reputation, nurtured by competing agents and the trade press, as a typically 'cheap and nasty' American automobile. By 1913 Ford was selling more cars in England than the five largest British companies in aggregate – Wolseley, Austin, Singer, Rover and Morris. About 29 per cent of all cars produced (including those assembled in Britain) consisted of Model T Fords. This was a reflection, above all, of price, for the vehicle was identical with that designed for American users, the only concession to the British market before 1927 being a right-hand drive, introduced in 1919. By pointing the way to a marketing strategy dominated primarily by price, the Model T heralded Phase II in Britain. This explains why, shortly before the war, a handful of British motor manufacturers perceived the commercial potential for a vehicle which tapped a utility market, and began to manufacture low-horsepower, two to four seater models selling for less than £250. Even among those companies, however, either the scale of production necessary in order to compete with Ford was seen to be far beyond their financial resources, or success in selling medium-powered, medium-priced cars in higher profit margins limited the incentive to take the plunge into the mass production of utility small cars (Church 1982: 4).

The reasons which explain why the Model T Ford did not propel Britain into Phase II are partly the disruptive effects of the war and its aftermath, but mainly Henry Ford's myopic policy towards the British market after the war ended. The McKenna Tariff imposed a 33 per cent duty on imported motor vehicles and parts from 1915, while the £1 horsepower tax introduced in 1921, which effectively penalized the American type of large, high-powered, high-fuel-consuming cars (of which the Model T was a low-cost version), placed an artificial premium on the production of high-speed, small-bore engines of low horsepower, which were characteristic of European cars. Henry Ford's disregard for the character of the British market and his refusal to design a vehicle suited to the legal and environmental circumstances contributed to Ford's failure to maintain dominance in the British market for mass-produced vehicles, as did his disastrous distribution policy (Church 1981: 69–71).

II

Phase II commenced in earnest in 1920–1 when William Morris, producing barely 1,000 cars slashed prices by one-third. By 1929 Morris was the market leader holding approximately 35 per cent of the market, which compared with about 25 per cent held by Austin, the second largest manufacturer (Rhys 1976: 246). Morris's low-cost assembly methods enabled him to sustain prices at levels low enough to squeeze most other producers out of the popular car market. However, at the same time, while price was the principle method of market penetration, Morris's promotion and advertising campaigns stressed quality, individuality and performance (Overy 1976: 17–23).

Explaining his commercial policy in 1924 William Morris referred to price as a vital element in his company's success. In this respect Morris's philosophy resembled that of Ford, while the former's two-model policy (though in the mid-1920s over 80 per cent of sales were the lower-priced Morris Cowleys) also resembled Ford's marketing strategy. Where it differed was in Morris's promotion and advertising campaigns which stressed that Morris cars were *not* mass produced. (Overy 1976: 23–33). The Austin Motor Company likewise pursued a policy after the 1920s of focusing investment and effort on the development and sales of an even lower priced car, the Austin Seven, which achieved over 60 per cent of the company's sales figures during the 1920s, falling to 50 per cent in the 1930s. Like Ford, Herbert Austin also stressed the qualities of the functional car:

> The fancy day is brief and spasmodic. The utility day is with us always. We have innumerable fads and fancies in matters of shape, size, colour and trimmings, but when we get down to our bedrock need, . . . then we find that what we are looking for is transport.
> (quoted in Church and Mullen 1989: 196)

During the 1920s a tolerable level of mechanical reliability, an accepted basic body shell (from the mid-1920s of steel pressings rather than the metal-clad ash frame employed by coachbuilders) and the stability of a dominant model design which resulted saw both Austin and Morris concentrate on the production of increasingly standardized, relatively low-priced cars. Their design characteristic was a combination of engineering efficiency, a degree of basic comfort and value for money, rather than aesthetic appeal. Both companies promoted car purchase through deferred payments. By 1929 Morris, Austin, and in third place Singer, dominated the market, price competition having reduced the number of producers from 96 in 1920 to 47 by 1926, and to 41 three years later (Ministry of Supply 1947: 22). The late 1920s thus heralded the end of Phase II in Britain, as oligopoly superseded a period of intense price competition.

This marked the beginnings of a transition from initial to mature demand. That process had taken place earlier in the 1920s in the United States, when factors other than those arising from the demand for a new product as reflected in the relationship between first-time and other buyers, came to exercise the greatest influence on the overall demand for vehicles. Although real price reductions in the British market continued in the late 1920s and early 1930s further significant *new* owner sales did not materialize. In Britain, therefore, the transition to a mature market, dominated by replacement sales and the emergence of a used car market, occurred in the mid-1930s, after the Slump. The process was protracted, as witnessed by the relative stagnation of home sales for nearly a decade after 1925, and by views widely expressed by contemporaries that saturation had been reached in the home market for motor cars. In the late 1920s marketing methods failed to overcome barriers to purchase presented by inadequate levels of real income, a factor encouraging the postponement of vehicle replacement, which also contributed towards market stagnation in the late 1920s. A further check to the value of car sales resulted from consumers trading down to lower priced vehicles rated below 12 horsepower, a trend which favoured the popularity of the 'Baby' Austin Seven, and the purchase of used cars (Maxcy and Silberston 1959: 38–9; Miller and Church 1979: 189). Market stagnation, therefore, was the trigger which ushered in Phase III of market development some ten years after it had occurred in the United States.

Technical innovations adopted by British volume car producers in the mid-1920s had provided the basis for the new form of competition which emerged during the 1930s, similar to those introduced by Sloan at General Motors ten years before. The introduction of stamped steel bodies involved a new approach to design in which supports and panels were integrated to form body construction; paints and varnishes were displaced by cellulose sprays. These developments contributed to an increasing emphasis by manufacturers on styling and accessories. In the late 1920s the trend in motor car design and construction was described by *Autocar* reporters at the Motor Show as showing new consideration for the 'owner-driver', by attention to closed saloons, easy access to engine and simpler maintenance, and concern to provide greater comfort for the driver – who could no longer be presumed to be a chauffeur (Church 1981: 68). The phase of mature demand, when it emerged after the Slump, was characterized by model price competition, in which the strategy of market segmentation took the form of model proliferation and product differentiation. Given the technology of volume production achieved in Britain in the early 1930s, and given the minimal scope for price competition within each horsepower category in a stagnant market, success depended more than ever upon modifications in design, styling and effective overall marketing in the search for hitherto unidentified market segments. A condition for survival by the small and medium-scale producers was a similarly marketing-oriented strategy to discover niches within the medium and large horsepower/quality segments, a development which increased the importance to manufacturers of cultivating brand loyalty even more than in earlier decades.

First in the United States and then in Britain, manufacturers recognized that in a mature market, compared with improved quality or appearance, absolute minimum price assumed diminishing relative importance. This became apparent even in the economy car classes, as the experience of Ford and Morris demonstrated. When in 1931 the Morris Minor was offered to the market as the first £100 car, it was the sales of the slightly modified version, costing around £110, which boomed. As Sir Miles Thomas, Morris's sales manager, later remarked: 'No one wants to keep down with the Jones's' (Thomas 1964: 168). A similar lesson could be learned from Ford's attempt to capture the market dominated in the mid-1930s by the Morris Minor, by slashing the price of the 8-horsepower Ford Popular by 20 per cent. The price cut secured an immediate impact in the market and sales rose, but still the cheap Ford cars were outsold by dearer cars which offered more comfort, performance and perceived individuality (Church and Miller 1977: 173).

III

There were, however, important differences in the character and consequences of market segmentation in Britain compared with the United States. General Motors' product policy in the early 1920s had been to offer 'a car for every purse and purpose', each make of car targeted on a separate set of customers (Sloan 1967: 67). Annual model changes evolved initially as technical improvements became available, but from the 1930s were 'regularized' as part of an explicit strategy aimed at stimulating trade-in and replacement sales. Each segment of the market was so defined by General Motors' managers as to support output levels sufficient to yield economies of large-scale production, an achievement which the limited social depth of the market in Britain rendered impossible within the existing structure of the industry. Nonetheless, in order to counter the inroads on Morris sales by the Austin Seven and the threat, premature in the event, of renewed competition from a revived and reorganized Ford Motor Company in Britain (which in 1928 recalled the formerly successful British manager, Sir Percival Perry, to plan a model and marketing strategy appropriate to the British market), Morris ended his two-model policy based on minimum visible alteration. The replacement was a policy of 'flexibility' intended to accommodate public taste for variations in demand for different types of cars: 'A car for every need' (Overy 1976: 49–50, 73). Such a policy was facilitated by the acquisition of the ailing Wolseley Motor Company from the Receiver in 1927, for Wolseley cars were aimed at the higher priced (though below luxury) segment of the market; Morris M.G. Cars Ltd was formed as a separate company in 1930, marking the beginnings of quantity production of the popular sports car. The Wolseley takeover also brought a new executive manager into the Nuffield empire in the person of Leonard Lord, to whom Morris not only gave responsibility for reorganizing and re-equipping the company but also for implementing a new diversified product policy. Between 1926 and 1929 the Nuffield-owned companies developed five new models, four more between 1929 and 1932. By 1933 the Nuffield group was producing 23 basic models and 12 engines, whereas Austin and Ford each produced 7 models and 4 engines (Church and Miller 1977: 177).

The failure of Nuffield to develop models sufficiently attractive to first-time purchasers or to ensure loyalty to a marque is evident in his company's inability to retain market share, which fell from 35 per cent in 1929 to 21 per cent by 1938. Simultaneously, Austin's share fell from 25 per cent to 21 per cent. The principal gainer during this period was Ford, which under Perry's leadership, backed by Henry Ford, undertook large-scale investment in mass production facilities at Dagenham to ensure low-cost production and a low-priced model. The new Y model, a 4-cylinder 8-horsepower model which was the first car designed in Detroit engineered and styled to meet the requirements of foreign laws and consumer preferences, proved a huge success, increasing Ford's share of the British market from 4 to 18 per cent between its introduction in 1933 and 1938 (Wilkins and Hill 1966: 238–40; Sedgwick 1975: 279).

However, Ford was not the only beneficiary from model price competition, for Rootes, Standard and Vauxhall, much smaller vehicle producers by comparison, also increased their aggregate market share from 8 to 31 per cent during the same period. In effect, in contrast to the structural market stability of the industry in the United States, during the interwar years the 1930s saw a relative decrease in concentration in the British volume car industry (Rhys 1976: 246, table 1). The quantity production methods of British manufacturers, faced with a much more limited market than their US counterparts and critically dependent on assembly rather than large-scale vertically integrated manufacture, enabled well-managed medium-sized car producers to match costs and prices of cars made by the volume producers; consequently in the 1930s especially sales depended increasingly upon non-price factors, appropriate selling and promotional policies, credit facilities and, critically, upon design.

IV

Already by the late 1920s Britain's major car producers were employing what an American government official described as 'modern intensive selling methods', including promotional campaigns, advertising and deferred payments (US Bureau of Domestic and Foreign Commerce 1928: 18–24). The same American observer reported a cooperative advertising campaign being conducted in the British press by car manufacturers urging the public to buy British products. Austin in particular emphasized the 'all-British' feature and the employment generated for British workmen ('Buy British and be proud of it'). Both Austin and Morris produced journals intended for dealers and owners, the *Austin Advocate* from 1911 and the *Morris Owner* from 1924. By 1927 instalment buying accounted for 60 per cent of car sales in Britain, compared with 75 per cent in the US in 1925 (Church 1981: 69–80).

The marketing methods adopted by smaller manufacturers were less developed. Three years after General Motors had acquired the little Vauxhall Motor Company in 1925, a new marketing strategy was introduced, beginning with the introduction of a British version of the *General Motors News*. Richard Grant, a General Motors' marketing executive, visited Britain and lectured to Vauxhall staff and dealers. Emphasizing that the basis of all successful selling was 'the right model, in the right place, at the right time' he offered advice on selling methods. He recommended salesmen to prepare a two-minute 'sound product talk' for delivery to potential car buyers; he advocated prize offers for successful salesmen, and regarded a fortnightly circular containing ideas for selling ('a sales speeder') as a useful aid. Also quite novel to British marketing was the introduction of systematic market research, carried out by a newly established statistics department. James D. Mooney, one of the three American directors on Vauxhall's board, regarded British salesmen's 'individualistic' approach as superior in its way, whereas the superiority of American salesmen's approach lay in knowing 'how to mass his forces. He defines the task to be done and then organises to it' (Holden 1984: 100–14).

When Colonel Frank Searle was appointed managing director of Rover in 1928, a company then beset by serious financial difficulties, he reorganized the salesforce, recruited new 'young and virile' salesmen, some possessing experience in the United States, and introduced American-style hard-selling methods to push sales of the new Rover model called 'The Scarab'. At the large sales conference held at Henlys in 1931, dealers received a booklet entitled 'A Golden Year for Rover Dealers', a lavishly produced suede green and gold-covered booklet, which informed them: 'You will know it as the Scarab, and this will symbolize to the motorist in a modern way, as it did to the Egyptians in ancient times, the "phenomenal" and the "marvellous"'. Agents, however, rejected this 'kind of motor cycle-sidecar on four wheels', (the equivalent of an American 'lemon'), for probably fewer than a dozen – rather than the mooted 30,000 – were actually made (Oliver 1971: 10–12, 111–14).

Crawfords Ltd became the leading agency handling advertising for car manufacturers during the 1920s, when advertisements began to appeal less to gentlemen's sporting needs or love of the countryside (both associated with elevated social status) and more to the performance and special delights of particular cars. Nonetheless, advertisements from the mid-1920s onwards often also contextualized the cars in accordance with their price range. A comparatively ordinary but solid, highly priced vehicle, the Armstrong Siddeley for example, was pictured in magnificent settings conveying an image of luxurious lifestyle; whereas the Austin Seven, one version of which was called 'the Nippy', appeared as an ideal car for runabout shopping (Frostick 1979: 20–5, 45–77). Selling methods in Britain differed from those in the United States in the absence among British manufacturers of any systematic segmentation of the market through market research, though in the 1930s the leading British advertising agents were beginning to mount sizeable technical media market research projects rivalling those of their American counterparts (West 1988: 490).

The production of sports and sporty cars, utility vehicles, family saloons and luxury cars, implicitly acknowledged an appreciation of the heterogeneity of the British market. A report by Claud Johnson, managing director of Rolls Royce in the 1920s, analysed the difficulty facing his company in the American market. He clearly felt that the scope for social segmentation not entirely based on price was greater in Britain, placing the Rolls at a disadvantage. Reporting that 'three or four fine American cars could be purchased for the cost of a single Rolls' he continued: 'the American citizen has a great fear of being laughed at locally by his neighbours as being a pretentious ass. Our big competitors in America have been most industrious and inventive in rubbing in these views' (Lloyd 1978: 52–7, 167).

In the volume car market, both in Britain and in the United States, aggressive selling methods, marketing techniques, and the use of hire purchase were pursued by the major manufacturers, though they differed in extent and character. One difference in the approach to selling by British and American manufacturers is captured by the imagery employed in car advertisements. Compare, for example, Austin's slogan 'You buy a car but you invest in an Austin' with the copy advertising the Jordan Playboy, described as 'eleven hundred pounds of steel and action' (Tedlow 1990: 180). Language of this kind was not to be found in the pages of British journals for dealers and owners, such as the *Austin Advocate*, the *Morris Owner* or the *Rover Mirror* 'devoted to sound trading and good fellowship' (Oliver 1971: 100).

V

One key contrast between the major manufacturers in the United States (including Ford by the 1930s), and the British car makers was their approach to investment in, and organization of, design. This is one aspect of Phase III marketing which Tedlow refers to in the American context but the importance of which, in the absence of international comparisons, is overlooked. Except in terms of mechanical engineering, the concept of overall car design hardly existed before World War I. The chassis was built separately from the body, the construction of which, with few exceptions, was carried out by the erstwhile woodworking carriage-making firms turned bodybuilders. The responsibility for car design during this period was typically that of the inventor–engineer–entrepreneur, or in the case of the large firms sometimes a consultant engineer who either worked for several companies or contracted to a single company and moved from one to another (Church 1979: 184). In the pioneering stage a car's final appearance was left to the customer or bodybuilder and was secondary to mechanical performance, which was the concern of the chassis manufacturers who chose bodies on offer. By 1913, when the first Morris Oxford car was built, it was the result of an aggregate assembly of components. Through assembly of parts and components Morris built up a flexible manufacturing organization, a form of enterprise enabling medium-scale producers to survive during the very different market conditions of the 1930s (Andrews and Brunner 1955: 62–71).

A condition of survival, and the basis for an increased share of the market for the medium-sized firms – Standard, Rootes (formerly Hillman and Humber) and Vauxhall – was low-cost development of cars in the popular price range, but critically possessing an appearance attractive to buyers – most of whom by the 1930s were not purchasing their first car (Maxcy and Silberston 1959: 108; Church and Miller 1977: 174–5). The widespread acceptance of the closed car shortly after its introduction in the mid-1920s further increased the scope for styling as an integral part of car design, as aesthetics (under the influence, in Austin's opinion, of women's needs and taste) assumed greater importance to sales (Kennington 1934–5: 67).

In 1924 Sloan's acknowledgement of the increasing importance of styling and design in the mature American market resulted in the setting up of a 'colour section' at General Motors. Two years later he proposed to extend this innovation by adopting a styling programme:

> I am sure we all realize how much appearance has to do with sales: with all cars fairly good mechanically it is a dominating proposition and in a product such as ours the individual appeal is so great, it means a tremendous influence on our future prosperity. . . . beauty of design, harmony of lines, attractiveness of colour schemes and general contour of the whole piece of apparatus [were seen to be equally important as] soundness of workmanship and other elements of a mechanical nature.
>
> (Sloan 1967: 290)

Despite initial opposition from GM's engineers, hitherto entirely responsible for design within the process of auto engineering construction, by 1927 the enlarged art and colour section employed ten industrial designers and forty other employees. They worked under the direction of Harley Earl, a Stanford graduate, the son of a carriage maker, and formerly a custom car body designer in Hollywood. He was recruited by Sloan to create styling ideas for the entire line of GM automobiles. Henceforward the annual model changes, consisting of body changes every four or five years, with 'face lifting in between', were based on elements of visual design and later incorporated planned obsolescence (Sloan 1967: 291–2, 300).

In 1935 the 'product-approval procedure' which had evolved was formally set down in manual form for the first time, the purpose being 'to provide a definite and orderly method for submitting the essential data required in order that the economic financial, engineering and commercial, position of proposed new products may be evaluated' (Sloan 1967: 263). In 1927 Ford reluctantly conceded the need to replace the ageing Model T with a new design, in the shape of the different, though less than innovative, Model A in order to remain competitive. Nonetheless it was not until after World War II that Ford and Chrysler set up systems of styling and integrated styling into the production planning process on the model well established at GM. By 1941 Sloan was speculating whether during the 1930s the appearance of a motor car had become the most important style factor in sales success. In planning for production after the war Sloan assumed that consumers would rank styling first, automatic transmissions second and high compression engines third (Sloan 1967: 299–300).

Among British engineers and company directors scepticism towards industrial as distinct from engineering design was much more deep-rooted. However, faced with one-dimensional sales, (of the low profit margin Austin Seven), in an overall stagnant market, Herbert Austin recruited Ricardo Burzi, the Italian engineer who designed Lancia cars for the luxury sports car market in Europe. After seeing his work at the Paris Motor Show Austin decided that Burzi was the person to re-style cars produced at Longbridge (Turner 1971: 9). The 1934 models bore the stamp of Burzi's work. Body lines had been altered by fitting a newly designed sloping radiator shell, bonnets were lengthened, projecting fittings eliminated; the boxy appearance of the 1920s was replaced by sweeping body lines, emulating to a degree the streamlining introduced by American manufacturers in 1931 (Church and Mullen 1989: 197). Morris also followed this trend. For a short period during the early 1930s slight alterations in the outward appearance of existing models occurred as a response to – or in anticipation of – what Sir Herbert Austin called 'The public's ever changing moods' (Overy 1976: 49; Church 1979: 116). However, as sales expanded in 1935, Sir Herbert announced that his company would make a 'bold stand against the fetish of change for change's sake', thereby avoiding expenditure which the model change policy had involved (Church 1979: 116). He promised that future models would remain virtually unchanged except for minor (real) improvements. Simultaneously, Morris adopted a similar policy, and instead introduced the concept of a 'series', making replacements only when necessary (Sedgwick 1975: 255).

The market strategies of General Motors suggest that one consequence of the major British manufacturers' policies in this respect may have been to enable other, smaller car makers to increase market shares. In the United States the annual model changes introduced from the mid-1920s by General Motors had the effect of increasing the minimal survival size as a result of the additional capital expenditure which such a policy involved (Thomas 1964: 121). The rising high levels of industrial concentration in the United States which followed contrasts with the falling levels of concentration in the British industry during the 1930s, as Morris, spectacularly, and Austin lost market shares to Ford, Standard, Vauxhall and Rootes.

VI

British manufacturers' brief flirtation with a systematic design strategy was exceptional and shortlived. Pevsner described the process in 1935:

Almost everywhere the ideas for new models originate with the director or manager, and incidentally within eighteen months before a car is put on the market. He may make some rough sketches or more careful drawings according to his ability, or else describe to the body engineer or coachwork manager what he means, only after this are more detailed drawings made by the designer and submitted to a board of experts (in one factory called the Elegance Committee) in which the sales manager has a particularly important voice.

(Pevsner 1937: 130)

A survey of motor companies in 1950 revealed that in the interim the process of design in the larger organizations had involved a three-dimensional project, the full-scale wood and plasticine models superseding the two-dimensional plans produced on the drawing board which was the traditional method. However, the professional industrial designer continued to be a peripheral figure within the corporate organization. The managing directors took responsibility for, and in some cases personally initiated, new designs. At one of the big three car makers in 1950 the practice was for the managing director to decide on the type of design, leaving chassis and body engineers to develop it over a period of two years, the services of an American consultant designer being called upon to improve the appearance of a new model at a late stage. The industrial design input, therefore, was inevitably superficial. At the other two major manufacturers the body engineers did enjoy authority to build their own prototype: 'As they possessed the production experience and technical ability to work out their own ideas, they were able to present a convincing case to the chassis and body engineers' (Farr 1955: 137–8). However, the researcher also concluded that in large firms a lack of sympathetic collaboration between the technical, production and sales departments led to clashes of inter-departmental interests, leaving the body designer, lacking a factory constituency, as the least influential in the design process (Farr 1950: 139–40).

Apart from the brief appearance during the early 1930s the professional industrial designer played little or no part in British motor factories. The engineering, architectural and aesthetic features of models were essentially the conception and creation of engineer–entrepreneurs and managers, to some extent suspicious of consumer-led design. It is in this critical respect that the design process differed from its history in the US; furthermore, British subsidiaries of American companies perpetuated this difference. At Ford's Dagenham factory the involvement of English engineers in car design was 'strictly forbidden', though their informal suggestions accepted by Sorenson did affect the conception of the Ford Anglia and Prefect in 1937 (Wilkins and Hill 1966: 191–2). At Vauxhall, taken over by General Motors in 1925, the new model, the Cadet, was a modified version based on the drawings used in designing the Opel Kadet for the German GM subsidiary. Under the British managers' influence subsequent models were of a lower horsepower – culminating in the 'Vauxhall Ten' in 1938, the first mass-produced monocoque car to be made in Britain. Thus, while new models produced by Vauxhall benefited not only from the greater financial and technical resources of its parent company, from GM's extensive design departments, and from a planned strategy of annual model variation and model replacement at three-year intervals, Vauxhall lacked a basic design capacity (Holden 1984: 53–8). Neither in British companies nor in American subsidiaries did design or styling become a separate corporate function.

Characteristically, British manufacturers (and Ford until World War II) thought in terms of model replacement and alterations in styling only when sales of existing models showed an appreciable downward trend. Nuffield's commercial director, Miles Thomas, described Morris as an adaptor rather than a creator: 'it was terribly hard to persuade him to let the drawing office start from the clean sheet of paper stage' (Thomas 1964: 160; Overy 1976: 49). At Nuffield's factories this principle resulted in intra-factory competition between models even within the same price bands (Nixon 1949: 111–12). A market strategy which did not envisage regular replacement precluded the development of an appropriate design and innovation structure.

When the Austin Seven was created by Herbert Austin in 1921–2 it had occurred on his own personal initiative outside the company's committee structure and took place initially on a billiards table at his home in the Lickey Hills. Many years later when Alec Issigonis, a senior engineer at Cowley, designed the Morris Minor, the design function did not yet figure within the organizational structure of the Nuffield empire. Issigonis, who was given responsibility for developing an effective suspension system for a new post-war model, as yet to be created, argued that a car should be designed as an integrated whole and persuaded the senior managers to give him support in so doing, with a clean sheet of paper and two senior draftsmen (Skilleter 1988: 48). A scale model of the car designed entirely by Issigonis was built in 1942 (scale models and clay models were not introduced at

Longbridge until the 1950s). Prototypes of 'the Mosquito' were put in hand in 1945 and simultaneously with the fixing of a launch date for mass production of the Mosquito, the sales director, Miles Thomas, somewhat belatedly asked for a breakdown of the costs of the production model in order to price it – a curious sequence of product planning.

Even at this late date Lord Nuffield blocked the launch, on the grounds that orders for the Morris Eight were still buoyant and that, regardless of the improvements and change in styling incorporated in the Mosquito, there was no need to replace it. On Nuffield's instructions the Series E (Morris Eight) was to continue in production without basic changes, 'but when sales showed definite signs of flagging the model will be fitted with independent front suspension and new front styling'. Nuffield and his sales director were in absolute disagreement on model policy. Thomas eventually secured the board's approval to proceed with a wide-bodied Mosquito by agreeing to incorporate the old 8-horsepower engine bored out to 950–980 cc instead of the 1100-cc engine originally envisaged; but frustrated by Nuffield's negative obstructionist approach, Thomas resigned before production commenced in November 1947. Four weeks later the directors of the Nuffield organization renamed the Mosquito the Morris Minor, the ultimate responsibility for its design resting with Issigonis (Skilleter 1988: 52–3). At a very late stage he took personal responsibility for widening the body from 50 to 60 inches purely on aesthetic grounds: 'Proportions are everything,' he later reflected, 'when I study a car to assess its looks I don't say . . . "its well styled", I say "does it look elegant?"'. In other words, are the proportions right?' (Barker 1970: 303–4). The Morris Minor took the Nuffield organization back to the premier position among British car producers.

After the Austin–Morris merger to form BMC in 1952 Leonard Lord became the chief executive, an irascible autocrat whose lifetime in car production engineering had left him with the philosophy 'make proper bloody products and you don't need to sell 'em'. (Turner 1971: 90). When in 1956 Lord decided that the ageing Morris Minor was unable to withstand European competition in the same range – notably the Volkswagen – he placed Issigonis at the head of a small experimental design team that circumvented the existing decision-making structure, instructing him to devise the Minor's replacement. The brief from Lord was to design a small, economic car to carry four people in relative comfort yet offering the same standards of serviceability of normal cars (Church and Mullen 1989: 200). Thus, neither the Morris Minor (nor, later, the Mini) were much influenced in their design either by market research or contemporary styling conventions. Like Austin, Issigonis associated styling (which he dismissed as designing for obsolescence) with fashion, which he despised as an unwholesome influence for which (again like Austin) he blamed women. Within his lifetime Issigonis was to see himself as a dinosaur: 'the last of the Bugattis, a man who designed whole cars. Now committees do the work' (Hope 1979: 34).

The history of car design in Britain's largest companies reveals a tension between the trend towards bureaucratic management structures and the distinctive corporate cultures created by the aspirations, assumptions and attitudes of their strong-minded founders, who particularly in the matter of design and product strategy were dominant influences. The administrative structures in these companies failed either to develop a continuing process of differentiation or to create a design capacity which, when required, might transform the company's product range within an overall, rather than an *ad hoc*, marketing strategy. In part this reflected the incompleteness of reorganizations following first the formation of the Nuffield empire through acquisitions between the wars, and second, the merger which formed BMC in 1952 (Church and Mullen 1989: 203).

VII

The contrasting international history of styling and design in the United States compared with the motor industry in Britain suggests that there is some justification for elaborating Tedlow's paradigm in order to acknowledge the critical importance of the design function and the changes it underwent in America in the late 1920s. The systematization of design and styling and their place in the sequence of strategic managerial decision-making were developments not transferred to Britain until after World War II. Other aspects of marketing, notably selling, advertising, credit facilities, even market research did develop in Britain, later and less systematically intensive, but unlike the case of design the differences were those of degree. There is a case, therefore, for introducing an additional Phase IV.

During the third phase, between 1921 and the late 1920s, model price competition in the US superseded price competition as the dominant marketing characteristic; this included segmentation of the market by balanced model range, the introduction of market research, and targeted selling methods, including advertising and time payments. The fourth phase can be identified in the US in the late 1920s when, in Sloan's words, American production engineers began to 'yield to market considerations' (Sloan 1967: 287) and became more sympathetic to changes in design. In part this explains why, although even from 1921 General Motors' policy had begun to emphasize the importance of styling for selling it was not until after 1926, when closed bodies became the norm, that Sloan implemented his policy by establishing and expanding a special department, the art and colour section, staffed by industrial designers. In 1927 Sloan wrote of the future of General Motors resting on the attractiveness of car bodies to consumers: 'the luxury of appointment, the degree to which they please the eye, both in contour and in colour scheme, also the degree to which we are able to make them different from competition' (Sloan 1967: 295). By incorporating styling as a staff function, charged with the task of continually reviewing research and proposing automobile design, it may be argued that the industry entered a new stage in the evolution of marketing. GM designers acknowledged that in order to anticipate consumer tastes in the longer term continuing systematic research was needed. Forecasting and planning became one of the functions of the General Motors Research Laboratories, which became the locus for research aimed at increasing 'consumer appeal' of GM products through improvements in design, functioning, serviceability and style. Through a combination of literature searches, surveys and interviews conducted on a large scale GM introduced 'systematic change-making' with the objective of long-term marketing leadership as an integral part of the corporate structure (Kuhn 1986: 216–18).

By the 1930s the role of the product engineer had become more a matter of solving problems created by the stylist, for the latter had become central rather than peripheral in the formulation of product policy. Describing the process by which in the 1930s new models were created, Sloan explained that the initial meeting of the Engineering Policy Group which started the formal planning sequence was to

> determine the cars' general appearance and size characteristics and to indicate the direction of further styling and divisional development. . . . The Styling Staff displays full-size styling drawings . . . develops full size clay models and seating bucks. . . . It is the Styling Staff's responsibility to set the basic appearance of each kind of car.
>
> (Sloan 1967: 264)

Meanwhile, the engineering departments of the car divisions and of Fisher Body worked with the styling staff in order to reach agreement on chassis dimensions so as to enable them 'to firm up' the concept of a new model. Harley Earl's designs achieved adequate levels of differentiation despite the proliferation of interchangeable parts, chassis and bodies among GM cars. Before the 1950s British manufacturers failed, where the American producers succeeded, in striking the right balance between making too few models to satisfy market demand yet not making so many chassis types as to hamper economic production and effective control over manufacturing processes (Kuhn 1986: 94). The British industry failed to develop an organizational capacity for the design of mass-produced vehicles, the missing – fourth – dimension from the mass marketing of motor cars in Britain during the first half of the twentieth century.

BIBLIOGRAPHY

Andrews, P.W.S. and Brunner, Elizabeth (1955) *The Life of Lord Nuffield*, Oxford: Basil Blackwell.
Austin, Sir Herbert (1930–1) 'The future trend of automobile design', *Proceedings of the Institute of Automobile Engineers* XXV.
Bardou, Jean-Pierre, Chanaron, Jean Jacques, Fridenson, Patrick and Laux, James M. (1982) *The Automobile Revolution: the Impact of an Industry*, translated by James M. Laux, Chapel Hill, USA: University of North Carolina Press.
Barker, Ronald (1970) *Automobile Design*, Newton Abbott: David & Charles.
Bayley, Stephen (1979) *In Good Shape: Style in Industrial Products*, London: Design Council.
Church, Roy (1979) *Herbert Austin: The British Car Industry to 1940*, London: Europa.
—— (1981) 'The marketing of automobiles in Britain and the United States before 1939', in Akio Okochi and Koichi Shimokawa (eds) *Development of Mass Marketing*, Tokyo: University of Tokyo.
—— (1982) 'Markets and marketing in the British motor industry before 1914; with some French comparisons', *Journal of Transport History*, Third Series, 3.
—— with Miller, Michael (1977) 'The big three: competition, management and marketing in the British motor industry 1922–1959', in Barry Supple (ed.) *Essays in British Business History*, Oxford: Oxford University Press.
—— with Mullen, C. (1989) 'Cars and corporate culture: the view from Longbridge', in Barbara Tilson (ed.) *Industry and Design in Birmingham 1889–1989*, Studley, Warwicks: Brewin Books.
Farr, Michael (1955) *Design in British Industry: a Mid-Century Survey*, Cambridge: Cambridge University Press.
Frostick, Michael (1979) *Advertising the Motor Car*, London: Foulis.
Gloag, John (1946) *Industrial Art Explained*, London: Allen & Unwin.
Holden, L.T. (1984) 'A history of Vauxhall Motors to 1950: industry,

development and local impact on the Luton economy', unpublished MPhil thesis, Open University.
Hope, A. (1979) 'The genius today', *Autocar*, 25 August.
Kennington, W.O. (1934–5) 'The utilitarian aesthetics of automobile body design', *Proceedings of the Institute of Automobile Engineers*.
Kotler, Philip (1988) *Marketing Management* (6th edn), Englewood Cliffs, NJ: Prentice Hall.
Kuhn, Arthur J. (1986) *G.M. Passes Ford, 1918–1938*, Pennsylvania: Pennsylvania University Press.
Levitt, Theodore (1960) 'Marketing myopia', *Harvard Business Review*, July–August.
Lloyd, Ian (1978) *Rolls Royce*, 3 vols, Basingstoke: Macmillan.
McCarthy, Fiona (1979) *A History of British Design 1830–1970*, London: Allen & Unwin.
Maxcy, G. and Silberston, A. (1959) *The Motor Industry*, London: George, Allen & Unwin.
Miller, Michael with Church, Roy (1979) 'Growth and instability in the British motor industry between the wars', in N. Buxton and D.H. Aldcroft (eds) *Instability and Industrial Development 1919–1939*, London: Allen & Unwin.
Ministry of Supply (1947) *National Advisory Council for the Motor Manufacturing Industry: Report of Proceedings*, London: HMSO.
Nixon, St John (1949) *Wolseley: A Saga of the Motor Industry*, London: Foulis.
Oliver, George (1971) *The Rover*, London: Cassell.
Overy, Richard (1976) *William Morris; Viscount Nuffield*, London, Europa.
Pevsner, N. (1937) *An Enquiry into Industrial Art in England*, Cambridge: Cambridge University Press.
Plowden, W.J. (1971) *The Motor Car and Politics*, London: Penguin.
Rhys, D.G. (1976) 'Concentration in the inter-war motor industry', *Journal of Transport History*, New Series, III, 4.
Saul, S.B. (1962) 'The motor industry in Britain to 1914', *Business History* V.
Sedgwick, Michael (1975) *Passenger Cars 1924–1942*, London: Blandford Foulis.
Skilleter, Paul (1988) 'The Thomas Papers', *Thoroughbred and Classic Cars*, June.
Sloan, Alfred P. Jnr (1967) *My Life with General Motors*, London: Pan Books.
Tedlow, Richard S. (1990) *New and Improved: The Story of Mass Marketing in America*, Oxford: Heinemann.
Thomas, Miles (1964) *Out on a Wing*, London: Sidgwick.
Thomas, Robert Paul (1973) 'Style change and the automobile industry during the roaring 'twenties', in L.P. Cain and P.J. Uselding (eds) *Business Enterprise and Economic Change*, Kent, Ohio: Kent State University Press.
Turner, Graham (1981) *The Leyland Papers*, Birkenhead: Eyre & Spottiswood.
Turner, P. (1981) 'The paradox of Sir Herbert Austin', *The Motor*, 10 January.
US Bureau of Domestic and Foreign Commerce (1928) 'Automotive industry and trade of Great Britain'.

West, Douglas (1988) 'Multinational competition in the British advertising agency business, 1936–1987', *Business History Review* 62 (autumn).

Wilkins, Mira and Hill, Frank Ernest (1966) *American Business Abroad: Ford on Six Continents*, Detroit: Wayne State University Press.

4 The rise and fall of mass marketing?
Food retailing in Great Britain since 1960

Leigh Sparks

Food retailing is central to most economies, whether the retailing is undertaken through a producers' market in Kenya or via a food court in a consumption 'palace' such as West Edmonton Mall, Alberta, Canada. The requirement to eat to live is a fundamental one recognized throughout the world. The ways in which food retailing and marketing are organized are therefore important pointers to the fabric of any society and indeed, the effectiveness and efficiency of mass food retailing has been taken as a measure of governmental ability. The consumer, retailer and producer relationships involved in a Chinese wet market in Singapore, or a bazaar in Tunis, or a drive-in McDonalds anywhere in the United States, say much about the respective economies and societies, as well as their consumers' beliefs, actions, motivations and desires (see, for example, McClelland 1962; Fanselow 1990). The central role of food retailing and production provides a critical 'mirror' on society itself. In practice, however, this is a two-way mirror, with retailers and consumers being inextricably linked and changed in this symbiotic relationship.

Changes in both retailing and consumers are crucial to any understanding of the development of the retail sector. What mediates this relationship is the 'marketing' that retailers and producers undertake to persuade consumers to visit and patronize their outlets and purchase their products. In order to study food retailing in Great Britain since 1960, therefore, it is necessary to consider both how retailers and retail practices have changed and also how consumers and consumer behaviour has changed. This is complicated by the fact that the date chosen here (1960) is selected for a variety of reasons. It is used both to fit in with the case study and because the 1960s saw the first decade emerging from the rationing shadow of World War II which distorts food retailing, marketing and consumption. Whilst useful in this regard, it cannot be claimed that 1960 witnessed the

The rise and fall of mass marketing? 59

introduction of marketing into food retailing, and is thus somewhat arbitrary.

Richard Tedlow (1990) identifies three phases of marketing (fragmentation, unitization and segmentation) and illustrates these through a number of case studies, which include both a food (A & P) and a non-food (Sears) retailer. Underpinning the successful companies are a number of themes (Tedlow 1990): profit through volume, entrepreneurial vision, vertical system, first-movers and entry barriers, competitors' options and managing change. Various timings for these phases are put forward; in food retailing the emergence of brands and the supermarket are seen as important events which shaped modern American food retailing. For Great Britain, there is little doubt that marketing and food retailing were in a fragmented phase, albeit with elements of modern marketing practice in use, in the previous century and earlier (see, for example, Jefferys 1954; Mui and Mui 1989). Self-service methods and supermarkets had to wait effectively until the 1950s when developments were hindered by the state of the country and consumers after World War II (McClelland 1963; Mathias 1967; Dawson 1981). This is not to say that there was no mass marketing in food retailing before that date, there undoubtedly was. This is well-illustrated, for example, in the company 'history' for Tesco (Powell 1991). However, it is fair to argue that the real revolution in British food retailing took place from the 1950s onwards. As consumers have changed, so too retailers have changed, with arguably a movement first towards a unification of the mass market and more recently a segmentation of this market. However, delineating precisely these phases and identifying a clear timescale is not the aim here.

This chapter examines the changing nature of food retailing and marketing since 1960. This is undertaken to answer a number of questions. The first of these is a relatively simple one: how have food retailing and the consumers it serves changed over this period? Secondly, the chapter looks at these changes in the light of the phases identified by Tedlow (1990) and assesses their 'fit'. Finally, the chapter reviews and assesses the six elements presented by Tedlow in his proposition of movement from pre-modern to modern marketing.

The timing of the Tedlow phases is moveable depending on the scale and the subject of enquiry. In the space available here it is not possible to present a history of food retailing in Great Britain. This would be a massive undertaking. However, such a study would, I believe, be able to identify the 'progression' that Tedlow's phases imply. Instead, and in the knowledge of the limited aims discussed above, this chapter examines in particular the development of one company, Kwik Save Group plc, which is one of Britain's leading food retailers. This choice allows the crucial period of the last thirty years to be studied through the development of one company, but also allows an assessment of whether Tedlow's phases and propositions are, in fact, a manifestation of business development generally rather than marketing or retail development.

The chapter has been divided into four main sections, in addition to this introduction. First, it is important to set the scene by examining the changes that have occurred in both consumers and society. This is followed by a review section on retailing and marketing change. In both cases, food retailing is the focus of study. Whilst these are separate sections it is important to note the interdependencies between them (as indicated earlier). These reviews are followed by the main section of this chapter. This is a case study of Kwik Save Group plc which charts its development from its entrepreneurial beginnings to its position now as one of the leading food retailers in Britain. Finally, the concluding section attempts to pull the strands together from the two review sections and the case study and in particular to answer the questions posed in this introduction.

CONSUMER AND SOCIAL CHANGE

The British consumer of 1990 is very different to the British consumer of 1960. There have been changes in both the consumers themselves and their ability and willingness to consume, as well as changes in the social fabric of Great Britain (Gershuny 1978, 1983; Marwick 1982; Bowlby 1984; Halsey 1988). Both these topics are reviewed here, commencing with consumer change. The structure for this discussion is taken from Dawson and Broadbridge (1988). In examining consumer change it is useful to disaggregate what is a large and complex issue. Here, the disaggregation is into consumption, consumer behaviour and shopping behaviour.

In terms of consumption, defined here as the volume and value of the types of goods and services consumed, there have been considerable changes. At a simple level the degree of consumption has increased as the economic level of affluence has risen between 1960 and 1990. This is demonstrated by Fig. 4.1 which presents the volume and value of retail sales since 1957. This should not be taken as the definitive series as it has been recalculated from data from several sources. However, the trend is clear from the figure and also the relative underperformance of the food element. In volume terms,

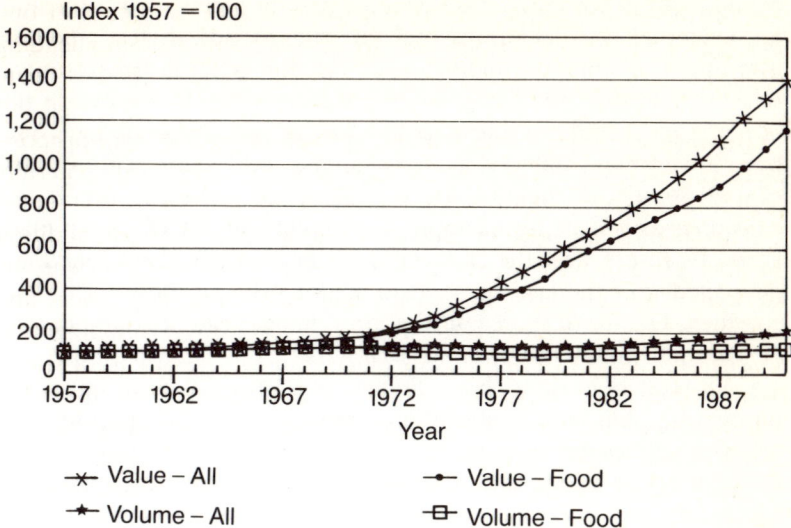

Figure 4.1 Retail sales in UK, 1957–91

food retailing has been relatively static over this timescale although there have been notable fluctuations. Such figures and their simplistic use have been questioned by Thorpe (1990) who argues cogently about the problems of comparing such data over this period given the quality changes in retailing and consumption.

Nevertheless it is clear that British consumers as a whole are far better off in consumption terms than ever before, although this is not to deny the undoubted sectors of the community that are not affluent and well-served. As a generalization consumers can now afford more and better products and have shown a willingness to consume such items. However, it is not just the general level of consumption that has changed, but the elements that make up this level. For example, there have been differential changes in consumption levels of food and non-food products (see Fig. 4.1). New products have been brought to the market and have become standard household products. The clearest examples have been in consumer durables such as colour televisions, video recorders and home computers, but the same argument is true in food retailing with products such as chicken Kiev, imports such as mango or starfruit and new sectors such as microwave-prepared meals. There is now a greater range of food products available for consumption. Some 'traditional' products have declined, often for a variety of reasons. The transfer of consumption of red meat to white meat is a change based on new ideas of health, for example; the decline in real fur sales is due to the emerging awareness of animal cruelty issues and for general 'environment' reasons; and the rise of vegetarian products is due to the emergence of new concerns about 'lifestyle' in a basic sense. Some changes have been government induced as, for example, in the differential taxing of petrol or the 'health' tax on cigarettes, whereas others are consumer driven as, for example, in the removal of CFCs from many aerosols. In essence, the consumption patterns have broadened and deepened over the last thirty years, making the position much more complex. Details of these consumption changes can be found in IGD (1990) and Mintel (1991) amongst others.

Consumer behaviour, here defined as a series of decisions about purchasing, has also changed enormously over this period. The relative balance between price, service and quality has moved away from price decisions and towards decisions based on quality or service. Price competition in many sectors of British retailing is less than it was before, although as current recessionary pressures mount, price competition is mooted again as a saviour for volume-based businesses. Food retailers have changed their approach over the last thirty years to move away from price competition and towards non-price competition. This has meant extensions to the service provision and the perceived quality of the products (Gardner and Sheppard 1989). Consumers have led the way in this by being attracted to retailers who demonstrate choice and value rather than those based solely on price. Many consumers have made purchasing decisions based not on the prices of products but on their quality or, more particularly, value, the service provided and the way in which it fits their 'lifestyle'. As consumers have become more affluent and their horizons have broadened and their values changed, so they have been more willing to 'trade-up' in product terms. Rather than being solely motivated by price decisions on individual products or shopping trips, the decisions have been based on the less tangible elements in a purchase or a shopping trip. That is not to say that price does not enter the decision, but rather that price is but one of the factors considered, rather than the only factor.

Similarly, change has also taken place in shopping behaviour, which is here defined as who buys what, where and in what shopping group. Consumers have shown themselves very willing to alter their shopping behaviour as opportunities have arisen. These opportunities have arisen through changes in retail locations and the change in mobility of the consumers as a whole. The mobility changes have seen an increasing willingness and capability to use the car as a mode of transport to shop. The personal emancipation afforded by cars has increased both actual and perceived mobility in terms of general movement, but particularly for retail trips. Consumers are now willing, and able, to travel further in their shopping trips, be they the once-a-week food shopping trip or the visits to local or neighbouring town centres. With a wider choice, the quality of experience becomes important in individual shopping trips, for maintaining patterns of patronage. Once again, therefore, the price issue is being replaced by non-price aspects of competition. The composition of the shopping group has also altered over time, with shopping no longer being the prerogative of females alone, but rather being shared either through single trips or by group trips. As the experience of shopping has developed into an end in itself, so shopping associated with or as a leisure activity has increased. Again, this is not to say that this is the case for all consumers. However, it is true that for many groups choice has increased and there is more freedom to choose the time, place and 'experience' of shopping.

These processes of consumer change are clearly interlinked and are also associated with wider changes in the economic environment of the country and in retailing. In addition, the changing consumer is a reflection of the changing social patterns in this country. Social change is a large and complex topic, but here the review is aided by disaggregating social change into individual or household, group and societal levels. The details of these changes are not given here, but can be found in any issue of *Social Trends*.

At the individual or household level the changes have been quite dramatic. Overall income levels have risen at the same time as time opportunities have altered. With a shorter working week, people have more leisure time. Being more mobile and affluent they spend this time in new ways and locations. This is also true of consumers at the end of their working life, where the retirement age is reducing, not through legislation but through practice and custom. Such individuals are more affluent, more mobile and healthier than ever before and exploit their opportunities in retirement. In terms of personal attitudes, these have changed dramatically over the last thirty years with increases, for example, in concepts such as personal gratification and awareness of health and fitness. The most recent extension of these areas has come in concern about the environment. As these attributes have developed, changed and matured in British society so fragmentation in the market place can be identified and targeted, as for example by the Body Shop.

64 *The rise and fall of mass marketing*

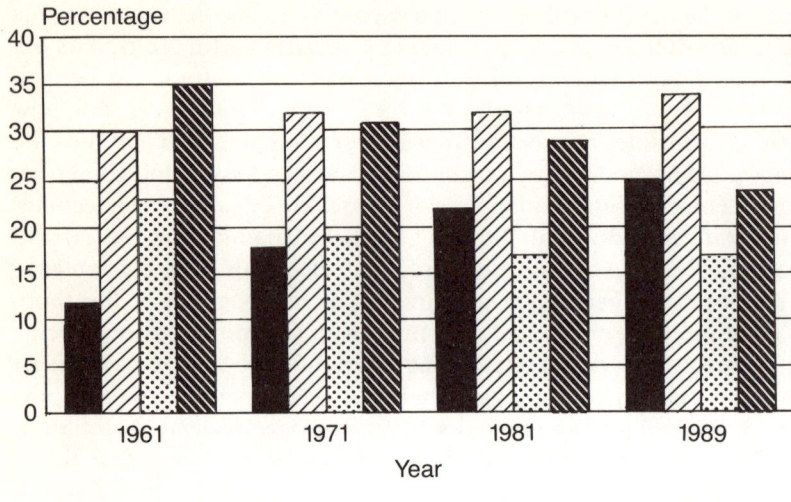

Figure 4.2 Household composition (UK), 1961–89

There have also been dramatic changes in terms of household composition. The standard nuclear family is now a minority of British households with instead a greater variety of household types and structures being found. Figure 4.2 provides some evidence of the changing household composition within an increasing number of households (from 16.1 million in 1961 to 19.4 million in 1981 and 22.7 million in 1989). The 'traditional' lifecycle is now not such a common one and instead revised ideas about household formation, dissolution and reformulation have had to be introduced (see Burt 1989 for a review). The basic argument is that complexity and complication has increased over the period.

Group behaviour changes are also apparent. Some of these arise from the individual changes discussed above, e.g. income changes. However, group changes arising from demographic change (Fig. 4.3) and the cohort of early house-owners passing on their 'estates' have provided similar opportunities for groups across society. In turn, groups within society have broadened their experiences in similar ways. The most obvious example of this is holidays abroad, where whole generations have replaced 'Blackpool' with 'Benidorm' and whilst replicating past experiences to some extent, have no doubt been exposed to elements of a different culture. These experiences have been brought back to British society in terms of a willingness

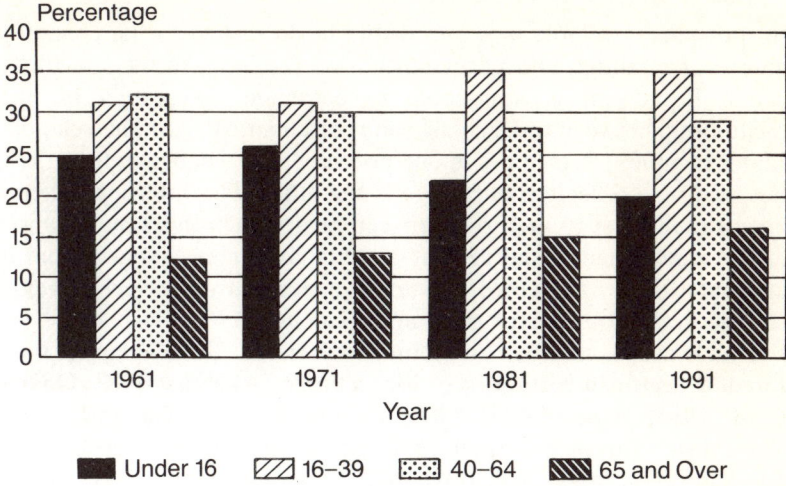

Figure 4.3 Age structure of the UK population, 1961–91

to experiment with different cultures and lifestyles, even if only at the level of purchasing and consuming frozen pizza. At the same time, immigration into Britain and realization by immigrant groups that food retailing is a relatively easy sector to enter (be it fresh produce or cooked) has ensured a further widening of cultural experiences for the population.

There are also changes occurring in society as a whole. The location of activities, including residence, has moved through a process of counter-urbanization. Society is now more information-rich than ever before, as well as being information-hungry. The social fabric of the country has changed with more practices and occurrences being tolerated or accepted than in the past, as, for example, with divorce, single parents and the other components of changing household formation. In particular, however, there has been a movement away from formal consumption and relationships to household consumption and relationships. Examples abound, but the take-home alcohol or food trade has replaced or augmented external social behaviour. Video rental or purchase has replaced or augmented external cinema-going. External behaviour patterns of thirty years ago with public consumption have been replaced by internal consumption and behaviour, allowing further individualistic development. This process simply enhances the tendency to fragmentation that is apparent.

RETAILING AND MARKETING CHANGE

In the space available it is impossible to do justice to the changing nature of retailing, and particularly food retailing, in the last thirty years. Equally it is impossible to comment adequately on the relationship between retail change and consumer change. This relationship is complex, as changes in one not only force change in the other, but are also a reflection of change in the other. This interdependency means that the success of retailers can be driven both by the reaction to consumer change and also by leading consumer change. What is attempted here, therefore, is simply a descriptive review of retail change in the food sector since approximately 1960.

There are a number of commentaries on the changing food retailing sector in Britain (see, for example, Akehurst 1983; Davies et al. 1985; Baden-Fuller 1986; Beaumont 1987; Dawson, 1987; Manchester Business School 1987; Lewis and Thomas 1990; Davis and Kay 1990; Moir 1990; IGD 1990; Duke 1991; Burt 1991; Mintel 1991). What they all show is that the food sector is one where change has been dramatic and concentration ratios have increased strongly. The sector is seen as being at the leading edge of retail change and the leading companies are amongst the largest in the United Kingdom. The UK component of J. Sainsbury, for example, had sales of £8.2 billion in 1991, made profits of £555 million from 469 stores with a total of 10 million sq ft, and the group as a whole employed over 108,000 people. The sector is now vastly different to the position in 1960.

Growing concentration has been associated with the increasing power of multiple retailers and a decline correspondingly in the strength of the cooperatives and independents. Table 4.1 provides overall figures for retailing for the period since 1961 and a clear growth of the power, if not the number, of large firms can be seen. Table 4.2 provides similar details for food retailing in the 1980s. The rise of the multiple retailers, particularly through economies of scale (Shaw et al. 1989; McClelland 1990) and replication, has produced a situation where only a handful of companies dominate food retailing, through their development of food superstores in particular. Currently the leading food retailers are Tesco and Sainsbury with Safeway in third place. These are followed by the troubled chains of Gateway and Asda. The cooperative movement as a whole is large, but the individual elements are often widely different in their performance. In the discount sector the dominant player is Kwik Save. There are also a small number of regional multiples such as Wm Low and Wm Morrison (Table 4.3). The market shares of these leading companies

Table 4.1 General comparisons of retailing in Britain, 1961–88

	1961	1971	1980	1988
No. of businesses ('000s)				
Total	394	351	256	237
With single store	356	327	225	212
With over ten stores	1.9	1.3	1.0	0.8
No. of establishments ('000s)				
Total	540	480	368	338
With over ten outlets	96	79	66	64
Average no. of stores in businesses with more than ten stores	51	61	66	77
Percentage of sales in businesses with more than ten stores	40	44	56	61
Percentage of capital expenditure in businesses with more than ten stores	63	73	69	78

Note: Precise comparisons for 1961 and 1971 with later years are not possible.
Sources: Business Monitors, Retail Inquiry 1988.

Table 4.2 Comparisons of food retailing in Britain, 1980, 1988

	1980	1988
No. of businesses ('000s)		
Total	90	68
With single store	82	62
With over ten stores	0.3	0.18
No. of establishments ('000s)		
Total	122	88
With single store	82	62
With over ten stores	18	12
Average no. of stores in businesses with more than ten stores	55	70
Percentage of sales in businesses with more than ten stores	65	75
Percentage of capital expenditure in businesses with more than ten stores	70	88

Source: Business Monitor SDA25, Retail Inquiry 1988.

have risen sharply over the last thirty years as the mass market has been unified. The basic changes have seen growth of the larger leading companies at the expense of smaller competitors, through both organic growth and takeovers. Until recently there has been little differentiation in the food marketplace. Whilst there may have been more fascias or trading names, the 'offer' was virtually the same.

Table 4.3 Market shares of leading UK food retail companies[a] (percentage)

	1970/1[b]	1979[c]	1989/90[d]
Sainsbury	6.1	11.9	12.1
Tesco	7.2	13.6	12.0
Safeway (Argyll)		1.2	8.9
Asda	1.5	7.3	8.0
Gateway			6.6
International	3.2	5.2	
Fine Fare	4.8	5.0	
Allied Suppliers	7.9	4.8	
Marks and Spencer		1.9	5.0
Kwik Save	0.3	4.9	2.4
Waitrose		1.3	1.9
Morrisons			1.6
Iceland			1.6
Other large grocery multiples		3.3	3.0
Specialist food retailers		15.9	17.7
Cooperatives		17.4	9.9
Others (including symbol groups)		6.3	9.3

[a] The columns in this table are not comparable but indicate here the trends rather than the quantitative changes. This is particularly the case for 1979–89.

[b] Market shares of the leading companies in the grocery market (*Source:* Akehurst 1984: 193).

[c] Market shares in the grocery market (*Source:* Akehurst 1984: 195).

[d] Market share of sales through all food retailers (*Source:* Mintel 1991: 75).

A review of the changes in food retailing since 1960 suggests that a number of common themes can be identified:

1 There has been a massive rise in the average size of stores, associated particularly with the growth of the food superstore

(Davies and Sparks 1989; Thorpe 1991). The average floorspace of new food superstores built for Tesco in 1991 was 41,500 sq ft for example. This increase in unit size has been associated with a ruthless pruning of smaller shops in established companies. For example, Tesco have reduced their number of stores from 790 in 1972 to 384 in 1991, but in the process have extended sales floorspace from 3.7 million sq ft to 9.7 million sq ft, increasing average store size from 4,700 sq ft sales area in 1972 to 25,100 sq ft in 1990. In addition to the growth in superstores, there has also been a massive rise in the number of large supermarkets (IGD 1990).

2 There has been a move towards out-of-town or off-centre locations, again linked to the superstore and the need for a large site for both the store and the associated car parking (Dawson 1984; Davies and Sparks 1989). Food retailing by mainline food retailers has been withdrawn from the majority of high streets (Dawson 1988), although there is evidence of a resurgence or re-interest in some locations for new formats, as food superstore saturation beckons (Duke 1991). One such example is the interest in various forms of convenience stores. A good illustration of these first two trends of scale and location is afforded by Lord and Guy (1991).

3 There has been a steady increase in the percentage of own-brand food products (McGoldrick 1984; Davies et al. 1986). Sainsbury always had a high level of such products but Tesco and the predecessors of Gateway and Safeway moved into own-brands in the 1970s. More recently, Asda has developed its own brands as a method of improving its margin and competitive position. In each case the positioning of the own-label is not as a cheap generic or fighting brand, but as a premier product. The retailer to all intents and purposes has become the brand.

4 There has been financial availability to enable the expansion to take place. The costs of single superstores are very high, with land costs and building costs rising continuously. The expansion policies of the major food retailers has required them to borrow money, often substantially. In some cases, this borrowed finance is now a millstone, e.g. Asda, Gateway.

5 The physical distribution system of the major food retailers has undergone massive changes, particularly in the last five years. This process of change is still not complete. In particular, physical distribution systems have become increasingly centralized with a high level of subcontracting. This process was started by Sainsbury (Quarmby 1989) and Kwik Save, but the other major food retailers

have all moved in the same direction (McKinnon 1985; Sparks 1986, 1992).

6 Finally, and from the point of this chapter, fundamentally, the major food retailers have become increasingly reliant on service and added value to sell to customers, rather than a strict reliance on price competition. Prices are generally competitive, but it is the quality, value, environment and service provided that have become important. The concept of customer service and care is now critical to many food retailers, as seen in staff training and development and product development. Whilst price is important to segments of the population, a factor exploited in the current recession, it is undeniable that the overall thrust of British food retailing has been towards service and value extensions and away from pure price competition. Examples of this concern can be seen in the product range extensions in new food superstores and the wide variety of counter service elements now being introduced to such stores (IGD 1990; Mintel 1991).

When these changes are examined it can be seen that they provide a picture of the changing British food consumer since 1960. From a position where food retailing was conducted primarily through small retail outlets, run mainly by independents and cooperatives, based on a corner shop model with counter service dominating (or just being replaced by self-service) and daily shopping trips predominant (as shown by McClelland 1963; Stacey and Wilson 1965, for example), we can see a transformation. Food retailing today is focused on large-scale, off-centre, self-service-based food superstores operated by multiples. Quality, value and choice have become the by-words. The rationing and utility of the 1950s has been replaced by the choice and quality of the 1980s and 1990s with an intermediate stage of price consciousness in the 1960s and 1970s.

The position for retailers in marketing terms between 1960 and 1990 is very different. The power of the food retailers is now substantially greater *vis-à-vis* the manufacturers and this power has been exploited in operational terms. By virtue of their closeness to the consumer, retailers have been able to adapt to their changing attitudes, tastes and desires and develop their own knowledge and power. This has meant that their operational decisions such as location, scale, product range and distribution have, over time, pressurized manufacturers, and given retailers an edge in the marketing channel. It must be emphasized, however, that it is the ability to lead and to reflect consumer attitudes, tastes and choice that has

The rise and fall of mass marketing? 71

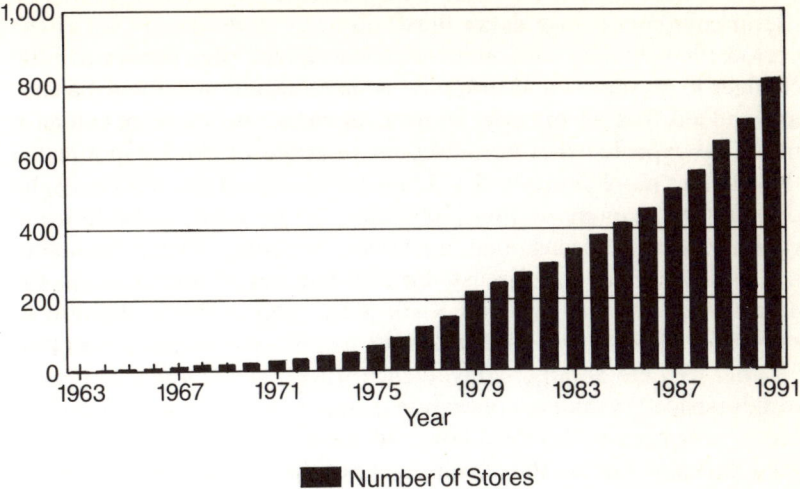

Figure 4.4 Kwik Save Group plc: number of stores, 1963–91

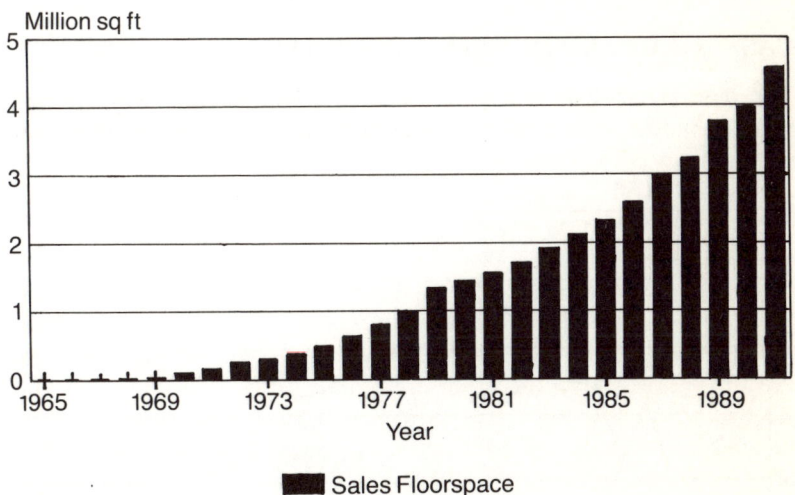

Figure 4.5 Kwik Save Group plc: sales floorspace, 1965–91

given the retailers this advantage. A knowledge of, and understanding of the consumer has been crucial.

It is these changes that are illustrated above and below by using the example of Kwik Save Group plc. Whilst not one of the leading two

72 The rise and fall of mass marketing

food retailers in market share terms (Table 4.3), Kwik Save is a useful company to use as an illustration, as it effectively spans the period 1960–90. As a discount retailer it has not been immune to the changes in consumer and shopping behaviour outlined above earlier, and indeed it is an effective case to demonstrate these points as it might be expected that non-discount oriented retailers experienced the changes more severely. Kwik Save were one of the leaders of the discount movement of the 1960s and 1970s, which reflected and capitalized on key consumer concerns of the time. This again makes it a useful company to discuss. From a number of precursors in the early 1960s and one original Kwik Save shop in 1965, the annual report for 1991 shows that Kwik Save has 745 Kwik Save stores plus another 69 Late Shopper convenience stores, giving 4.6 million sq ft of floorspace (excluding concessions), made profits of £101.7 million on a turnover of £1.895 billion and have 13,211 FTE employees. Figures 4.4–4.7 detail the development of the business in commercial terms. The current trading philosophy of the company is neatly encapsulated in Table 4.4, which lists the elements of the Kwik Save Charter.

CASE STUDY: KWIK SAVE GROUP PLC

The case presented here is a shortened, summarized and updated version of the case reported in Sparks (1990). It is possible now

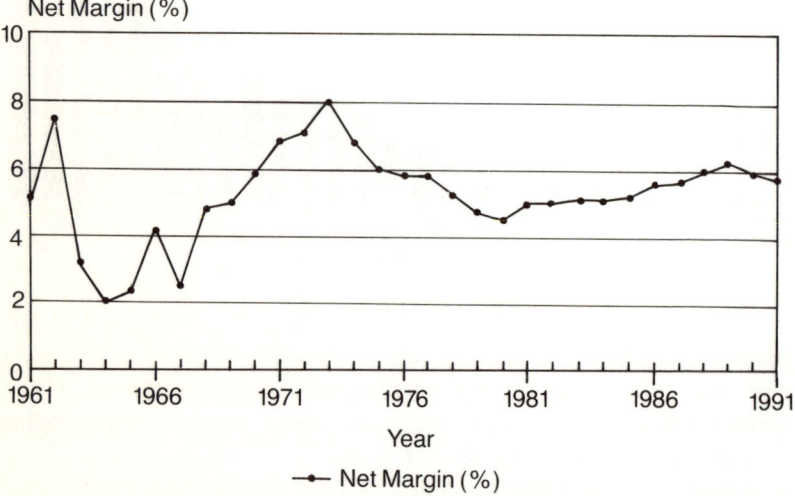

Figure 4.6 Kwik Save Group plc: net margin, 1961–91

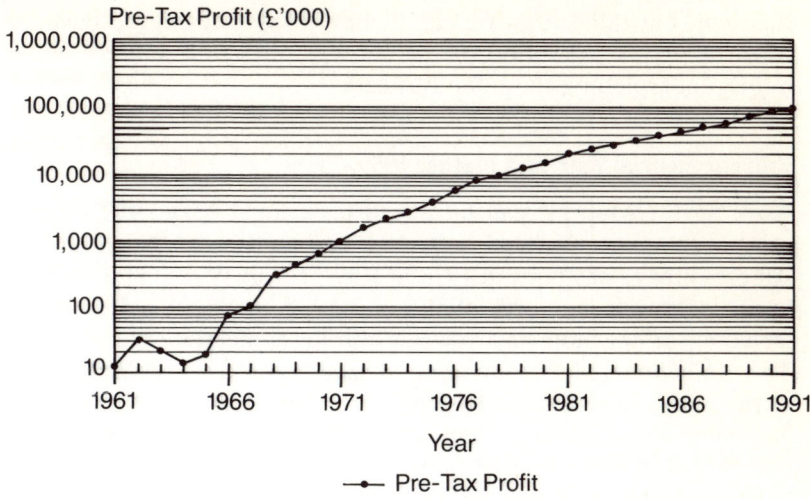

Figure 4.7 Kwik Save Group plc: pre-tax profit, 1961–91

Table 4.4 The Kwik Save Charter

- The more efficiently we operate the more our customers benefit from the best prices.
- We only sell top brands and top sellers, and never compromise on quality.
- We will always use our buying power to keep costs to a minimum and pass on the savings through our everyday low prices.
- We will operate smaller, efficient stores that are easy to shop at and easy to get to.
- We will not insult you with frills or gimmicks which the customer ends up paying for.
- We believe that all this adds up to the best value grocery shopping in the country.

Source: Kwik Save Advertisements, e.g. *Daily Mail*, 21 November 1991, p. 51; Annual Report 1991, p. 5.

(admittedly with an element of hindsight) to see a change in the company around 1987 which makes the disaggregation of the case into three rather than two sections as previously more logical. These sections are:

1 entrepreneurial flair and hiatus, 1959–73;
2 maturation and ageing, 1973–87;
3 new blood and new challenges, 1987 to date.

74 *The rise and fall of mass marketing*

It is not suggested that the timings of these phases or sections are clear-cut, but rather that we can identify tendencies in the business which allow consideration of the strategic direction and consumer trends underpinning the retail business.

Entrepreneurial flair and hiatus, 1959–73

Kwik Save Group plc can be traced back to 11 May 1959 when a private company, Value Foods Ltd was registered. The founder, Albert Gubay, was born in 1928 in Rhyl, North Wales, and began a business career in North Wales involving a variety of activities including selling non-sugar sweets during confectionery rationing. The confectionery business began to have difficulties in the late 1950s as rationing ended and Gubay moved into retailing via market stalls and then a rented grocery shop in Rhyl. Value Foods Ltd represented a further step down a retail path.

Value Foods Ltd was based in Prestatyn in North Wales and opened its first traditional-style grocery shop in Rhyl in July 1959. The first supermarket operated by the company opened in Prestatyn in 1962 and was claimed to be the first drive-in supermarket in the UK. Supermarkets then became the main business of the company. These stores were nothing exceptional in size or turnover, although there was a reliance on the provision of car parking and the (then) dubious activities of late night opening and price cutting below the manufacturers' recommended re-sale price (Fulop 1964).

The real starting point, however, for Kwik Save came after a trip by Albert Gubay, Ken Nicholson (another Value Foods director) and Ian Howe to the United States in late 1964/early 1965. In the USA they learnt about 'baby shark' retailing, the selling at very low prices but high volume of a limited range of nationally branded goods, from small 'stripped-down' stores, particularly in the drugstore market. Enthused by the possibilities Gubay translated the idea, together with some operating ideas gained from Aldi food stores in West Germany, into a 2,000 sq ft food supermarket at Colwyn Bay trading as Kwik Save Discount. So successful was this unit that the remaining stores were converted to the format and the company moved over totally to limited-range food discount retailing. With growth coming in the next five years from new stores in converted garages, cinemas, showrooms and churches the company moved steadily forward. Growth was aided by the abolition of resale price maintenance in the mid-1960s, which helped retail entrepreneurs develop their skills in buying and selling. Store size also increased towards an average of 7,000 sq ft. By 1967 there were thirteen discount stores trading as Kwik Save, based particularly in North Wales and Cheshire. These stores carried groceries, household soaps/cleaners, toiletries, sweets, bakery and textiles. Butchery and fruit and vegetable sections in some stores represented the beginnings of the use of concessions to retail certain goods (Singer and Friedlander 1970).

The company's conversion into a public company in November 1970 was preceded by a name change in July 1970 from Value Foods Ltd to Kwik Save Discount Group Ltd. Kwik Save Discount Group Ltd, at the time of flotation had twenty-four stores based in North Wales, Cheshire and Shropshire. These twenty-four outlets had 115,000 sq ft of selling space and made profits of £643,000 on turnover of £11 million.

The basic idea behind the Kwik Save retail operation was a classically simple one. The company believed that customers could be attracted and their needs satisfied by offering basic goods at very competitive prices. This pricing stance was particularly appealing to low-income customers. It is difficult to obtain price data for this early period, but figures from a variety of sources (Thorpe 1972; Livesey 1979) mention Kwik Save as being cheap, whilst since 1977, when *Which?* included Kwik Save in their surveys for the first time, the company has always been at or very near the top (cheapest). Thorpe (1972), in a study of prices in discount stores and superstores, found Kwik Save to be the cheapest. The competitive pricing policies were enabled by a number of interconnected factors.

The first element was the 'stripped-to-basics' approach of the stores. Fixtures, fittings and fascias were basic with the goods sold from manufacturers' cardboard boxes placed on pallets or wooden shelving designed, built and fitted in-house. Stock was often held above the shelves, allowing easy restocking and minimizing warehouse and storage space. There was nothing sophisticated or fancy about the stores. As Tanburn (1974: 51) notes 'Kwik Save offer a very limited range of products . . . and literally dump them in opened outers for customers to help themselves. The grocery area . . . looks like a warehouse or shed'.

The second element was that of control, with the company dedicated to tight control of operations. Computers were an integral part of the company from almost the beginning, and the company also moved early into central distribution, a process enabled by the technology. Both centralized distribution and extensive computerization were innovations in food retailing at this time. In particular, the company introduced a sophisticated computer-based stock control system, again developed in-house which enabled stock levels to be kept to a minimum and orders and deliveries to be computer processed. Centralized buying and particularly centralized distribution produced further cost savings, through better deals, less pilferage, lower stock levels and better use of stock space. Control of costs produced low overheads, low operating costs, low staffing costs including management and a dedication to low levels of shrinkage (Singer and Friedlander 1970). Kwik Save also operated its own fleet of vehicles, garage facilities, joinery and waste-paper baling stations, further reducing costs. By controlling the business centrally as much as possible and by standardizing operating procedures across the outlets, Gubay de-skilled the store management task.

The third element was that of buying muscle combined with a reliance on manufacturer branded goods. In spite of being small, the company had considerable buying muscle through the very rapid stockturn and large volume on a small number of items. This was linked to a decision not to use own-brand or generic products but to buy aggressively from manufacturers and pass on the savings to the customers. Only a very limited range of packaged goods (about 450 lines), all manufacturer brands but mainly second-line national brands, was sold. Stocking policy for goods was dependent on the price deal to be obtained. If this was not good enough then the line was not stocked. Cheapness was the driving motivation. There were no tailored promotions or special offers in the stores and manufacturers' representatives were not permitted to merchandise. The strategy of 'loss leaders' was not often pursued but rather prices were discounted across the entire range, with all goods being sold very cheaply (Singer and Friedlandler 1970; Thorpe 1972) at a price equivalent to or better than other companies' 'specials'. The idea, as Gubay stated, was 'not to sell cheap groceries but to sell groceries cheaply'. The limited-range approach allowed the removal of item pricing, replacing it with shelf-edge pricing and requiring the check-out operators to memorize the prices, through the use of a limited number of pricing points. Staff costs were kept low and the trolley-to-trolley checkout operation allowed rapid flow through the checkout.

The final element was that of risk reduction through the use of concessions in the store to cover the goods that Kwik Save itself did not want to and could not handle, i.e. the non-packaged sectors such as fresh meat, fruit, vegetables and bread. This approach reduced the risk by allowing Kwik Save to concentrate on the procedures it did best, but also provided the company with a range of products in the store and as importantly, with rental income. The rental paid to Kwik

Save by a concession was based on the turnover of the Kwik Save unit, which was an unusual practice. In the main the concessions were run by independent traders or small companies.

Kwik Save introduced discount food retailing as an innovation in Britain, although discounting itself was being practised by several food retailers including superstore operators. The difference for Kwik Save and other northern-based discounters (e.g. Asda and Wm Morrison) was that they offered price cuts on far more products than established retailers and did not use selective price cuts, loss leaders or trading stamps (Thorpe 1972). At a time of high inflation this was to give them a clear advantage over the other food retailers, which were changing and were forced to change prices regularly (Livesey 1979). These discount companies were at this time minor parts of the British food retailing scene (Thorpe 1972; Akehurst 1983, 1984; Livesey 1979; Davies and Sparks 1986).

At flotation in 1970, Kwik Save, whilst small, had a proven formula that apparently suited the needs of particularly working-class consumers in North Wales, Merseyside and Lancashire. The problem was to translate that success into a retail company for the 1970s and 1980s. Much of this success in the 1960s can be attributed to the chairman Albert Gubay. His retailing know-how had begun and driven the company, overcome problems of operation (as shown by the data in Figs 4.6 and 4.7 for the 1960s), and the flotation was as much a statement of confidence in 'the controversial Welshman' Gubay as in Kwik Save.

Albert Gubay was a very high-profile and controversial director who was perhaps too individual, forthright and independent to be 'shackled' by institutional investors. He very much wanted to be his own boss. At the same time he wanted to turn his paper profits into capital and also felt alienated and penalized by the tax structure. At the time of flotation, control of Kwik Save rested firmly in Albert Gubay's hands with his family retaining about 45 per cent of the shares. In April/May 1972 the Gubay family sold about 27 per cent of the total Kwik Save shares worth approximately £7.4 million although Albert Gubay remained as a director and declared his intention to retain the remaining shares (about 15 per cent) as a permanent holding. In December 1972, Gubay stepped aside from the chairmanship and became a non-executive director. This move was symptomatic of Gubay distancing himself from the business and in early January 1973 Gubay's remaining shareholding was disposed of and he left the country to go to New Zealand. These last sales and emigration apparently came as a shock to the company and their financial advisers (Department of Trade and Industry 1974). His position as the '*bête noire*' of British food retailing was confirmed. Since leaving Britain, Gubay has founded, run and sold retail chains in New Zealand, Ireland and the USA (Lord *et al.* 1988).

For the Kwik Save Discount Group the immediate problem in 1973 was that the perception of the company was synonymous with Gubay and few institutions or shareholders believed that there was life after the founder. Gubay's 'walk-out' forced Kwik Save to manage a crisis of confidence, if not operations, where control was really invested in the systems. It took several years for the company to convince the City that Kwik Save could survive and, more importantly, prosper. Gubay's departure also came at the time of the peak per cent profit margin and subsequent decline reinforced the City's suspicions. In the longer term Kwik Save had to convince investors and the public that their brand of retailing could be developed beyond the North Wales/Cheshire area, and that the company could manage this expansion.

Maturation and ageing, 1973–87

The company that Gubay left behind had to convince the City of its value and its operating performance. Immediately after flotation and Gubay's departure, the net margin was driven lower as Kwik Save came under pressure both within the company and through the more difficult and government restricted trading conditions of the 1970s. In one sense the 1970s was beneficial to Kwik Save's brand of discount retailing as consumers were more price conscious, but on the other hand inflation and product shortages as well as government controls made trading difficult. Food price inflation was above 10 per cent per annum for the majority of the period 1972–82, being particularly high in 1974–7 when annual food inflation reached 25 per cent (Figs 4.8 and 4.9). Price-consciousness amongst consumers rose considerably at this time, especially among the lower paid.

Kwik Save steadily increased its store numbers (Fig. 4.4); in the 1980s, for example, on average at least one store per fortnight opened. The expansion over this period was mainly organic growth with the exception of a 1978 takeover of the forty-nine unit strong Cee-n-Cee supermarket chain. More recently there has been the acquisition of Tates (1986) which bought twelve food shops, fourteen wine shops and six convenience stores and also the purchase of twenty-three Dee Corporation units (1987).

The change in the company was marked. From its entrepreneurial

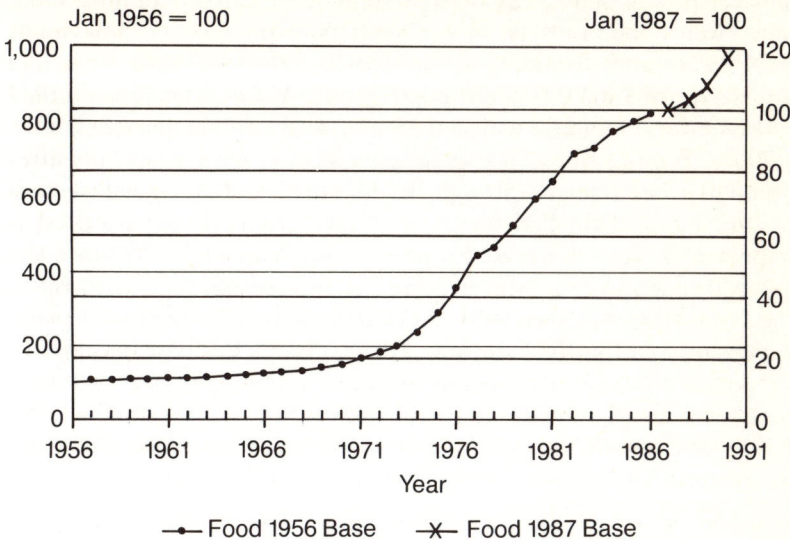

Figure 4.8 Retail prices in UK, 1956–90

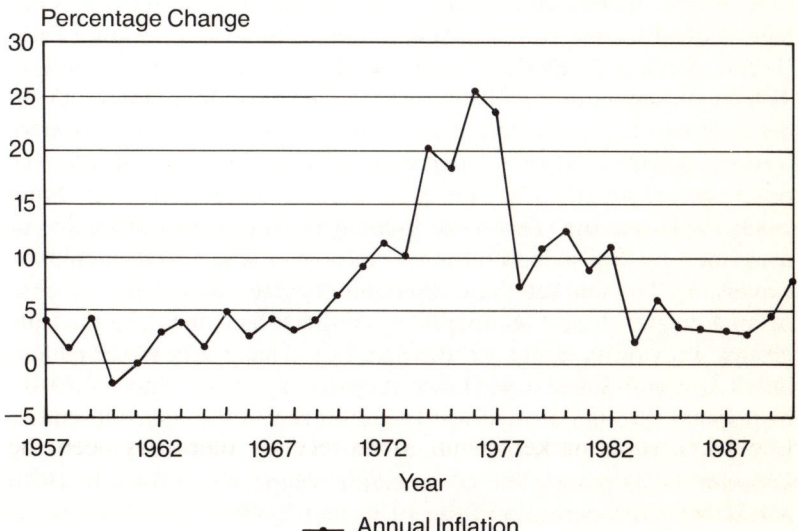

Figure 4.9 Food price inflation in UK, 1957–90

beginnings, Kwik Save had grown to have a turnover of £11 million and net profits before tax of £0.64 million in 1970. It retailed from only twenty-four outlets with a sales floorspace of 115,000 sq ft. There were approximately 450 employees. By 1987 Kwik Save had a turnover of £862.0 million, made profits of £46.6 million, retailed from almost 590 units, with 3.0 million sq ft of floorspace and over 7,700 FTE employees. The management of change from the entrepreneurial beginnings, through the hiatus of Gubay's goodbye to a mature retail chain had been safely and profitably achieved. It is important to consider how this process was managed. This is undertaken through first, a brief overview of the general food industry in the 1970s and 1980s, secondly, an examination of Kwik Save's spatial expansion and thirdly, a review of Kwik Save's business operations.

Akehurst (1984) has examined food retailing in the 1970s in particular and has pointed to the difficulties many retailers were facing. Such problems led to the introduction of Operation Checkout by Tesco in 1977 which, as Bamfield (1980: 41) states:

> marks a change in retail techniques, particularly promotional methods, rather than being a temporary phenomenon after which retail prices might return to normal . . . the response to a change in consumer buying habits as reflected in the rapid growth of low cost discounters.

The success of discounters such as Asda with superstores and Kwik Save with discount stores brought conflict to food retailing. Their success produced imitators from established food retailers through Tesco with superstores and Shoppers Paradise and Key Discount with discount stores. Expansion of Asda and Kwik Save brought conflict through spatial expansion of trading areas and traditional selective price cutters began to stand still in market share terms (Akehurst 1983, 1984). Across the board discount pricing, whilst attractive to consumers, also provided business efficiencies which in turn enabled expansion. The market share discounters gained was at the expense of independents and cooperatives rather than the big multiple groups. Previously, however, this gain would have gone to companies like Tesco and Sainsbury. Hence the need for Tesco and Sainsbury to respond through a price war based on across the board discounting. The success of Kwik Save at this time is well-marked by the adoption of its pricing stance by major companies in the late 1970s and its style of operation in the 1970s and 1980s.

Kwik Save was imitated by many operators. Some were limited-range discounters from the 1960s. Most of these did not expand as fast as Kwik Save and were taken over or failed, such as Discount Foods Ltd which became one of the bases for Oriel Foods and thus Argyll and finally Safeway. Of the discount operators listed by Thorpe (1972) only three of nine companies remain in operation, and two of these operate superstores. Other imitators were set up as trading arms of major retailers. This does not mean that imitation brought success, as the problems of KD Discount (Key Markets), Pricerite (International), Shoppers Paradise (Fine Fare) and Victor Value (Tesco, Bejam and finally Kwik Save) amongst others show. All of these operations have been sold or closed down. Limited-range discount operations are difficult to run profitably and successfully and the success of Kwik Save is impressive. This emphasizes the importance of being the first and the best.

The expansion of the Kwik Save Discount Group can also be viewed in spatial terms. In 1967, when the discount store format had been fully accepted by the company, as has been seen there were thirteen branches trading as Kwik Save Discount, mainly in North Wales, but with some expansion into Cheshire. By 1970 the company had twenty-four units trading in North Wales, Cheshire and Shropshire with the headquarters and distribution depot remaining at Prestatyn. Expansion was also aided by the further extension of the motorway network. It is often forgotten that at this period, physical distribution could not rely on good infrastructure and spatial expansion was often geared to infrastructure investment. By 1974 the beginnings of the move away from the 'heartland' of Prestatyn, North Wales can be clearly discerned and by 1977 there was a clear drive southwards and into South Wales, continuing the spatial transformation of the company. The late 1970s and the 1980s saw further expansion southwards and northwards within England and Wales. Since 1985 Kwik Save has also entered the important London and South-East area. At the same time Kwik Save's strategy encompassed the 'in-filling' of existing trading areas with newer and more stores.

Kwik Save also expanded away from its 'traditional' food supermarket. Since 1984 a freezer centre component – Arctic – has been operating, initially adjacent but now within existing Kwik Save units. There are also Late Shopper convenience stores which were originally part of Tates; relatively limited expansion of this format (1991 – sixty-nine stores) has occurred. The previous reliance on outside concessions has been reduced with a subsidiary, Colemans Meat (purchased in 1980), and an in-house drinks unit, Best of Cellars, being common concessions.

The transition from an entrepreneurial-led small company to a significant corporate retailer has also seen changes in structural elements of the business as well as spatial expansion. However, at a broad level the company has remained faithful to Gubay's original principles. This may be due in part to the presence on the board of several directors who started out with Gubay in the 1960s and early 1970s. In two particular aspects, Kwik Save has remained faithful to the original principles. First, Kwik Save still operates out of small units. The average selling space of a Kwik Save supermarket is only approximately 6,250 sq ft. This is against the trend in food retailing which is for polarization into large superstores and small specialist stores (Dawson 1985). Kwik Save occupies a middle size range which many other companies ignore. Secondly, the company maintains its reliance on manufacturer branded goods and avoids the widespread trend towards own-brands. This has seen Kwik Save welcomed by manufacturers and a stocking policy based on national brands developed rather than an earlier reliance on secondary brands. As the Annual Report of 1985 states, the trading policy is one 'of offering the lowest possible prices on our range of top branded names'.

There is one other way in which Kwik Save has gone against the trends in UK food retailing; that is in its locational policy. Kwik Save is reliant on convenient locations which are often relatively central. This is against the trend generally which is to segregate food shopping away from high streets into suburban superstores. The approach of Kwik Save is to take the shops to the customer, allowing Kwik Save to run several shops in a town where other retailers have been withdrawing to the edge of town or closing their presence completely. This also reflects the smaller catchment area and greater walk-in trade generated by Kwik Save compared to other food multiples. This site location strategy is illustrated, for example, through the cases reported by Watkin and Joseph (1976), Guy (1987), Lillywhite (1987) and Rees (1987). The polarization of retailing and the move to out-of-town locations by other operators is seen as providing opportunities for Kwik Save to expand its operations and to fill a gap or niche in the marketplace.

In a number of other ways, however, the company has moved away from the principles of Albert Gubay and instead has followed developments in the market. First, the stores have expanded to have considerably more lines than in the past, often 1,000+ compared to the previous 450. This is still, however, vastly fewer than in a food superstore. This extension to the number of lines has caused problems with checkout operators' abilities to memorize the prices. This is particularly acute in areas where it is difficult to ensure staff quality and reliability. Laser scanning systems are now the norm, allowing further range expansion. Perhaps a more noticeable change, however, is the extension to service and design that occurred in the 1980s. Whilst it is not true to say that Kwik Save has moved completely upmarket in its positioning or as far as most superstores, it certainly has 'traded-up' in response to consumer changes. The consumer emphasis on quality and value and the new consumer perceptions which have steadily broadened have seen most firms in food retailing improve quality and value. The most notable change is Tesco's drive upmarket (Akehurst 1984), but other chains, including Kwik Save, have moved in the same direction. For Kwik Save this has meant new design, decor and layout and refurbishment of stores and staff attitudes. Whilst prices are still keen, and the differential with other chains has probably been maintained, the emphasis is less on discount, a fact recognized by a change in name in January 1986 to Kwik Save Group plc (from Kwik Save Discount Group plc) and the disappearance of 'Discount' from all store fascias.

New blood and new challenges, 1987 to date

With hindsight it is possible to see that Kwik Save was beginning to stagnate in the mid-1980s. The profit growth, whilst still acceptable, was beginning to show strains and it can be suggested that new blood was needed. This was introduced in the form of a 25 per cent stake acquired by Dairy Farm International Limited, a Hong Kong company mainly owned by Jardine Matheson, and operators of retail chains in Hong Kong (Wellcome), Australia (Franklins) and Spain (Simago) amongst others, and in the persona of Graeme Seabrook who became managing director and subsequently and concurrently chief executive. Substantial board changes and restructuring occurred, with new, young management being brought into place, and the retirement of people who began with Gubay in Kwik Save in the 1960s and early 1970s. Whilst Kwik Save continues to develop along similar lines to the previous period, it is clear that the approach to the business has been overhauled and the restructuring needed to make the most of the format has been undertaken.

It has been stated that Kwik Save's current approach is based on three main areas (County NatWest WoodMac 1991): first, building on existing strengths, second, expanding sales, and third, investing in the future.

There is no question but that Kwik Save have formidable existing strengths on which to base future development. The geographical spread of the stores is now into almost every county in England and Wales, with still considerable scope for in-filling in most areas. Newspaper advertisements are running currently (November 1991) announcing the opening of the 750th Kwik Save store. The customer base is therefore considerable and there is loyalty to the company. This base is drawn from a wider social spectrum than for other companies in food retailing. The low-cost base of the operation has been important in the past, and remains a major strength. The lack of debt and the ability to extract productivity gains from labour and other assets are important underpinnings of the discount offer. With demand increases stemming from this offer, the company obtains increased efficiencies of operating which are in turn fed not into margin expansion, but into discount pricing. This virtuous wheel (County NatWest WoodMac 1991) drives the business forward.

The expansion of sales as described above in terms of existing strengths, has been a feature of the business for some time. However, sales expansion is also coming from other activities. First, the introduction of scanning systems, whilst not as important for labour productivity for Kwik Save as for other food retailers, has been important in allowing range expansion. Rather than the very limited range enforced by price memorization, laser scanning allows an expanded range of approximately 2,500 lines to be introduced into appropriate stores. At the same time, developments in marketing and in obtaining control over wines and spirits through the purchase of Liquorsave (previously an in-store concession) have enhanced sales in particular lines.

The introduction of scanning is in many senses an investment for the future, but investment is also being undertaken in other aspects of the business. Investment in people has already been noted in terms of the board and the development of a young management team. In association with scanning, investment has also taken place in systems and logistics, as for example with Kwiknet which is an integrated voice and data network which offers a high-speed digital link amongst distribution centres (the locations and facilities of which are also being upgraded). Investment is also being undertaken in stores, with older stores being replaced or refurbished and newer stores being opened at an increasing pace. In particular, opportunities to purchase the Victor Value chain (fifty-three stores) in 1989, and a portion of the Gateway chain (forty-two stores), seven Grandways outlets and eighteen R. T. Willis stores in 1991 have been grasped, providing evidence of the commitment to expansion.

Since 1987, therefore, the new blood brought in to Kwik Save has tackled the problems that were beginning to manifest themselves. The company was not in a bad way, but needed in essence a refocusing on the basics of running the leading low-cost food retailer in the country. This has been undertaken in the ways set out above. At the same time, however, it has also been a changing and challenging time in the British retail food market as a whole. New blood has entered the discount market in the form of Aldi and Netto from Continental Europe and Shoprite from the Isle of Man and new discount fascias have appeared from existing retailers such as Pioneer from the Co-operative Movement and Food Giant from Gateway. What is different about this influx is that this activity is concentrated at the lower cost end of the market, attracted by the recession in the country at large, the margins achieved in British food retailing compared (possibly unfairly) to elsewhere, and the realization that Kwik Save was essentially having the discount/low-cost market to itself.

The new challenges are therefore different to those of the past in that a direct assault on Kwik Save's position is underway. The effective polarization and segmentation of the British food market is seeing growing competition for the price-conscious shopper by new chains and formats as well as the revitalized and expansionary Kwik Save. The threats to the market are clear, and only time will tell if Kwik Save has been revitalized in time to meet the more thorough challenge of the 1990s. It does have to be remembered, however, that Kwik Save has seen off imitators and competitors before! As the Annual Report for 1991 states:

> In the last year some other UK supermarket operators have experimented on a limited scale with discount formats. . . . We believe this increased focus on discounting will lead to a growth in the discount grocery sector, and we are committed to remain the clear leader of that sector.
> (Kwik Save Annual Report 1991: 7)

DISCUSSION AND CONCLUSIONS: THE RISE AND FALL OF MASS MARKETING?

It has been argued here that in any study of marketing, retailing has to loom large as the retailers and consumers are embraced in a symbiotic relationship that encourages dependency. In understanding marketing, therefore, we have to understand retailing and consumers. It is relatively easy to identify the facts about consumer change and retail change. The study here has commented briefly on the changing consumers and food retailers between 1960 and today. The changing relationship has been explored in particular through the case study of Kwik Save Group plc. What is interesting now is to reflect on two topics: first, the relationship between this company and changing society, and in particular how the changing retailers help 'explain' the changing consumers. Secondly, it is important to reflect on the various ideas put forward by Tedlow (1990) and in particular on his three-stage model of marketing development and his six-element proposition about the movement from pre-modern to modern marketing.

Kwik Save, when it began in the late 1950s and early 1960s, was but one of many such developments, being small and relatively inconsequential. The business, however, was in tune with consumer demands of the moment. Consumers wanted to forget about the rationing and utility of the 1950s and to be able to feed the family 'properly'. Whilst rationing was one straitjacket, resale price maintenance was another and consumers wanted to be able to buy what they wanted at the cheapest available price. Kwik Save grew and prospered because it was recognized that the mood of the times was price and self-service rather than the 'traditional' approaches to food retailing. As the affluence of the 1960s expanded, so the desire was to try the products that were now available, and because of the price orientation, affordable. This movement continued in the 1970s, reinforced by periods of high inflation and the emergence of more cost-conscious consumers. As the 1970s ended, however, the 'mood' was changing and the 1980s became radically different. It is ironic that this change can be laid at the door of 'Operation Checkout' by Tesco, which began as a price-based response to the discounters, but ended up as providing the base in terms of control and systems, for Tesco to satisfy the demands of the 1980s which were reliant much more on individual rather than mass consumption and quality of life rather than price of product.

Kwik Save in the 1980s, therefore, had the role of 'shadowing' the leading retailers by providing a price-based option that enabled them to develop steadily and progressively. The symbolic dropping of 'Discount' from the group name reflects the recognition that cheap was being viewed as bad rather than sensible if pushed too hard. It has to be noted, however, that throughout this period Kwik Save found a ready market, suggesting that segments of the population valued their brand-based, locally focused, cheap but sensible approach. The overriding tendency in British food retailing, however, was towards a unification of the market, with only 'shades' of differentiation.

The rise and fall of mass marketing? 87

The recession of the late 1980s and early 1990s has produced another change in 'mood', or so the newcomers to the discount market hope. Lured by the possibilities in the cases of Shoprite, Aldi and Netto and driven by necessity in the cases of the Co-operative Movement and Gateway, the discount market is currently the focus of much activity. In fact, however, it can be suggested that a polarization (segmentation) of the food marketplace is taking place. Whilst there always have been low-cost and high-price operators in food retailing, the position now is that a schism may be occurring. Tesco, Sainsbury and Safeway are on the extensive-range, high-quality end of the spectrum with Kwik Save and the newcomers on the low-price, value-for-money end. In the middle are Gateway and Asda who will need to make hard decisions. A real segmentation is now emerging (see Table 4.3). The interesting questions are whether the discounters can attract consumers away from the high-quality end of the market as well as their 'natural' market and whether the high-quality end will be sucked into a potentially seriously damaging price war. Much will depend on the consumers' perceptions of their economic position and their commitment to continuing the quality lifestyle of the 1980s.

As Kwik Save provide an illustrated guide to the changing fortunes of food retailing and consumers since 1960, so too they provide a mechanism to test Tedlow's propositions. Tedlow's three phases of marketing see a move from fragmentation through unification to segmentation. In terms of food retailing generally it is possible to see this progression for Britain. The initial fragmentation and the ensuing unification are very clear. The argument is that it is at this time that real segmentation is emerging. Previous segmentation strategies in food retailing have not had this national focus, being more restricted in their aim. If, however, the discount market is the scale of enquiry then this progression becomes less clear as there is now an element of segmentation emerging (Aldi versus Food Giant which have different branding, scale and other characteristics for example), but at the same time it is possible to argue that the current changes are really the elements of unification falling into place. In this model, the current changes herald the emergence of a national discount sector and the unification of this marketplace. This potential variation depending on the scale of enquiry is interesting as it focuses attention on the possible inter-linking mechanisms of the scales of enquiry, and also on the belief that the phases are a reflection of business imperatives.

Tedlow's second proposition is that there are six elements that are important in the development of modern marketing. It is useful to look at Kwik Save in the light of these. These elements are profit through volume, entrepreneurial vision, vertical system, first-movers and entry barriers, competitors' options, and managing change. Each of these can be examined in turn.

The source of profit for any business is important and Tedlow argues that it is profit from volume sales that is essential for modern marketing. Kwik Save has built its entire business around this element. The volume base for the business was recognized as crucial from the outset, and today it is clear that it is the volume generated that underpins the strategy and the performance. The second element. entrepreneurial vision, is very clear in the study of Kwik Save. It is embodied in Albert Gubay in terms of founding the business, and there can be little doubt that Gubay was critical in its development. However, the performance of the business after his departure is testimony both to the strength of the vision and also the people remaining who carried it out. It is only in the mid-1980s that the vision begins to falter and the need for new blood and restructuring are recognized. Again, one person, Graeme Seabrook, is in place to implement the new vision, which whilst not entrepreneurial in the real sense, is a continuation of important entrepreneurial principles.

The need for a vertical system is the third element of Tedlow's proposition. Vertical systems can take many forms (Dawson and Shaw 1989; Traill 1989), but the Kwik Save case illustrates the importance that company placed on links and relationships with product suppliers and on the early development of central distribution. The reliance on branded goods enhances their stature with the main brand manufacturers and the volume generated ensures good buying and distribution terms. The fourth element of first-movers and entry barriers can be combined with consideration of the fifth, competitors' options. Kwik Save, as a company early into the marketplace, certainly gained some first-mover advantages, particularly when combined with the publicity abilities of Albert Gubay. As the virtuous circle of prices improving volume improving efficiencies improving prices turns, so too the problems for any competitor mount. This circle provides barriers to entry in the form of business efficiencies. In one sense this entry barrier is akin to the strategy proportion of Michael Porter; that it is necessary to be *the* low-cost operator in the market if price is the strategy (see Sparks 1990, for a discussion of Kwik Save in this context). In this case, once this could be demonstrated, the barriers were up for entrants. As time progressed and the market moved, so the offer could be amended to reflect the changing circumstances. In terms of competitors, the early Kwik Save attracted imitators and there were examples of 'me-too'. However, in such an industry, the lowest cost operator is key, and business efficiencies sustained over a long period faced down many of the competitors. In food retailing generally, the 'competition' made itself distinct with the range extensions etc. of food superstores. As the market has changed again in the late 1980s with new entrants to the discount/low-cost end of the market, similar distinctions can be drawn. The competition has avoided Kwik Save to some extent, although this avoidance will not last. Food Giant from Gateway is different in size and range; Aldi uses Continental brands to ensure price leadership; Shoprite has a locational avoidance strategy focused on Scotland. In most cases too, the decor of the store is modelled on early Kwik Save operations rather than current ones.

Finally, Tedlow focuses on the need for managing change. What the Kwik Save case shows is that the general change in the marketplace is managed satisfactorily for a long period. Eventually, however, there comes a time when new blood and a new approach is needed. Without the changes introduced in the late 1980s it is doubtful whether Kwik Save could be the force it is now. The future is interesting for the company because of the changes going on in its marketplace. Without the restructuring the battle would be a lot harder.

In terms of the six elements, it can be seen that Kwik Save illustrates the importance of all of these through their development as a business. What perhaps is underplayed in the list of elements, however, is the focus on understanding the customer that is essential to any business involved with marketing. Whilst not explicitly an element, it can be seen that the issues of consumer change and requirements flow through these elements of modern marketing. This leads on to another consideration for the phases of marketing. The major requirement for any business is understanding and knowing its customers. To do this properly, particularly in a segmented marketplace, will probably require moving towards personal knowledge of consumers. Is there a fourth phase of individual (micro) marketing to follow the segmentation phase? Certainly the technology is in place in food retailing to allow such a move at a cost-effective level.

Food retailing is a critical sector of the economy both for consumers and retailers. The efficiency and effectiveness of the food retail sector has also been seen, rightly or wrongly, as a test of government ability. Mass marketing has developed in the food industry, but may now be breaking down as the market segments and changes. One thing is certain: food retailing is so critical that the current changes are unlikely to be the last.

REFERENCES

Akehurst, G. (1983) 'Concentration in retail distribution: measurement and significance', *Service Industries Journal* 3(2): 161–79.
—— (1984) 'Checkout: the analysis of oligopolistic behaviour in the UK grocery retail market', *Service Industries Journal* 4(2): 198–242.
Baden-Fuller, C.W.F. (1986) 'Rising concentration in the UK grocery trade 1970–80', in K. Tucker and C.W.F. Baden-Fuller (eds) *Firms and Markets*, London: Croom Helm.
Bamfield, J.A.N. (1980) 'The changing face of British retailing', *National Westminster Bank Quarterly Review*, May.
Beaumont, J. (1987) 'Trends in food retailing', in E. McFadyen (ed.) *The Changing Face of British Retailing*, London: Newman Books, pp. 52–63.
Bowlby, S.R. (1984) 'Planning for women to shop in post-war Britain', *Environment and Planning D* 12: 179–99.
Burt, S.L. (1989) 'Trends and management issues in European retailing', *International Journal of Retailing* 4(4): 1–97.
—— (1991) 'Trends in the internationalisation of grocery retailing: the European experience', *International Review of Retail, Distribution and Consumer Research* 1(4): 487–515.
County NatWest WoodMac (1991) *Kwik Save Group PLC: The Choice is Obvious*, London: Authors.
Davies, B.K. and Sparks, L. (1986) 'ASDA-MFI: the superstore and the flat-pack', *International Journal of Retailing* 1(1): 55–78.
Davies, B.K. and Sparks, L. (1989) 'The development of superstore retailing in Great Britain 1960–1986', *Transactions of the Institute of British Geographers* 14(1): 74–89.
Davies, B.K., Gilligan, C. and Sutton, C. (1985) 'Structural changes in grocery retailing: the implications for competition', *International Journal of Physical Distribution and Materials Management* 15(2): 1–48.
Davies, B.K., Gilligan, C. and Sutton, C. (1986) 'The development of own label product strategies in grocery and DIY retailing in the UK', *International Journal of Retailing* 1(1): 6–19.
Davis, E. and Kay, J. (1990) 'Assessing corporate performance', *Business Strategy Review*, Summer, 1–16.
Dawson, J.A. (1981) 'Innovation adoption in food retailing – the example of self-service methods', *Service Industries Journal* 1(2): 22–35.
—— (1984) 'Structural–spatial relationships in the spread of hypermarket retailing', in E. Kaynak and R. Savitt (eds) *Comparative Marketing Systems*, New York: Praeger, pp. 156–82.
—— (1985) 'Structural change in European retailing: the polarisation of operating scale', in E. Kaynak (ed.) *Global Perspectives in Marketing*, New York: Praeger, pp. 211–29.
—— (1987) 'The evolution of UK food retailing: inventory, prospect and research challenges', paper presented at the Twelfth Annual Macromarketing Conference, Montreal.

—— (1988) 'Futures for the high street', *The Geographical Journal* 154(1): 1–12.
Dawson, J.A. and Broadbridge, A.M. (1988) *Retailing in Scotland 2005*, Institute for Retail Studies, University of Stirling.
Dawson, J.A. and Shaw, S.A., (1989) 'The move to administered vertical marketing systems by British retailing', *European Journal of Marketing* 23(7): 42–52.
Department of Trade and Industry (1974) *Kwik Save Discount Group Limited*, London: HMSO.
Duke, R. (1991) 'Post-saturation competition in UK grocery retailing', *Journal of Marketing Management* 7: 63–75.
Fanselow, F.S. (1990) 'The bazaar economy or how bizarre is the bazaar really?', *Man (N.S.)* 25: 250–65.
Fulop, C. (1964) *Competition for Consumers*, London: André Deutsch.
Gardner, C. and Sheppard, J. (1989) *Consuming Passion: the rise of retail culture*, London: Unwin Hyman.
Gershuny, J.I. (1978) *After Industrial Society*, Basingstoke: Macmillan.
—— (1983) *Social Innovation and the Division of Labour*, Oxford: Oxford University Press.
Guy, C.M. (1987) 'Accessibility to multiple-owned grocery stores in Cardiff: a description and evaluation of recent changes', *Planning Practice and Research* 2: 9–15.
Halsey, A.H. (1988) *British Social Trends Since 1900*, Basingstoke: Macmillan.
IGD (1990) *Food Retailing '90*, Watford: Institute of Grocery Distribution.
Jefferys, J.B. (1954) *Retail Trading in Britain, 1850–1950*, Cambridge: Cambridge University Press.
Lewis, P. and Thomas, H. (1990) 'The link between strategy, strategic groups and performance in the UK retail grocery industry', *Strategic Management Journal* 11: 385–97.
Lillywhite, J. (1987) 'Equity considerations in the location of retail food outlets', paper presented at Planning Practice and Research Conference, Cardiff, January.
Livesey, F. (1979) *The Distributive Trades*, London: Heinemann.
Lord, J.D. and Guy, C.M. (1991) 'Comparative retail structure of British and American cities: Cardiff (UK) and Charlotte (USA)', *International Review of Retail, Distribution and Consumer Research* 1(4): 391–436.
Lord, J.D., Moran, W., Parker, A.J. and Sparks, L. (1988) 'Retailing on three continents: the discount food store operations of Albert Gubay', *International Journal of Retailing* 3(3): 1–54.
McClelland, W.G. (1962) 'The supermarket and society', *The Sociological Review* 10: 133–44.
—— (1963) *Studies in Retailing*, Oxford: Blackwell.
—— (1990) 'Economies of scale in British food retailing, in C. Moir and J.A. Dawson (eds) *Competition and Markets*, Basingstoke: Macmillan: 119–40.
McGoldrick, P.J. (1984) 'Grocery generics – an extension of the private label concept', *European Journal of Marketing* 18(3): 63–76.
McKinnon, A.C. (1985) 'The distribution systems of supermarket chains', *Service Industries Journal* 5(2): 226–38.
Manchester Business School (1987) *UK Grocery Retailing*, Manchester: Authors.

Marwick, A. (1982) *British Social Trends since 1900*, Basingstoke: Macmillan.
Mathias, P. (1967) *Retailing Revolution*, London: Longmans.
Mintel (1991) 'Food retailing', *Mintel Retail Intelligence*, issue 1.
Moir, C. (1990) 'Competition in the UK grocery trades', in C. Moir and J.A. Dawson (eds) *Competition and Markets*, Basingstoke: Macmillan: 91–118.
Mui, H.-C. and Mui, L.H. (1989) *Shops and Shopkeeping in Eighteenth Century England*, Montreal and London: McGill University and Routledge.
Powell, D. (1991) *Counter Revolution: the Tesco Story*, London: Grafton Books.
Quarmby, D.A. (1989) 'Developments in the retail market and their effect on freight distribution', *Journal of Transport Economics and Policy* 23(1): 75–87.
Rees, J. (1987) 'Social polarisation in shopping patterns: an example from Swansea', paper presented at Planning Practice and Research Conference, Cardiff, January.
Shaw, S.A., Nisbet, D.J. and Dawson, J.A. (1989) 'Economies of scale in UK supermarkets: some preliminary findings', *International Journal of Retailing* 4(5): 12–26.
Singer and Friedlander (1970) *Offer for Sale: Kwik Save Discount Group Ltd.*
Sparks, L. (1986) 'The changing structure of distribution in retail companies', *Transactions of the Institute of British Geographers* 11(2): 147–54.
—— (1990) 'Spatial–structural relationships in retail corporate growth: a case study of Kwik Save Group PLC', *Service Industries Journal* 10(1): 25–84.
—— (1992) 'Physical distribution management', in W.S. Howe (ed.) *Retailing Management*, Basingstoke: Macmillan, chapter 7.
Stacey, N.A.H. and Wilson, A. (1965) *The Changing Pattern of Distribution* (2nd edn), Oxford: Pergamon.
Tanburn, J. (1974) *Retailing and the Competitive Challenge*, London: Lintas.
Tedlow, R. (1990) *New and Improved: the Story of Mass Marketing in America*, Oxford: Heinemann.
Thorpe, D. (1972) 'Food prices: a study of some northern discount and superstores', *Retail Outlets Research Unit Report* no. 5.
—— (1990) 'Economic theory, retail output and capacity in British retailing', in C. Moir and J.A. Dawson (eds) *Competition and Markets*, Basingstoke: Macmillan: 153–206.
—— (1991) 'The development of British superstore retailing – further comments on Davies and Sparks', *Transactions of the Institute of British Geographers* 16(3): 354–67.
Traill, B. (ed.) (1989) *Prospects for the European Food System*, Barking: Elsevier.
Watkin, D.G. and Joseph, M.E. (1976) 'The day of the discounter', *Retail and Distribution Management* 4(4): 24–9.

5 Marketing and business history, in theory and practice

T.A.B. Corley

INTRODUCTION

As business historians increasingly face the problem of how to turn their subject into an academic discipline, with its own methodology and analytical tools, one question above all will concern them. Have some of its basic elements so altered over time that they are not amenable to overall analysis?

To give one or two examples of such elements: was the firm on the eve of Britain's industrial revolution radically different from the large corporation of today, so that the workshop discussed by Adam Smith (1776) had little in common with the very much more elaborate entity which Chamberlin (1933) or, say, Scherer (1980) analysed? Have the functions of the entrepreneur changed so greatly that the individual described by Cantillon (1755) or Say (1803) bears scarcely any resemblance to the subject of Casson's theoretical work (1982)? If corporate size, the scope of the market, the competitive environment, the sophistication of technology, the types of raw materials, the methods of organization and control and managerial techniques of the typical enterprise have changed out of all recognition over the past two centuries, then any theory that tried to offer explanations and predictions would have to be so general as to yield few, if any, worthwhile findings. Such an outcome would greatly reduce the opportunity of forging links between business historians – except for those covering relatively brief time periods – and economists.

This dilemma seems particularly acute in relation to marketing, which in most people's minds is essentially a twentieth-century phenomenon. In earlier times, was there an absence of marketing practices that could be usefully related to those of today? Alternatively, are there certain fundamental principles which underlie all marketing activities, from those of the huckster at the local market calling his own wares, to those of giant firms with globally celebrated products, as described by Richard Tedlow in Chapter 2?

Tedlow's exposition there of the four phases of consumer product marketing in the United States since independence is the latest example of the way in which American business and economic historians have tended to concentrate on marketing developments over time rather than to seek common principles applicable to all phases. Among these were two pioneering works of the 1970s. Porter and Livesay (1971) showed how greatly the marketing of manufactured products changed in the US during the nineteenth century, from being undertaken by sedentary merchants in all but local markets to being increasingly taken over by the manufacturers themselves, as the characteristics of both products and markets altered. Chandler (1977: 485) carried the analysis further by exploring in depth the organizational changes from which the modern American business enterprise evolved, namely the coordination of flows of goods down the vertical sequence of production and distribution. The marketing revolution sprang from the need for multi-unit enterprises to ensure the sale to final customers of the greatly expanded volume of goods, made possible by technological developments.

In an authoritative survey of marketing from the economic and business historians' viewpoint, Porter (1980) helpfully summarized relevant changes in the US. While he cited Levitt's definition, 'Marketing is not just a business function. It is a consolidating view of the entire business process' (Levitt 1969: vii), as a very mild exaggeration, he did not offer any marketing principles as such. Tedlow, in *New and Improved* (1990: 5) has admitted that marketing is an elusive subject, 'difficult to discuss because it is difficult to define', comprehending as it does such a wide range of activities from logistics to the 'purest speculation' regarding people's wants and willingness to pay for the gratification of such wants. Hence Tedlow sought generalizations along historical lines of broad 'tendencies in the evolution of market strategy' rather than about the fundamental roots of marketing conduct.

In Chapter 2, Tedlow admits (p. 10) that 'some aspects of marketing never change', since the basic bargaining system between 'someone who has a need to be filled and someone else who claims to have just the thing to fill it' has remained the same ever since the exchange economy developed. However, he also states (p. 25) that consumer product marketing in the US in 1970 was fundamentally different from that in the 1920s, the difference being 'not only in degree but in kind', given the large increase both in the number of products on offer and also in techniques such as market segmentation, springing from advances in psychology as well as in statistical methods which turned marketing research into such a powerful tool.

While it is indeed true that very far-reaching changes have taken place, the questions which Tedlow asks seem to be of universal validity. Why have a few products achieved success with consumers while most fail? What was the secret of these rare successes? Can some firms, by astute marketing, 'foist a product on unwilling customers and change the will of the customer'? Alternatively, was success due to, say, the entrepreneur spotting the potential advantage of bucking a trend and using skill and intelligence to secure that advantage? So far, international 'business history' comparisons of marketing practices have been rare. Iwata (1974: 177ff.), although specifying his model in the conventional economic terms of competition and monopoly, found that mechanistic connections between such market forms and marketing policies, or between strategies and structures in marketing, were less significant than entrepreneurial initiatives, especially those designed to overcome institutional and other obstacles.

To date, the view of business historians seems to be that the momentous developments in marketing are of greater interest and significance than the pursuit of any all-encompassing generalizations. In the next section, the opposite viewpoint of economists will be investigated. Then the basic principles of marketing will be discussed, followed by a section showing how the application of these principles could play a role in strengthening business history. After two illustrative case studies of British consumer goods firms, the final section offers some tentative conclusions on this important topic.

ECONOMIC THEORY AND MARKETING

In the present chapter, the topic of marketing is examined in the context of its possible use in helping business history to become a discipline. What contribution could economics make, for instance, in providing an analytical framework? Regrettably, during most of this century, mainstream economists have tended to neglect marketing. The reason has been given in a widely used textbook on 'the firm in a modern context' (Koutsoyiannis 1982: 51–2). This discussed corporate behaviour in the various market forms. In conditions of perfect competition, marketing was unnecessary, since by definition a firm could sell as much as it chose at the competitive price, which it was too small to affect. Marketing was of limited use to pure monopolists, who might resort to advertising so as to make the demand for their products less elastic, thus seeking to increase monopoly profits by raising prices. Only in the case of oligopoly would advertising be attractive as a weapon against rivals. 'However, because all oligopolists have the same incentives for advertising, a substantial part of it becomes self-cancelling; defensive advertising has become a routine for oligopolists . . . [and] essential for maintaining one's market share' (Koutsoyiannis 1982: 52).

This bleak picture of advertising as ultimately futile has been made even bleaker by those economists whose object has been to demonstrate its harmful effect on consumer welfare. Cowling and Mueller (1978: 733, 745) showed how the social costs – in terms of welfare forgone – of corporate monopoly power were relatively heavy in both Britain and the US, amounting to about a 7 per cent and a 13 per cent loss respectively. Giant firms incurred such costs in efforts to secure and retain monopoly power, most notably through advertising, intended also to deter potential entrants. In reply to a critic, Cowling and Mueller (1981) admitted the need for case study evidence on the costs and benefits of non-price competition. However, they anticipated that studies of marketing, advertising and packaging would uphold their conviction that such activities resulted in heavy welfare losses.

All these, and many other, negative views of advertising and marketing basically sprang from a structural approach to competition: whether a firm operated in a perfectly or less than perfectly competitive market system was shown by the shape of its own sales or average revenue curve. That curve, relating the quantity of the product demanded to its unit price, could only be drawn on the assumption of certainty, both about consumers' future reactions and about the behaviour of rivals in the same market. Although, as business historians know well, real-life firms have to contend with uncertainty, so that goods often have to be priced according to their total unit cost, economists have argued that most business men have a reasonably good idea of the elasticity of demand for their products, thus providing approximate slopes for their average revenue curves. Selling costs would be allowed for in either overheads or the conventional addition for profit.

Thus the current mainstream economic approach to these questions can be seen as essentially production-based. The firm is faced with a given consumer demand schedule for its good(s), so that corporate decisions are made on the production side, sometimes involving the alteration of product quality. As the next section will show, this is the converse of the marketing approach. However, work by earlier economists has contributed some helpful ideas on the subject, to be discussed next.

Where the older tradition, extending from Adam Smith (1776) to Alfred Marshall (1890 [1961], 1919), basically differed from the analysis just outlined, was in the way it handled competition. That was not along structural lines, distinguishing perfect from imperfect competition; instead, competition was seen as an activity or process, involving firms' rivalry with one another through time (Richardson 1975: 359). Marshall's ideas were particularly apposite to business history research, as he was a mathematician with both a deep sense of history and a first-hand knowledge of business in his day. Thus he emphasized that firms' decisions on how to sell goods were as important as those on how or what to produce (O'Brien 1990: 70). To him, production and marketing were 'parts of a single process of adjustment of supply to demand'. His analytical stance was therefore essentially marketing-based.

Indeed, the only example he gave of an individual enterprise being in static equilibrium was that of a statutory monopoly such as a gas undertaking. By definition, there was no acceptable substitute for its output and no product lifecycle or technological development (Marshall 1961: I, 480). While he would not draw an average revenue curve for an ordinary commercial firm, he did admit that consumer goodwill, built up through satisfaction with a product over a long period, would induce many customers to continue to buy even if the unit price rose, which indicated a sloping curve. This natural goodwill needs to be contrasted with the artificial product differentiation, through advertising, branding and packaging, portrayed by the 'structural' economists.

Marshall also differed from his mainstream successors over the role of knowledge. While the latters' world was one of 'costless omniscience' (O'Brien 1984: 26), where the appropriate amount of knowledge was assumed to exist, Marshall stated categorically that knowledge was 'the most powerful engine of production'. Although a firm's capital – which he defined as all stored-up provision for the making of material goods – was often in the tangible form of plant, machinery and so on, to him knowledge was a vital element of capital.

Not until fairly recently has knowledge – nowadays often called information – been brought back into the forefront of corporate analysis, as part of the theory of the multinational enterprise. As Buckley and Casson (1976: 33) have pointed out, over and above the routine production of goods and services, firms undertake many activities which are interconnected by flows of intermediate products. Some of the latter are tangible, such as semi-processed materials or components traded between firms; yet more often they are categories of knowledge and expertise, most notably managerial, marketing and technological skills (Caves 1982: 3ff.). This new approach to knowledge invites the comment that, as long as economists view firms as no more than production functions in a static world, then marketing skills can be dismissed as trivial if not economically wasteful (cf. Niman 1991: 174).

In Chapter 10, Casson does not develop these important ideas, but defines marketing as a system of interdependent entrepreneurial activities, linked with such functions as innovation and research and development. He distinguishes four main aspects of marketing: market research (to identify new opportunities); promotion (to offer customers a 'problem' and thereby manipulate their preferences for a good or service to overcome that problem); transactions management (to make the required contacts and arrangements with customers); and distribution (to ensure physical delivery to the final destination).

Casson stresses the entrepreneur's manipulation of customer preferences, which may be 'honest' or 'dishonest'. While Tedlow, as quoted earlier, believes that a business cannot foist its product on an unwilling customer, Marshall recognized that marketing had both benign and harmful sides, by distinguishing two kinds of advertising: the constructive, or information-providing, and the 'combative', which strives to persuade by over-repetition and sometimes by denigrating or 'knocking' rivals' products, the latter kind being socially wasteful (Marshall 1919: 304ff.). Even so, Marshall was convinced that no amount of advertising would allow a product to secure a permanent hold on consumers unless it was 'fairly good' in relation to its price. This runs counter to the opinion of economists such as J.K. Galbraith (1962: 133ff., 1967: 203–10), that advertising over-persuades people to buy goods they do not really want.

To be sure, there might be truth in both sides' arguments, with some large firms being able to use market power through their marketing strategies, even though much marketing takes place through highly competitive channels. To uphold the former view, successive reports of Britain's Monopolies Commission have found certain firms indulging in excessive marketing outlays in the way suggested by Cowling and Mueller (Rowley 1966: 169, 299). A very well-publicised example of this strategy was that manufacturers of washing powders and dishwashing liquids incurred wastefully high promotional expenditure, which the commission strongly recommended should be reduced (Shaw and Simpson 1989: 16–17, 59–74). In the event, these manufacturers' market power was eroded by the growth of own brands in large distributors such as supermarkets. Thus when the element of time is introduced, so far from enjoying a permanent advantage, giant firms may possess no more than quasi-rents capable of being eventually competed away. Business historians should be able to furnish first-hand evidence from corporate archives to throw light on this important question.

After the above broad discussion of how economists have regarded marketing, some basic marketing principles, of relevance to business history studies, are offered in the next section.

PRINCIPLES OF MARKETING

So far, it appears that marketing as a subject has hitherto attracted inadequate attention among business historians, and of late has found little favour on the part of academic economists. This negative perception may be due to the fact that the rationale of marketing still remains to be presented in a form acceptable to these groups of scholars. As to an introductory definition, Tedlow has neatly provided one, as follows: 'Marketing is about the interplay between company and customer, within the context of competition'.

Here Tedlow highlights the fundamental interactive, and competitive, aspects of the entrepreneur's task (Tedlow 1990: 375). Much, indeed, depends on what are the latter's overall objectives. Academics usually assume that he seeks to maximize profits, or else sales revenue or market share. However, he may choose to exchange profit for leisure: a similar trade-off to that allowed to units of labour able to vary their hours of work. Some entrepreneurs are known to put in only enough effort to keep their families, sleeping partners or shareholders happy. Others in their turn pursue entrepreneurial utility, not only by taking time off for leisure or public service activities, but also by excessive spending on inessential items such as over-ornate offices.

The business historian should thus be able to assess firms and individual entrepreneurs according to how closely they adhered to the optimizing goal, or fell short of it. This would not involve sitting in judgement on them, but should help to deepen our understanding of their conduct, and also assist in the search for regularities and lay down a standard of inter-firm comparison. For example, were departures from optimization more common in some industries than in others, or at specific periods, say after 1870, compared with before? Almost certainly, the more intense the desire for optimization, the greater the marketing effort will tend to be, with entrepreneurs who seek merely to 'satisfice' or to gratify their own utility having low marketing consciousness.

Tedlow's definition can now be complemented with another, namely: 'Marketing, in modern terms, involves deciding marketing objectives in relation to a firm's products and then integrating research, production, advertising, selling and distribution into a policy and programme designed to secure these objectives' (Alford 1981: 328). Here Alford does not regard marketing as just one of several interacting functions of equal weight within a firm, as Casson does in Chapter 10. Instead, if the firm is to maximize its opportunities, and use its scarce resources in the most effective way to achieve overall corporate goals, the wants and needs of the final consumer should properly dominate every corner of its organization. At the same time, as the firm is a collection of opportunity costs (namely, those costs incurred in using resources in a given way rather than in alternative ways which have to be forgone), methods of satisfying perceived wants or needs have to be reconciled with available resources. It would be as inappropriate to over-gratify consumers as to neglect their wishes altogether.

This view of marketing allows entrepreneurs' attitudes to the consumer to be categorized in three different types of firm:

1 *Production-orientated.* Here firms subordinate the consumer's interests to their own chosen aims. By turning out the kinds of good they are happiest at producing, they are unlikely to optimize consumer satisfaction. Rather, they may only make themselves vulnerable to competition from more wide-awake rivals.
2 *Sales-orientated.* Such firms go to great lengths to meet all their customers' demands, even to the extent of straining their resource capabilities. They may spend excessively on advertising, sometimes in clearly wasteful forms – for instance, by too much undifferentiated and poorly segmented advertising (see below) – or they may offer too wide a range of each good. Where any given variety is demanded by an uneconomically small number of customers, a campaign of persuasion might divert their demand to more popular varieties and permit the firm longer production runs, thus yielding economies of scale and of stockholding.
3 *Marketing-orientated.* To avoid the mistakes of the other two

Marketing and business history 101

categories, these firms attempt to supply goods within the constraint of existing resources. That involves having from the outset a clear marketing concept or strategy, to include all corporate activities (Doyle 1984: 134ff.; Trustrum 1989: 48ff.).

Arising out of this marketing concept, there are a number of marketing functions, sometimes known as the marketing mix (Christopher *et al.* 1980: 8). Their object is to analyse, plan and control the process of matching human, financial and physical resources with the wants of consumers. The respective marketing functions are known as the four P's, standing for Product, Price, Place and Promotion (Doyle 1984: 136; Christopher *et al.* 1980: 61ff.). These will be considered in turn.

1 *Product.* Goods and services can be looked at either as entities or as bundles of attributes or characteristics. Until fairly recently, economists saw no need to draw such a distinction, since what mattered to them was the anticipated utility, reflected in the shape and slope of the demand curve. The amount actually purchased would therefore depend on the unit price. However, the work of Lancaster (1966, 1979), in developing the concept of product characteristics, has had an impact on industrial economics: for instance, the price of goods can be usefully related to the collection of characteristics embodied therein (Hay and Morris 1979: 84–5).

Marketing scholars can taken this novel approach a stage further in their analysis. If biscuits or chocolate, say, deliver satisfactions such as assuaging hunger, providing convenient forms of nutrition, or gratifying the palate, an understanding of these characteristics could help marketing-conscious firms to discover alternative types of food if ingredients such as sugar are subsequently attacked as harmful. Again, petrol is merely a substance which has the sole merit of making a motor car run. Since the motorist seeks to maximize the pleasure or minimize the disutility of a car journey, a service station owner will offset the tedious chore of petrol buying by offering for sale complementary products from audio tapes and magazines to food and drinks.

2 *Price.* Mainstream economists derive the equilibrium price from the intersection of marginal revenue and marginal cost. In practice, as suggested earlier, oligopolistic firms may be compelled by uncertainty to fix price according to full-cost principles, perhaps shading it upwards or downwards depending on the general state of the market. However, if an integrated marketing strategy were being sought, then the price chosen would need to take account of

where, for instance, the product stood in its lifecycle, and what was the firm's overall policy. Since most firms are, in practice, multi-product, any of its products should therefore be priced in accordance with the sales and market share objectives, and the optimum revenue sought from products as a whole. Thus well-established goods may be priced at a high enough level to subsidize the development of others that were still struggling. Moreover, the firm's aggregate market profile needs to be considered. If it has built up a reputation in a certain segment of the market, say with a luxury range of goods, then fixing a low price for a new product could be unwise since many consumers – especially in Britain – tend to equate price with quality.

3 *Place*. Until fairly recently, economists have shown comparatively little interest in spatial or locational questions. This has changed now that the theory of the multinational enterprise has been developed. Insights from that theory have helped to explain how multi-regional and multi-plant firms are organized and run. In consequence, both multinationals and uninational firms are now regarded as special cases of a general theory of the enterprise in space (Casson 1987: 1).

The marketing interest in this topic centres on how to get the right product to the right place at the right time (Christopher *et al.* 1980: 91). This entails recognizing the importance of the marketing channel, which leads to the outlets through which consumers can acquire the products they want. Making the best use of this channel basically involves deciding whether to use 'push' or 'pull' methods. The goods can be pushed down the vertical sequence of production and distribution through special terms to distributors, advertising in trade journals, merchandising or setting up displays in retail stores, or similar tactics. This may be especially effective with a luxury product, sold through a limited number of high-class outlets.

For mass markets, the alternative 'pull' route of appealing directly to the final consumer may be more appropriate, so as to persuade that consumer to pull the good down the sequence. The question of product availability will clearly be vital, especially for goods often bought on impulse such as confectionery.

4 *Promotion*. Economists go no further than to recognize that oligopolistic firms have to decide on selling costs and the quality of the products, matters which complicate the simplicity of models of monopolistic competition (Hay and Morris 1979: 13ff.). For marketing scholars, on the other hand, promotion is complementary

to the other P's as part of the marketing mix (Christopher *et al.* 1980: 121). There is a range of options on how to communicate with customers. This 'communications mix' includes personal contact – through the direct approaches mentioned above – and the more indirect route of mass advertising campaigns. Thus promotion and the communications mix, of personal sales initiatives and more impersonal publicity, would interact in an appropriate manner with price, product and place.

To sum up on these four P's, a marketing-orientated firm would be expected to achieve a suitable mix, to form part of the marketing audit (Trustrum 1989: 51). That audit comprises three parts, as follows:

1 *Resource audit.* To ensure that its goals are capable of realization, the firm will need to assess its present and future resources, including management at every level, skilled and unskilled manpower, production potential, and finance, both for current activities and for programmes to develop products and markets. This may be done quantitatively, with budgets, or qualitatively, with broad targets period by period, or with a mixture of the two.
2 *Market audit.* This examines the market in general and the characteristics of potential buyers in this market. Historical data can be compared with forecasts, allowing for contingencies such as expected government actions and demographic and environmental trends, which might affect future demand patterns. An element in this audit is consideration of the anticipated behaviour of rivals.
3 *Position audit.* The foregoing investigation of the current and likely state of the market as a whole provides the framework within which the firm's position can be assessed. Here again, historical evidence and forecasts can be married, both of actual sales performance and of market share. Since the extent of available and potential resources have to be borne in mind, the firm needs to look at its financial strength, especially as compared with that of rivals, as well as ratios such as that of profit to turnover.

One vital tool here is that of marketing research. Although some surveys of this kind were made in Britain during the 1920s and 1930s, they did not become common until after 1945 (Corley 1987: 70–1). Applied economists, like earlier theorists such as Marshall, were well aware of the uncertain world in which firms had and have to operate. This uncertainty can be reduced by marketing research, which seeks to identify market opportunities, to enhance the understanding of market processes, and to provide data for the control of marketing programmes. Marketing research may take the form of sample surveys, retail sales audits or customer panels. When new products are being launched, test marketing can usefully be carried out (Christopher *et al.* 1980: 155ff.).

Within this overall framework of measures to reduce uncertainty, there are market, sales, product, advertising and other categories of research, depending on what aspect is under particular scrutiny. Market research, for instance, seeks to find out the extent and characteristics of the market according to consumers' age, sex, income, occupation and social status, and to their geographical locations, as well as the structure, composition and organization of the distributive channels. Advertising research looks at attitudes to the firm and to publicity put out, and the relative effectiveness of their different forms.

Thus to a considerable extent, marketing research and the use of computers to process relevant information have replaced the intuition and hunches of old-style entrepreneurs. They have also allowed marketing to become far more sophisticated. To take an example, undifferentiated marketing entails marketing research over the total population of would-be consumers and a marketing mix applicable to the market as a whole. This is costly and also neglects the fact that markets, far from being homogeneous, comprise various categories of consumers, differing both in perceptions of product benefits and appropriate prices, and in their preferences for channels of distribution. To deal most effectively with this spectrum of ideas and preferences, the firm needs to differentiate the market, by breaking it up into segments; for cars there are the cheap-with-no-frills segment, the status-conferring expensive one, the showy sports-type, and so on, each requiring its own marketing strategy. A small firm could choose the single market segment which suited it best, and devise an appropriately economical marketing mix.

The marketing principles outlined in the present section clearly have important implications for the future development of business history. These implications will be pursued in the next section.

MARKETING AND BUSINESS HISTORY STUDIES

In this section, it is argued that the application of marketing ideas to business history opens up a radically new agenda for scholars in this discipline. Indeed, in a real sense it renders obsolete most of the existing attempts to generalize on the subject. Business history cases will need to be looked at anew, and fresh theorizing carried out, this time from the marketing perspective.

To sketch out some items in this new agenda, certain techniques can be introduced from historiography. Past events may be recounted from the outside or from the inside. The former approach is sufficient for, say, establishing a basic chronology of events; however, it will inevitably concentrate on what occurred rather than on why. Generalizations from such comparatively bald chronicles can only be of limited use in evolving any theory of business history.

On the other hand, once business historians are able to study their cases from inside, opportunities for generalizing and theorizing should be correspondingly more plentiful. The distinguished philosopher and historian, R.G. Collingwood, drew a distinction between unscientific scissors-and-paste history, where compilers were merely engaged in 'excerpting and combining the testimonies of different authorities' on the one side, and 'history as the re-enactment of past experience' on the other side. In the latter case, historians need both to weigh up the reliability and provenance of their documentary sources and to think themselves into the minds of the people involved. Collingwood took the example of Admiral Nelson at Trafalgar. A simple – and in a scholarly sense uncritical – chronology of the battle's successive phases is useful only for the record. However, it is possible to reconstruct and monitor the admiral's overall plan, particularly the extent to which it was followed through or modified as events unfolded, and how the outcome matched up with the original goals. The strategy of the opposing French admiral Villeneuve can be similarly assessed. From this exercise, broad comparisons may be drawn, *mutatis mutandis*, with other naval engagements from Salamis to Jutland (Collingwood 1944: 77–8, 1946: 257, 282).

If the above distinction is related to business history studies, any given firm's past can be narrated in a scissors-and-paste fashion. Admittedly, the archives of many firms are so sparse that this may very often be the best that can be done. However, where business correspondence and memoranda are plentiful, then the firm can be investigated from the inside by the historian mentally re-enacting past key events. In this investigation, the marketing framework set out earlier (pp. 94–104) should be of value. In every age, entrepreneurs could be expected to keep in mind four elementary questions, in the light of which they should be prepared to adapt themselves to ever-changing circumstances (Brech 1983: 175). These questions are as follows:

1. *What is the firm's basic character?* Alternatively, as a very influential marketing scholar has put it, what business is the firm really in? (Levitt 1977: 26). The recent shift in research emphasis by business economists from tangibles to intangibles can help here. A widely used concept has been the lifecycle of the product, which moves through various phases from invention to development to growth, to its peak, then to decline or to enter a period of revitalization and recycling (Brech 1983: 213). This concept has itself come under fire on the grounds that it is a good's characteristics, rather than the good itself, from which consumers derive satisfaction, and that these characteristics are not necessarily subject to a lifecycle. As shown earlier, this is why biscuit or chocolate manufacturers may diversify into other enjoyable snacks such as potato crisps, and pill manufacturers into other remedies to offer improved health, including ethical drugs. Such new products can often be marketed by the same sales teams and through the same outlets as the core product(s).
2. *How is top management exercised?* The entrepreneur should be prepared to do two things. He must take speedy decisions on major problems as they arise, and ensure that these decisions are put into effect. He must also plan for the future, in the light of the answers he reached on question 1 above, and once again see his plan fully implemented. If these operational and long-term tasks are carried out in a marketing framework, they should lead to correspondingly greater success than otherwise.
3. *What precisely is the source of the firm's income?* This acts as a salutary reminder that the final consumers provide the firm's revenue, and therefore should properly dictate what needs to be produced in order to gratify their wishes. Unless the entrepreneur not only subordinates corporate strategy to customer interests, but also unceasingly investigates means of improving that service, then the firm will not grow and prosper as expected.
4. *Is the management appropriate for the firm at its current stage of development?* An inadequate management structure will hamper marketing effectiveness; at the same time, too many managers, in relation to the marketing effort needed, would be wasteful. This question once again highlights the question of resources, especially of intangible skills, and serves as a reminder of the need to maintain an optimum size of marketing management.

To sum up on these four questions, Brech has stated that 'marketing as it is now known has evolved as a consequence of social and commercial conditions during the last thirty years [that is, since 1945] to become a specialist function of top management' (Brech 1983: 175). His statement is true as far as it goes. However, if the marketing principles set out in the last section are universally valid, then business history research should find that past entrepreneurs tended to succeed because they constantly bore in mind these principles, making their firms marketing-orientated, and vice versa. In order to follow up this point, in the next section the marketing histories of two British companies will be followed through from the early nineteenth century until recent times. These narratives may reveal some of the lessons that can be drawn from paying attention to marketing questions.

MARKETING IN PRACTICE: TWO CASE STUDIES

These cases can be considered in the framework of the successive phases of consumer marketing in Britain, comparable with those for America given by Tedlow. As he has shown, in the considerable land mass of the United States, the fragmented individual markets could not be unified until the 1880s, when the national railroad and telegraph systems were being completed (Tedlow 1990: 8). By contrast, Great Britain was relatively compact, having less than one-fortieth of the area of the US; very soon after 1800, a number of its specialities – low-priced branded and packaged goods (Chandler 1990: 239ff.), from patent medicines, sauces and proprietary foodstuffs to pottery – were being marketed throughout Britain. Although segmentation proper in Britain, as in the US, had to await the arrival of marketing research on a large scale in the 1950s, marketing-conscious entrepreneurs had much earlier adopted rough and ready – but still effective – forms of market segmentation.

The two British consumer product firms looked at here have continuous histories extending over a century and a half or more. While not being in any way representative, their branded and mass-produced goods have possessed trade names that have been very well-known at home and in the rest of the world. Since their records are fairly plentiful, it is possible to penetrate inside the two firms' workings and extract some useful marketing lessons.

Huntley & Palmers (Corley 1972)

Building on the local goodwill which Thomas Huntley had won for his handmade biscuits, George Palmer, who joined the partnership in 1841, set out to invent the first continuously running biscuit-making machinery in the world, moving to a factory five years later. He grasped the need for a strong marketing organization to sell the steadily increasing flow of biscuits which mechanization made possible. At first he sold through commission agents; then, to economize on marketing costs, from the 1850s onwards he built up a team of full-time salaried travellers. His brother Samuel, in London, dealt with marketing in the metropolis and in the non-European export field. The Continental market was in the hands of an agent, the very able Joseph Leete, who maintained sales in Europe despite high tariffs.

Until the late 1870s, the firm was clearly marketing-orientated. From 1874 onwards, seven Palmer sons joined the top management, each running a department; the sales department merely sold what was produced. Marketing was entirely 'push', through the reputable family grocers which retailed the bulk of these highly priced goods. Between 1870 and 1900, the number of different biscuit varieties rose from 130 to 400, a selection maintained (except in 1914–18) until 1939.

Failing to understand and implement marketing principles, Huntley & Palmers lost both national and international leadership in biscuit-making. The directors refused to enter the low-income market by introducing a cheaper range of biscuit, to diversify into sweeter and shorter-baked types which appealed to younger age groups, or to manufacture overseas in the face of steadily increasing tariffs. They reluctantly introduced 'pull' advertising only after the firm's main rival, Peek Frean, began seriously to erode its home market share, aided by Scottish and Irish competitors such as McVitie & Price and Jacob's which opened up factories in or near the great conurbations of England. Huntley & Palmers was steadily driven into the low-tariff export market, nearly 50 per cent of all output being sold overseas by 1914, a half to the Far East and to Africa.

This export trade was decimated by World War I and its aftermath, being reduced to 25 per cent of production by 1924 and 15 per cent by the late 1930s. Home biscuit sales plummeted as well, since its range was old-fashioned, with few, if any, novelties being introduced before the 1930s. Marketing was poor, with inadequate advertising, fewer travellers than in rival firms, a reliance on wholesalers and no depots outside Reading. The merger with Peek Frean in 1921 basically changed little, as the new combine of Associated Biscuits was only a holding company, the two units continuing to produce and market independently of each other. Both firms shunned the cheap end of the market, so that by 1939 they jointly provided only 15 per cent of all biscuits in Britain, while some newly established cheap manufacturers had gained 26 per cent. Although Peek Frean installed automatic biscuit-making plants in the early 1930s, Huntley & Palmers refused to follow suit until 1938.

After 1945 the Scottish manufacturers, merged in 1948 as United Biscuits, became the industry leaders, offering a limited number of very professionally marketed varieties. Jacob's joined Associated Biscuits in 1960; it acted as a catalyst in forcing the latter to become a multidivisional company controlled jointly by the three reigning families. A vigorous group marketing function was created, and this allowed it to hold its own in the rapidly expanding supermarket trade. However, United Biscuits, more powerful than ever through some successful diversification and enjoying 40 per cent of Britain's biscuit market as against Associated Biscuits' 20 per cent, was able to generate enough income to carry out the massive investment needed to keep down costs in a static market. With no hope of matching these strategies, in 1982 Associated Biscuits sold out to the American food corporation Nabisco.

Nabisco was later acquired by the US conglomerate R.J. Reynolds, which in turn became the subject of a management buy-out, and in 1989 its biscuit and snack interests were acquired by the French multinational food group BSN. Operations in Britain were renamed Jacob's Bakery Ltd, with an overall strategy of safeguarding the market strength of its leading varieties. The Huntley & Palmers and Peek Frean brand names were phased out, and those products marketed under the Jacob's name. With a continuing formidable competition from United Biscuits, Jacob's pursued a defensive marketing strategy, apparently with success.

Beecham (Corley 1983)

Thomas Beecham, having been an itinerant seller of his own hand-rolled pills in local Lancashire markets, moved in 1859 to St Helens. In Lancashire wages were relatively high and industrial pollution rife, thus creating both the means to buy and the need for his pills. There he branched out through press advertising and mail order. In about 1865 he changed from domestic to workshop manufacture, and soon afterwards installed his first steam engine. That year he had ninety-nine wholesale agents, encouraging their efforts with good discounts. This indirect selling enabled him to economize on office work, for he and his son Joseph ran the firm on their own. He also 'joined' the patent medicine industry by harmonizing his prices with those of rival firms; he reduced the range of his products to the two largest sellers, a digestive and a cough pill.

Beecham's leap from obscurity to industry leadership took place on the back of a remarkable surge in demand for 'health' products by British consumers. Between 1850 and 1913, average real wages rose by 70 per cent, while sales of patent medicines increased nearly seven-fold. His son, Joseph Beecham, was a rarity among the Victorian second generation of entrepreneurs, since he had a wider vision than his father. Effectively in sole charge from the early 1880s onwards, he and his Anglo-American general manager converted the Beecham firm into one of the foremost marketing-orientated enterprises in Britain at this time. Since pills were relatively high priced but cheap to make, gross profits were plentiful enough for him to increase advertising outlay from £22,000 in 1884 to £120,000, a national record, in 1891. He also achieved some *de facto* segmentation by concentrating press advertising on the cheapest papers and magazines, and on women's periodicals. By 1897, when turnover was about £210,000, there were no fewer than 2,500 wholesale accounts, and these were helped with various incentives.

This powerful marketing strategy was more sophisticated than that of his rival pill-maker Thomas Holloway, the pioneer of nineteenth-century advertising in Britain. Holloway's considerable advertising expenditure, rising to £45,000 in 1883, had been squandered on unmemorable copy which had largely ignored the substantial working-class market. When he died in 1883 and his successors sharply reduced advertising outlays, turnover fell by a third. By contrast, Joseph Beecham continued to spend over £100,000 a year on publicity to 1914, and offered 'fun' advertisements which attracted much public interest and editorial comment in the press. However, from 1900 onwards, with an ageing general manager and an inadequate son in the firm, Joseph began to lose interest in pill-making. Then between 1914 and 1924, a £2 million property deal, involving the Covent Garden estate in London, went awry. Joseph died in 1916 and left the firm without an effective leader.

In 1924 Beecham came into the hands of the property magnate Philip Hill (Corley 1985a, 1993) who effectively asked the question, 'What business is the firm really in?' His answer was to begin a series of mergers with rivals which created the largest patent medicine combine in Britain. He also diversified into cold and influenza powders, at a time when tastes were moving away from pills to liquid and other easily consumed home remedies. In 1938–9 he made three far-reaching acquisitions, of Macleans (toothpaste and powders), Eno's (fruit salt, with an extensive overseas marketing organization) and the makers of the hair preparation Brylcreem. Yet at his death, in 1944, Hill had done nothing to restructure the Beecham combine into an integrated group. Like Associated Biscuits at this time, it was no more than a holding company, in which the units were little coordinated.

Hill's immediate successors, far from overhauling the group, made matters worse by a totally inappropriate diversification into wholesale groceries, a step which later proved costly to undo. However, the Macleans purchase had brought in some able management, including Leslie Lazell, who was to become one of Britain's greatest marketing entrepreneurs in the second half of the twentieth century (Corley 1985b: 690).

Lazell, like Hill, enquired what business the Beecham group was in. As managing director from 1951, and then as chairman to 1968, he decided that while health care remained its core business, his primary object must be to transform the group into an international science-based and marketing-orientated company. After a huge expenditure of resources, he developed a range of very profitable ethical drugs, most notably penicillins. He also reorganized the group along multidivisional lines, the three divisions dealing with pharmaceuticals, food and drink, and toiletries.

His was the first British company to practise marketing in the American style, ensuring that marketing leadership was exercised from the top. (Lazell 1975: 199). It became the second largest advertiser in Britain, after Unilever. In 1989 the Beecham group, by then very powerful, merged on equal terms with the giant American pharmaceutical corporation SmithKline Beckman, to create the world's second biggest drugs combine. An important motive for the merger was to reap economies in expenditure on both marketing and research and development.

CONCLUSION

It would be premature to claim that even the first building blocks of a theory of business history had been put into place, and the marketing principles discussed here are on the whole not much more than sets of definitions. Yet, as shown earlier, they do raise some important if hitherto inadequately debated questions, and suggest how optimum marketing objectives might be realized. Given the constructive ideas available from marketing, it is a matter of surprise that, on the evidence presented here, neither recent economists nor business historians have paid as wholehearted attention to the topic as might have been expected.

To answer the questions posed at the beginning of this chapter, it does look as if there is a bedrock of immutable marketing 'laws' on which an analysis of corporate behaviour in a historical context might be built. This is notwithstanding the radical changes that have taken place in both marketing practices and the underlying conditions affecting these practices. Indeed, a lesson to be drawn from the case studies is that firms remain distinct entities over very long periods. Despite all the internal and external changes to which they are subject, their entrepreneurs throughout maintained very similar objectives, problems and opportunities, even though their marketing consciousness has varied over the years.

One further question remains to be addressed, in the light of the foregoing discussion. Is marketing simply the art of manipulation; that is, of inducing consumers to buy products that were essentially worthless? Lazell of the Beecham group echoed Marshall in rejecting that view, with the statement that 'No amount of marketing techniques will bring about a repeat sale to a customer who has decided that a product's performance does not measure up to the claims that were made for it' (Lazell 1975: 195). Both firms studied here had repeat sales in plenty. Between 1865 and 1914 Huntley & Palmers succeeded in selling a total of just over 900,000 tons of biscuits, since their high quality – if not their overexciting range – attracted affluent buyers at home and abroad.

Over the same period 1865–1914, Beecham marketed no fewer than 10,000 million pills. As late as 1938 the firm claimed to be selling 570 million pills in Britain alone, or double its sales in the early 1890s, when total pill consumption throughout Britain had been 2,070 million a year. The formula of Beecham's pills remained unchanged for well over a century, consisting half of aloes, a quarter of powdered ginger, and about an eighth of hard soap, with a sprinkling of essential oils to make the mass palatable. The ingredients cost only the equivalent of $\frac{1}{8}$p per box, which sold at 5p net of tax. Joseph Beecham admitted that he could have offered the pills at $\frac{1}{2}$p a box and still made a profit of more than $\frac{1}{4}$p, but he did not believe that anyone would have bought them at that price, regarding them as too cheap to be of any use (Francis 1968: 159). Much the same story could be told of consumers in the US, eagerly buying up Brandreth's, Carter's and Dr Williams' pills, and even less reputable nostrums pushed in rural areas by means of the notorious 'medicine shows' (Young 1961).

Were all these examples of the most notorious and longest running fraud perpetrated against the unsuspecting public? On the other hand, was there a not unreasonable balance of interest between the manipulators and the manipulated, the latter gaining their principal gratification from the advertisements and a placebo element in the products and regarding any improvement in their health as almost an uncovenanted bonus? Arguments on the welfare aspects, and ethics, of marketing are likely to persist until the end of time. This chapter has sought to do no more than open up some of the marketing issues for the benefit of business historians.

REFERENCES

Alford, B.W.E. (1981) 'New industries for old? British industry between the wars', in R. Floud and D. McCloskey (eds) *The Economic History of Britain since 1700*, vol. 2, Cambridge: Cambridge University Press.
Brech, E.F.L. (1983) *The Principles and Practice of Management* (3rd edn), London: Longman.
Buckley, P. and Casson, M. (1976) *The Future of the Multinational Enterprise*, London: Macmillan.
Cantillon, R. (1755) *Essai sur la Nature du Commerce en Général*, H. Higgs (ed.), London: Macmillan, 1931.
Casson, M. (1982) *The Entrepreneur: An Economic Theory*, Oxford: Martin Robertson.
—— (1987) *The Firm and the Market*, Oxford: Basil Blackwell.
Caves, R.E. (1982) *Multinational Enterprise and Economic Analysis*, Cambridge: Cambridge University Press.
Chamberlin, E. (1933) *The Theory of Monopolistic Competition*, Cambridge, Mass.: Harvard University Press.
Chandler, A.D. (1977) *The Visible Hand: The Managerial Revolution in American Business*, Cambridge, Mass.: Harvard University Press.
—— (1990) *Scale and Scope: The Dynamics of Industrial Capitalism*, Cambridge, Mass.: Harvard University Press.
Christopher, M., Kennedy, S.H., McDonald, M. and Wills, G. (1980) *Effective Marketing Management*, Farnborough: Gower.
Collingwood, R.G. (1944) *An Autobiography*, Harmondsworth: Penguin.
—— (1946) *The Idea of History*, Oxford: Clarendon Press.
Corley, T.A.B. (1972) *Quaker Enterprise in Biscuits: Huntley & Palmers of Reading 1822-1972*, London: Hutchinson.
—— (1983) 'From national to multinational enterprise: the Beecham business 1848-1945', *University of Reading Discussion Papers in International Investment and Business Studies*, no. 76.
—— (1985a) 'Philip Ernest Hill 1873-1944', in D.J. Jeremy (ed.) *Dictionary of Business Biography*, vol. 3, London: Butterworths.
—— (1985b) 'Henry George Leslie Lazell 1903-1982', in D.J. Jeremy (ed.) *Dictionary of Business Biography*, vol. 3, London: Butterworths.
—— (1987) 'Consumer marketing in Britain 1914-60', *Business History* xxix: 65-83.

—— (1993) 'Philip Ernest Hill 1873–1944', in C.S. Nicholls (ed.) *Dictionary of National Biography: Supplement, from the beginnings to 1985*, Oxford: Oxford University Press.
Cowling, K. and Mueller, D. (1978) 'The social costs of monopoly power', *Economic Journal* 88: 727–48.
Cowling, K. and Mueller, D. (1981) 'The social costs of monopoly power revisited', *Economic Journal* 91: 721–5.
Doyle, P. (1984) 'Marketing management', in J.F. Pickering and T.A.J. Cockerill (eds) *The Economic Management of the Firm*, Oxford: Philip Allan.
Francis, A. (1968) *A Guinea A Box: A Biography* [of Thomas Beecham], London: Hale.
Galbraith, J.K. (1962) *The Affluent Society*, Harmondsworth: Penguin.
—— (1967) *The New Industrial State*, London: Hamish Hamilton.
Hay, D.A. and Morris, D.J. (1979) *Industrial Economics: Theory and Evidence*, Oxford: Oxford University Press.
Iwata, R. (1974) 'Marketing strategy and market structure in three nations: the United States, the United Kingdom, and Japan', in K. Nakagawa (ed.) *Strategy and Structure of Big Business*, Tokyo: University of Tokyo Press.
Koutsoyiannis, A. (1982) *Non-Price Decisions: The Firm in a Modern Context*, London: Macmillan.
Lancaster, K. (1966) 'A new approach to consumer theory', *Journal of Political Economy* 74: 132–57.
—— (1979) *Variety, Equity and Efficiency*, Oxford: Basil Blackwell.
Lazell, H.G. (1975) *From Pills to Penicillin: The Beecham Story*, London: Heinemann.
Levitt, T. (1969) *The Marketing Mode: Pathways to Corporate Growth*, New York: McGraw-Hill.
—— (1977) 'Marketing myopia', in B.M. Ennis and K.H. Cox, *Marketing Classics* (3rd edn) Boston: Allyn & Bacon.
Marshall, A. (1890 [1961]) *Principles of Economics* (9th edn), London: Macmillan, 1961.
—— (1919) *Industry and Trade*, London: Macmillan.
Niman, N.B. (1991) 'The entrepreneurial function in the theory of the firm', *Scottish Journal of Political Economy* 38: 162–76.
O'Brien, D.P. (1984) 'The evolution of the theory of the firm', in F.H. Stephen, *Firms, Organisations and Labour: Approaches to the Economics of Work Organisation*, London: Macmillan.
—— (1990) 'Marshall's industrial analysis', *Scottish Journal of Political Economy* 37: 61–84.
Porter, G. (1980) 'Marketing', in G. Porter (ed.) *Encyclopaedia of American Economic History*, New York: Charles Scribner's Sons.
Porter, G. and Livesay, H.C. (1971) *Merchants and Manufacturers: Studies in the Changing Structure of the Nineteenth-Century Marketing*, Baltimore: Johns Hopkins Press.
Richardson, G.B. (1975) 'Adam Smith on competition and on increasing returns', in A.S. Skinner and T. Wilson (eds) *Essays on Adam Smith*, Oxford: Clarendon Press.
Rowley, C.K. (1966) *The British Monopolies Commission*, London: Allen & Unwin.

Say, J.B. (1803) *A Treatise on Political Economy*, New York: Augustus M. Kelley, 1964.
Scherer, F.M. (1980) *Industrial Market Structure and Economic Performance* (2nd edn), Chicago: Rand McNally.
Shaw, R. and Simpson, P. (1989) *The Monopolies Commission and the Market Process*, London: Institute of Fiscal Studies.
Smith, A. (1776) *An Enquiry into the Nature and Causes of the Wealth of Nations*, R.H. Campbell and A.S. Skinner (eds), Oxford: Clarendon Press, 1976.
Tedlow, R. (1990) *New and Improved: The Story of Mass Marketing in America*, Oxford: Heinemann.
Trustrum, L.B. (1989) 'Marketing: concept and function', *European Journal of Marketing* 23: 48–56.
Young, J.H. (1961) *The Toadstool Millionaires: A Social History of Patent Medicines in America before Federal Regulation*, Princeton, NJ: Princeton University Press.

6 The marketing of Scotch whisky
An historical perspective

Nicholas Morgan and Michael Moss

In any study of the whisky industry marketing, broadly defined, looms large. Many would argue that the dynamic of the industry has always rested less in its production process than in its marketing; this regardless of the romantic and alluring tales of illicit distilling, the heroic struggles of pioneer licensed distillers, and, of course, of the enduringly magical process by which water and barley are converted into aqua vitae, the water of life. We will argue here that marketing was of pre-eminent importance to the industry. We also stress the quality and complexity of the marketing effort which involves personalities and innovations far greater than those associated with the whisky barons, a handful of the most successful whisky blenders, whose place in history is itself largely a triumph of their self-marketing. Like others who have examined the subject (Weir 1990) we believe that the industry is largely exonerated from the strictures of Davenport-Hines (1986) in his collection of essays. But we also assert, paradoxically, the pre-eminence of the product, for it was the unique qualities and properties of the product that provided whisky men with an unrivalled marketing opportunity. This is not a detailed narrative of the development of the industry, for this can be found elsewhere (Wilson 1970; Weir 1974; Moss and Hume 1981).

THE PRODUCT

From the reform in the excise regulations under which the UK distilling industry operated in 1823, whisky was a differentiated product. There were already three discrete products on the market: whisky distilled from a mash of malt in small pot stills; whisky distilled in large pot stills or in the newly developed continuous or patent stills from a mash of grain with a small malt content; and mixtures. The mixtures might be vats, mixed malt whisky from a number of distilleries, or what later became known as blends, a combination of both, sometimes sold fraudulently, sometimes using a small amount of pot still malt whisky to cover (with varying degrees of success) the blemishes of sometimes low-quality patent still malt whisky. A third type of mixture was whisky covered with a variety of fruit cordials or spices, again to reduce the severity of the sometimes raw and immature malt or grain spirit. The market for the product was largely confined to Scotland and was very often local (Royal Commission 1908: 162). Distillers in Scotland had access to a wider market for their spirits sold not as whisky but rectified in a further distillation process into hollands, gin or geneva for the fast-growing English market. For large Lowland distillers this represented the biggest part of their complex market (Moss and Hume 1981: 47).

As the nineteenth century progressed, the three discrete products were improved and refined, partly due to improvements in distilling technology and agricultural practice, partly due to changes in markets as a result of two competing (but distinctive) Scottish processes, urbanization and emigration, and partly due to good fortune. The premium market for wine and spirits in the United Kingdom was opened after the commercial treaty with France in 1860 which brought chateau-bottled wines and labelled brandies onto most wine and spirit merchants' lists, encouraging whisky distillers to emulate the example of these new competitors. In bringing whisky to the market, wine and spirit merchants were assisted by the Excise Act of 1860 which allowed blending and vatting to take place in bonded warehouses without payment of duty, removing the fiscal constraints that had restricted blending to a cottage industry.

In the 1880s the premium market for whisky expanded dramatically after phylloxera beetle ravaged the French, Spanish and Portuguese vineyards. Wine and spirit merchants substituted whiskies for imported wines and spirits, looking in many cases either to the higher quality self-whiskies (both malt and grain), branded largely according to their place of production, or to blends, produced on a large scale from the mid-1860s and increasingly branded from the mid-1870s. The growing vogue for Scotch and soda was legitimized by the fashion for all things Scots, promoted by Queen Victoria and her family, who made highly publicized visits to Highland distilleries during their annual sojourns north, and who exhibited their undoubted taste for the product by the award of numerous royal warrants to blenders and distillers. In addition this royal endorsement played (and plays) an important role in marketing Scotch whisky, beginning with Queen Victoria's visit to John Begg's Lochnagar Distillery (subsequently, for many years, Royal Lochnagar Distillery) in 1848 (Barnard 1987: 263).

These three types of product were further differentiated as the premium market grew by an additional factor, the age of the product and the nature of its maturation. Pot still malt whisky was distinguished by its region of origin (generally characterized as Highland, Lowland, Islay, Campbeltown or Speyside), but also by its age and the type of barrel chosen for maturation; sherry-soaked barrels produced a rounder, smoother and more sophisticated whisky than plain or re-used oak. Blends also came to be differentiated by the age of their component whiskies, and by the ratio of pot still malt to patent still grain; brands were generally superior to own-label spirit shop blends, but were themselves differentiated by age and content into standard, premium, and liqueur (later deluxe) ranges.

Because of this, longevity (either actual or by association), allied to the product's rich Scottish heritage, became (and remains) one of the key platforms for marketing propositions. In addition to being the name of the flagship brand for John Walker & Sons of Kilmarnock in the last quarter of the nineteenth century, 'Old Highland Whisky' was a generic description used by blenders to describe whisky aged from one year (and possibly less) and upwards. *Auld Kirk, Ancient Stimulant, Antiquary, Centurion, Old Still, Old Moses, Old Gran's Special Toddy,* and *Old Mortality* are just a handful of the early whisky brand names that played around the theme of age (Munro 1899). Few blenders, however, were able to surpass the inspired choice of Thomas Parr as a name for a deluxe brand. Adopted by Greenlees Brothers in 1909 the label of *Old Parr* carried (and still carries) on the facing label (where blenders sometimes include age statements about their products), not only the motto 'Born 1483', but also the legend 'Aged 152 years'. It is hardly surprising that with their deep veneration of age *Old Parr* found a unique niche in the Japanese market, first in the late 1920s, and again in the 1950s.

As is shown below, many blenders used these opportunities to create a large range of highly focused brands for home and export trade, featuring range-extensions to premium and deluxe levels. Others steadfastly refused to follow this lead; Walkers preferring to concentrate on the mass marketing of only two brands for much of their history.

DISTRIBUTION

Distillers were prohibited by the 1823 legislation from selling their whiskies direct to consumers and were obliged to use retail or wholesale outlets whose premises were situated at a distance from the distillery. Demand for whisky developed largely through demographic change as Scots and Irish moved from rural areas into the fast-growing industrial towns and cities of the UK, or emigrated to North and South America, Australia and New Zealand and South Africa. The Colonial Officer, a Dewar's brand, and Bulloch Lade's The Old Colonist, were aimed directly at those Scots who had chosen the extensive opportunities offered by service in the Empire rather than outright desertion of the homeland. In addressing this demand, both in the UK and overseas, the whisky distillers, and later blenders with branded products, used agents or (as they were to become) distributors (Spiller 1984: 84). Agreements with agents were usually tightly drawn, specifying geographical boundaries, the rate of commission to be paid by the supplier to the agent, and sometimes to be paid by the agent to sub-agents charged with servicing discrete areas. Agreements covered also terms of sales of product covering the use of the name, the type of packaging and label, and allowances for and instructions for the preferred type of advertising. Agents for distilleries marketed and sold both new-make whisky for laying down or immediate consumption, and for blending and for sale as 'self-whiskies', as well as aged whiskies for the same purpose. Agents for blenders marketed and sold standard blends in bulk to be bottled as own label or sold in public houses from the cask, as branded blends in bottle or bulk, or as mixtures to be used by customers in making their own blends. Although of less importance to the larger blenders in the home trade by the turn of the century, agents were preferred even in those export markets deemed significant enough to warrant an overseas office.

The majority of agents in the UK and overseas held agencies for more than one distillery or blending house: other wines, spirits, beers and mineral waters all competed for resources and attention. Agents in the UK were often also blenders, not just of whiskies, but also of rums, brandies, ports and wines. Little is known in detail about this relationship of distillers and blenders with their agents in this complex market, largely because few historians, apart from enthusiasts, have explored the mechanisms of the wine and spirit trade, despite its size and international significance from earliest times.

There is certainly no paucity of source material in the archives of those firms whose records have been spared the ravages of time, takeover and business termination. Minute books contain details of appointments of agents, whilst letter-books frequently recite their failings and transgressions. Detailed distributor agreements and specific distributor files form the bulk of the archives of many blending companies from the early twentieth century. Financial records provide information about sales, not just to agents, but often to their customers. In some companies export records, or export managers' notebooks, contain statistical data on sales by brands and market that would rival any current number-crunching operation. These various sources all confirm that the agency system was far from a passive sacrifice of a product to a distant market. Leading brands could dictate their own terms in the marketplace, whilst margins were sufficiently generous to ensure that brands could make a distributor who played by the rules. Even for brands with large home trade sales, properly managed export markets offered the greatest margin of profit. Distributors were fiercely policed by blenders and their appointed salesmen, who oversaw the activities of agents in remote markets (sometimes from a regional office) and collected vital market intelligence, supplemented by information from agents themselves. Any deviation from established brand identities (maintained principally by label books which were produced and copied to distributors, the forerunners of current brand identity manuals) begged severe retribution.

However, there was a two-way relationship between distributor and blender; with a closer understanding of the local market, and an eye to the performance of the opposition, distributors were essential in feeding back consumer response to products. And despite its alleged enduring and changeless qualities the product, either self-whisky or blend, was very flexible. In the same way that brands (particularly in the deluxe range) were named and packaged to suit local cultural characteristics, producers could and did vary product to suit local taste and legal regulations, and if necessary introduce new product where opportunities were seen to exist. This was not a hopeless proliferation of brands, but rather a sophisticated matching of product to market needs.

If the distributor provided the mechanism for unlocking the market, then the key lay with the identity created for the brand naturally by the production, maturation, and blending process, and unnaturally by those intent on projecting its image to the market through packaging, pricing and advertising. Within the industry the highest rewards, and the highest profiles, were awarded to those who pursued this unnatural activity, which has created what is currently the UK's largest export earner.

THE THREE PHASES OF MARKETING – SCOTCH WHISKY AND THE TEDLOW PARADIGM

Richard S Tedlow's model of a three-phase history of marketing in the United States fits uneasily with the history of the Scotch whisky industry both in the UK, its Empire, and its worldwide emigrant community (Tedlow 1990: 4–8). Whereas in some respects Scotch whisky has always exhibited tendencies associated with all three of Tedlow's phases, in others it has failed until recently to move beyond his second stage. As we have demonstrated in the first half of this chapter, Scotch whisky is an unusually complex product; were it as simple as a bottle of Coca-Cola or a Model T Ford its experience might well match more closely Tedlow's model. In order to demonstrate both the similarities and differences we will address each of Tedlow's three phases.

Phase I

Tedlow's Phase I of a domestic market fragmented amongst localities, with absence of nationally supported brands, where small firms pursued high profits through high-priced low-volume sales, can only apply to Scotch whisky up to the events of the 1860s, which we have described. Even so it is doubtful if distillers and their sales outlets sustained a high-price regime except in exceptional circumstances like harvest failures or withdrawal of competition from other products during the French wars. The differentiation that was characteristic of whisky always ensured that high prices could be commanded by products of certain distilleries or localities selling into effectively premium markets of relatively high disposable incomes amongst the rural gentry and urban professional classes (whose links with the countryside were intimate). To this extent a distillery or locality could be regarded as surrogate for a nationally recognized brand (Royal Commission 1908: 162). The best example of distillery-specific recognition of this kind in the eighteenth century is Ferintosh which, for historic reasons, was manufactured duty-free until 1784; after this date the name was used as a generic brand for whisky from the small district (Moss and Hume 1981: 53). The distinctive whisky made on the island of Islay enjoyed a similar reputation from the late eighteenth century.

National reputations within Scotland in the premium market were achieved, as far as can be judged, by quality and consistency, which in the absence of any semblance of national advertising depended on word of mouth in fairly tightly knit groups where drinking was one of the principal forms of social activity. Highland distillers remote from the larger towns added value to their product after 1823 by adroit use of an illegal past and a highly crafted mode of production. Much Lowland whisky was of good quality, but suffered from being distilled close to urban centres where there was a ready market for poorer spirit. Whereas the generic reputation of Highland whiskies was founded on the exceptional quality of a small number of distillers, the reputation of the Lowland product was firmly based on that segment of producers whose product was at best indifferent and at worse poisonous.

Before 1860 firms were not, as Tedlow suggests, universally small. There were, particularly in the Lowlands, some very large producers whose business could compare with the largest manufacturers at that time. In the 1780s James Stein opened a gigantic plant at Kilbagie in Clakmannanshire with a potential capacity of 16 tons (nearly 5,000,000 gallons) of spirits a day. This plant included the first Boulton and Watt steam engine to be installed in Scotland. The product extended beyond whisky into gin and geneva sold largely on the English market (Moss and Hume 1981: 45). Highland distillers were smaller, but by 1860 a few had become, relative to the general scale of enterprise in all sectors (where despite the image of large mill, engineering shop or shipyard, small firms and small workshops remained the norm until the early twentieth century), large concerns (Rodger 1988). Examples are Macdonalds Ben Nevis distillery at Fort William (which was developing a national brand, *Highland Dew of Ben Nevis*), Lagavulin, the largest of the Islay distilleries, and Greenlees and Colvill's Hazelburn distillery, one of a number of large Campbeltown plants linked through a complex network of inter-family investments. Operating on this scale in the Highlands was fraught with problems of supply of raw materials, distribution of finished products and disposal of waste. Despite the rudimentary transport system these problems demonstrably did not of themselves impede growth. It would be naive to maintain that an underdeveloped transport infrastructure inhibited the growth of markets in a country which was, at least from 1745, peaceful, with a developing economy that was largely based on overseas (mainly Atlantic) trade in finished goods and commodities.

Phase II

Scotch whisky's national (within the UK) and international mass market dates from the 1860s due to the complex interaction which we have already described. From this date the trade witnessed the rise of bottled, blended and branded Scotch whiskies, which drove some existing distillers to expand production to sustain sales of self-whiskies and to meet the demands of a worldwide market of the blended product. In this phase the new product – proprietary blends, a more sophisticated version of the earlier often crude mixtures – was developed not by the distiller but by entrepreneurs whose expertise lay in the craft skills of the wine and spirit merchant and the business sense of the high street. These skills were learned in an environment where national boundaries were not barriers to interchange of different products. However, it should be acknowledged that the first producers of blended whiskies successfully to conquer the London market were the distilling Greenlees Brothers from Campbeltown, whose *Lorne* whisky was promiscuously promoted in the metropolis by a variety of conventional and unconventional means.

Rightly or wrongly, the growth of branded whiskies has been associated by historians with the rise of mass advertising. While some qualification should be offered to this view (not least because it was one soon promoted by the firms themselves) it was undoubtedly advertising that acted as a major tool in the marketing effort of the blenders (Weir 1974: 544–8). 'I attribute it [the growth of blended whiskies] to advertisements, to a large extent', claimed the London solicitor Arthur Bramall, giving evidence before the Royal Commission on Whisky of 1908. 'It has been advertised to a perfectly extraordinary extent and everybody knows how it is advertised through London even with these electric lighted things which go up and down.' However, as Bramall had recognized, it was not simply mass advertising that grew a brand; brand integrity based on specification, consistency, quality and careful price positioning was also important. Without these characteristics, no amount of brand promotion would succeed. He went on to say 'People do not know what Scotch whisky to get and these are largely advertised under highly respectable and well-known names and I think they are sold on the strength of those names'. (Royal Commission 1908: 29). James Greenlees, himself a blender, concurred: 'It is the name of the firm that gives the people the guarantee that the whisky is good' (Royal Commission 1908: 206).

Before promoting either a blended or self-whisky considerable care was taken to ensure that the product possessed the characteristics that research had shown were demanded by particular markets. It was well-known that certain styles of whisky were more acceptable in particular markets than in others. In 1881 the Mackenzie Brothers of Dalmore Distillery on the Moray Firth decided to 'push their brand to some advantage in England'. They found it hard to win orders for their self-whisky because of its distinctive style. Instead of abandoning the venture they responded by changing the style of their whisky to give it 'more body and Highland character of flavour'. After tasting the new product their Glasgow agent wrote enthusiastically: 'We are very much impressed with its quality and think it should hold its own against the best Highland whiskies, it comes out so rich, sweet, fine flavoured, and is altogether we think a powerful whisky' (Moss and Turton 1991).

The marketing effort of the Greenlees Brothers was focused around the production of a distinctly Scotch blend which nonetheless possessed those flavours and characteristics which made Irish whiskey such a popular drink in the capital. At the same time they sought to increase consumer awareness: 'We tried', said James Greenlees, 'to educate the public' (Royal Commission 1908: 204). When Francis Berry of the famous London wine merchants Berry Brothers decided to design a new whisky for the American market – Cutty Sark – he deliberately produced a light blend with the textures of the fine old brandies he knew so well (Johnson n.d.: 19–21). Within the price constraints of any market, this ability to tailor whiskies to the demand of segments as defined by taste preference allowed the blender to 'value price' their product. This was well-understood in the wine and spirit trade more generally, particularly at the premium end of the trade where very high prices could be commanded for certain products, like chateau-bottled wines and proprietary brandies and champagnes.

Having decided on the whisky for the chosen market, consistency had to be guaranteed if fickle customer loyalty was to be ensured. The pre-eminent and sometime romantic position attributed to the master blender within whisky companies was a result less of his ability to design new blends than of his skill in maintaining the characteristics of those already established. This was a difficult task, particularly where a blend had achieved high volume sales. In these circumstances the blender had to maintain the right 'nose' for the whisky but at the correct price. He had to do this using a range of whiskies whose individual characteristics could not be guaranteed from one distillation to the next and whose availability and cost could not be relied on. New make whiskies were checked in the blender's sample room and compared with others from distilleries in the same area.

In 1898 Tamdhu Distillery on Speyside was brought into production under the watchful nose of R.I. Cameron of Munro and

Cameron, an Elgin firm of whisky merchants with a wide range of distillery interests. He wrote to the distillery manager George Reid after the first month's production:

> I got back from Glasgow the sample all right but I do not think the fourth period sample as good as the former ones. You wrote me . . . you had given the fourth period more flavour but I think it is not improved. I also have a note from the Glasgow agents saying the fourth period is not so good as former ones. I have sent you today the samples of the new Minmore, new Mortlach and new Glenfiddich [all neighbouring distilleries].
>
> (Moss 1987)

These sorts of problems meant that the recipe for the blend lay in the blender's nose rather than in a cherished calf-bound notebook. Moreover, as the taste for whisky spread and became more discerning towards the end of the nineteenth century, the blender had to subtly change his product to reflect demand which was shifting towards lighter styles of alcoholic beverages. Highland Distilleries noted in 1897 that their blending customers were taking out 'whisky for use with considerable maturity in it', and refusing 'the fiery stuff once so popular in many quarters' (Moss 1987). This made whisky as brand very different from the other mass-produced commodities of the late nineteenth century whose marketing histories possibly fit more closely with the Tedlow paradigm.

Agents and distributors, particularly when introducing a label in a new market, pressed for whisky at the lowest price possible and in not a few instances got it. In February 1878 Mackenzie Brothers wrote to Neill & Co who had recently been appointed their agents in Dunedin in New Zealand:

> We spare no expense in distilling a spirit of finest quality and it cannot be sold by us to leave a fair profit under the price invoiced to you. We are fully alive to the difficulty of introducing a new brand and have to thank you for your fast services, but we think it best to state plainly how we are placed in our sales to others and hope now that the brand is getting known you will be able to get fair value for it to leave a profit to the buyer and seller.
>
> (Moss and Turton 1993)

Those companies who were pursuing the growth of strongly branded products were rarely prepared to compromise the integrity of their product by reducing the price, which would ultimately mean either trading at a loss or changing the specification. Arthur Bell, who was curious among the early blenders for his refusal to advertise his product, was adamant on this point. As he explained to his Melbourne agent:

> I should keep up the quality, and only export No 6, which you could push among merchants, clubs and private gentlemen, and, when once tried, would be sure to keep up its own owing to the quality being so superior to what is usually sold in Melbourne. You might also get orders by explaining to your friends that the reason I can keep up the quality is that I do not advertise.
>
> (House 1976: 30)

Price positioning and price ranges were well-understood in the wine and spirit trade by the mid-nineteenth century. In order to prevent brand compromise blending houses would create brands tailored to specific price positions; in the lower price range these would frequently be sold under the names of subsidiary companies in order to protect the integrity of the flagship brands which were always those that carried the name of the house. In 1884 Alexander Walker, the son of the founder of Walker's of Kilmarnock, created a new brand, *Glencairn*, for the Australian market, in an attempt to attack the lower end of the price range without interfering with Walker's main *Old Highland* brand. He wrote that he 'meant it to be totally different from OH so that it would not interfere with it & yet be a whisky in value which no other house could compare with' (Walker 1881–6: 47).

Flagship brands were themselves, in some instances, susceptible to range extension by using terms such as old, very old and extra special and by employing different coloured labels and numbers of stars. Mackenzie Brothers sold their Dalmore self-whisky in two varieties with different packaging; the better one filled in sherry wood and sold in bottles with white labels, and the other filled into new barrels – termed distillery wood – and sold in bottles under a tartan label (Moss and Turton 1993). Within a year of introducing his *Famous Grouse* brand in 1897, advertised to the well-to-do middle-aged sportsman who frequented the country as 'unique as an aid to digestion and preventive of acidity', Matthew Gloag of Perth was marketing a liqueur *Grouse* blend and a deluxe blend *Perth Royal*, an extension of his other standard brand *Brig O' Perth* (Moss 1987). Perhaps the most famous, and enduring, of these extensions was based on Walker's *Old Highland Whisky*. Dressed from the 1880s in a square bottle with a slanting black label the original brand was pushed upwards to become *Extra Special Old Highland*, and was joined by *Special Very Old Highland*, distinguished by a red neck label. In 1909 the firm increased the range to three, at the same time radically changing the identity of each. *Extra Special Old Highland* became *Black Label*, *Special* became *Red Label*, and the third (and cheapest) was *White Label* (Walker 1886–1920).

This clever and sophisticated price positioning at its best reflected an understanding of some of the demographic and psychographic techniques of marketing associated by Tedlow with the third phase of marketing; at worst it illustrated the tendency to produce brands thoughtlessly without any consideration of the sectors of the market to which they might appeal. No doubt some of the blenders did both. As we have seen, range extensions were one way of playing to demographic factors. The identities created for brands, which in an era before large-scale national advertising by the companies rested largely on brand name and dress (labels), were the key to other demographic and psychographic appeals. We have already discussed the importance of associations based on age, place, Scottish history (and, for that matter, literature) and royal patronage, but these were almost generic to the product as a whole. In addition to these, blenders deliberately exploited other well-defined themes in order to target groups and market segments, particularly as brands proliferated towards the end of the century.

The sportsman was one of the main victims: *Curler's Cheer* (1890), *Golfers Special* (1891), *Ramblers* (1895), *Anglers* (1898), *Athlete* (1898) and *The Trainer's Blend* (1898) were all aimed at the active outdoor type. *Invalid* (1884), *Doctor's Blend* (1885), *Comfortable Night-cap* (1891) and *Hygienic Elixir Vitae* (1896) were designed to reassure those concerned about the possible ill-effects of whisky consumption (a constant theme of temperance campaigners) by emphasizing its health-giving properties. Some brands emphasized masculinity and male companionship such as *Bachelor's* (1897), *Club* (1888), *Old Swells* (1898) and *The Glasgow Chappie* (1895). Others focused on modern pastimes, such as the *Bungalow* (1889), *The Cyclist's Friend* (1898), *The Record* (1896), *X Rays* (1897) or *The New Motor Car* (1897). A few appealed to professions, *Barrister* (1897), *The Doctor* (1881), *Old Vicar* (1892) and *Professor* (1891), a brand trademarked by a wine and spirit merchant whose premises were close by Glasgow University (Munro 1899).

Some of these attempts to pick-off potential market segments were as crude as they were laughable, and few were successful as long-term brands. But they do illustrate the relative sophistication of some of the blenders, and support the view that in some respects Scotch whisky's third phase of marketing arrived early. And although brands abounded there was something to be gained by a multiplicity of blends from which consumers could choose, for this promoted the notion of connoisseurship, a conceit which could be readily bought into play by the drinker faced with a shelf full of brands. George Mackay Brown, in *The House with the Green Shutters*, written in 1901, described the following conversation in the bar of the Black Bull, in the fictional Lowland Scottish town of Barbie, sometime in or before the 1880s:

> '. . . but no doubt a man who knoweth Edinburgh tho [the speaker has a lisp] as well as you, will have a favourite blend of hith own. I notice that University men have a fine taste in thpirits.'
> 'I generally prefer Kinblythmonts Cure', said Gourlay with the air of a connoisseur. 'But Anderson's Sting o' Delight's very good, and so's Balsillies Brig o' the Mains.'
> (Mackay Brown *The House with Green Shutters* 1985: 170)

Connoisseurs and experts were a self-generating market segment whose existence only served to enhance the marketability of the product.

Phase III

In the case of Scotch whisky the distinction between Phases II and III in Tedlow's model is blurred. As we have seen, the second phase of marketing Scotch whisky exhibited many of the characteristics of the third. In addition, a complicated conjunction of circumstances distorted the market in which whisky blenders operated after World War I.

The complexities of the market for Scotch whisky after World War I are perhaps unique. In the first instance, the introduction of prohibition in the United States after the passing of the Volstead Act in 1919, and a growing anti-spirits lobby worldwide, placed constraints on the actions of producers and distributors that were not experienced by other trades. The closure of one of the industry's largest and most profitable export markets witnessed the development of the 'Special Trade', the euphemism used by the blending companies for their dealings with Canadian and Caribbean distributors who, despite intergovernmental agreements, continued to illegally run Scotch whisky and other spirits into the United States for the duration of prohibition. The legal trade with the United States in blends for medicinal purposes was supported by imaginative promotions aimed exclusively at the elderly middle-class drinker 'with a heart problem' (Moss and Hume 1981: 149).

At the end of prohibition in 1933 the difficulty faced by domestic producers in rebuilding stocks left the premium end of the market open to foreign spirits. With their experience of dealing with existing distributors the Scotch whisky blenders were able to take advantage of this opportunity, supported (through carefully placed magazine advertising, direct mail campaigns and liquor store promotions) by careful targeting of clearly defined market segments, defined by both demographic and pyschographic criteria. They were aided by the social cachet that had developed around high-quality branded Scotch imported during prohibition. The success of the blenders in the North American market was almost self-defeating; it was a sign of confidence in consumer preference that prices could be raised when stocks became scarce without affecting profits (Moss 1990).

To a limited extent the difficulties in North America were offset by growing markets in the south, where (as in Venezuela) increased prosperity amongst professional and business groups created demand for prestige imported products, of which whisky was one of the most important. Here, carefully chosen distributors together with the blenders successfully contrived to project their products to meet the aspirations of the newly rich. If marketing Scotch whisky to old markets in the colonies was status or culture confirming, then marketing to these new territories was status or culture enhancing.

World War II confirmed whisky's presence in the export market for premium products. Whisky distilling was controlled by the British government from the outbreak of hostilities; however, because of the shortage of foreign exchange, sales of such stocks as were released were concentrated on overseas markets, particularly in North America. The end of the war witnessed the imposition of strict sales quotas on the industry, determined by pre-war export market share. This, combined with a scarcity of stock helped to increase the prestige of the product. Producers and distributors, keen to 'value price', targeted their stocks even more closely than before, particularly on segments of the American market, such as elderly whites. Because of the demands and profitability of the American market it was tempting to neglect other markets or focus specific minor liquor or deluxe brands on them, building on previous connections or experience. As a result only one whisky, Johnny Walker, could claim to be marketed as a worldwide range of brands by the 1970s, whereas with other branded goods, such as Coca-Cola or Levi jeans, the world market was always the sole objective.

CONCLUSIONS

Although this essay cannot claim to offer anything more than a superficial account of the marketing of Scotch whisky, a number of points should be apparent. Scotch whisky was a complex and differentiated product; it is hardly surprising then that the history of its marketing should differ so much from a model formulated largely around the experience of Coca-Cola. For the history of marketing Scotch does differ profoundly from Tedlow's model; the market for Scotch was segmented, and producers and blenders were able to exploit this from the second half of the nineteenth century onwards. Compared to marketeers today the Scotch whisky blenders and merchants were amateurs, but, despite the absence of detailed consumer analysis, they knew their markets. They were sometimes crude, their failures were spectacular, but their successes were prodigious. But if Johnny Walker had been 'born' in 1820, his whisky had been born two or three hundred years earlier. With this sort of lead on Coca-Cola is it surprising that Scotch whisky marketing should have been so advanced?

REFERENCES

Barnard, A. (1987) *The Whisky Distilleries of the United Kingdom*, Edinburgh: Mainstream Publishing.
Davenport-Hines, R.P.T. (ed.) (1986) *Markets and Bagmen*, Aldershot: Gower.
House, J. (1976) *The Pride of Perth: the Story of Arthur Bell & Sons Ltd. Scotch Whisky Distillers*, London: Century Bentham.
Johnson, T. (n.d.) *The Story of Berry Brothers and Rudd, Wine and Spirit Merchants*, London: privately published.
Moss, M.S. (1987) *100 Years of Quality: the History of Highland Distilleries Co plc 1887–1987* (unpublished typescript).
—— (1990) 'Scotch whisky: 1933–1988', in M. Chick (ed.) *Governments, Industries and Markets*, Aldershot: Edward Elgar.
Moss, M.S. and Hume, J.R. (1981) *The Making of Scotch Whisky*, Edinburgh: James & James.
Moss, M.S. and Turton, A. (1993) *Double Lion: the History of Whyte & Mackay 1843–1987* (forthcoming).
Munro, J.M. (1899) *Scottish Licensed Trades Directory*, Glasgow: J.M. Munro.
Rodger, R. (1988) 'Concentration and fragmentation: capital, labour and the structure of mid-Victorian Scottish Industry', *Journal of Urban History* 14: 178–213.
Royal Commission on Whisky and Other Potable Spirits (1908) London: HMSO.
Spiller, B. (1984) *The Chameleon's Eye: James Buchanan & Company Limited 1884–1984*, London: James Buchanan & Co.

Tedlow, R.S. (1990) *New and Improved. The Story of Mass Marketing in America*, Oxford: Heinemann.
Walker, J. & Sons (1881–1886) Letter Book, United Distillers Archive, Leith.
—— (1886–1920) Directors' Minute Book No. 1, United Distillers Archive, Leith.
Weir, R.J. (1974) 'The development of the distilling industry in Scotland in the 19th and early 20th centuries', unpublished PhD thesis, University of Edinburgh.
—— (1990) 'The export marketing of Scotch whisky (1870–1939)', in E. Aerts *et al.* (eds) *Production, Marketing and Consumption of Alcoholic Beverages*, Leuven: Leuven University Press.
Wilson, R. (1970) *Scotch the Formative Years*, London: Constable.

7 A machine on every desk
The development of the mass market in computers

Geoffrey Tweedale

Until the 1960s, as one mathematician and programmer highlighted, computers were

> so scarce and so expensive that man approached the computer the way an ancient Greek approached an oracle. ... A man submitted his request ... and then waited patiently until it was convenient for the machine to work out the problem. Only specially selected acolytes were allowed to have direct communications with the computer.
>
> (Augarten 1984: 253)

As everyone will be aware, within only a few decades that picture has been transformed dramatically worldwide. Computers have now become simply another product: 'personal computers' sit on our desks, send us our bills, cater for our recreational needs, and – at a business level – interact directly with the marketing process itself. Such has been their impact that even from the earliest days commentators have frequently talked of a 'second Industrial Revolution' (Bowden 1953: preface). In the 1990s computers are regarded in much the same way as any other consumer item: a mass-produced commodity, they roll off the production line in their thousands. They have not quite reached the ubiquity of other household products, but nevertheless they have become, in many respects, a consumer durable which now has to fight for its place in the market. Whilst doing so, the big companies – International Business Machines (IBM), Apple, Digital Equipment Corporation (DEC) and Amstrad – and their founders and chief executives have become almost as familiar in business and marketing folklore as Henry Ford and Pepsi.

No one can doubt the importance of marketing in the computer revolution and certainly the leading manufacturers have not done so. But the fact that the mass market in computers has appeared only very recently has meant that it has yet to be adequately researched by historians. Marketing itself, of course, is a subject that has received relatively little attention in business history, especially in the UK (Davenport-Hines, 1986). The books published by computer historians and their academic journal, the *Annals of the History of Computing*, are heavily weighted towards the machines and the people who built them (Williams, 1985). Thus we know in great detail about the technological genesis of IBM's electronic digital computers, but far less about how these machines were marketed (Bashe *et al.* 1986). At present, although several studies touch on the subject, only one journal article presents a scholarly study of computer marketing (Aspray and Beaver 1986).

This chapter, therefore, presents an overview of the subject. It briefly examines the pre-digital computer era up to the 1940s; describes the early marketing of modern electronic machines; and looks, as far as the sources allow, at some of the strategies adopted by leading computer manufacturers since the 1960s. The relationship of the computer to the mass market is also examined.

THE PREHISTORY

The modern computer is usually regarded as a development of the last forty years. In a sense that is correct, if we confine our attention to computers that are electronic, have a programmable memory (a stored program), and are digital (as opposed to analogue). By this yardstick the mass market in computers was late in arriving. On the other hand, it might be argued that from the broadest perspective the emergence of a unified market for calculating machines can be seen in the late nineteenth and early twentieth centuries. Indeed, perhaps it could hardly be otherwise. If it is agreed that modern mass marketing only became possible with the development after the 1880s in the USA of the telegraph and the railway, then it is also true to say that such developments would have been slower without better business machines: typewriters, punched-card tabulators and calculators. Business, the marketplace and computers have always been inextricably linked.

Computer historians have looked for the origins of the computer in ancient times with the invention of the first calculating machines, such as the humble abacus. From that starting point numerous philosophers, mathematicians and inventors through the ages devised increasingly sophisticated devices, amongst them the English mathematician Charles Babbage, who embarked upon the construction of his ill-fated Difference Engine in the 1820s.

Before the nineteenth century these mechanical calculators were not widely available and were often little more than curiosities. The first to sell in any numbers was the Arithmometer, designed in France and marketed in the 1820s: about 1,500 were eventually sold. Better engineered and designed machines were to appear later in the century, with American business expansion. In 1885 Dorr E. Felt, who worked as a mechanic for the Pullman Co. in Chicago, made the pivotal breakthrough with the invention of a 'key-set' calculator, which had a typewriter-style keyboard, allowing numbers to be entered quickly. From his crude prototype, he developed in 1886 the highly successful Comptometer adding machine. Hundreds, thousands, and eventually millions were sold, even though it was limited by its inability to produce a written record. This problem was solved by another American inventor, William S Burroughs, who in 1892 patented his 'adder-lister', an adding machine that printed out its results on a roll. It was to outsell every calculator on the market: sales were over 10,000 by 1907 and there were as many as fifty-eight different styles.

Of greater importance for the development of the computer industry was the development of punched-card machines. These received their greatest impetus from Herman Hollerith, the American inventor–entrepreneur, whose tabulators for the 1890 US Census Office made obsolete the laborious manual methods previously used for enumeration. Hollerith's census machines established the data-processing industry (Austrian 1982). In 1896 he founded his own company, the Tabulating Machine Company, to begin marketing his machines to customers other than the government. After some initial hesitation, private industry became interested: the New York Central Railway and Pennsylvania Steel bought the equipment for their accounting and inventory departments and soon found them indispensable.

The way in which these machines were marketed has not been researched, but certainly the actual selling of the machines was soon recognized as being of vital importance. Early attempts at using retailers had not been successful, partly because office machines were such specialized products. By integrating selling within their organizations Hollerith and other office machine manufacturers such as Burroughs and Remington soon established dominance in the market (Chandler 1977: 313). Integration was useful: not only did it break the ground for future expansion – the customers for office machines later became the buyers of computers – but the sophisticated selling and training operations made it difficult for rivals such as the

British to enter the market. Typically machines were leased – a practice followed by Hollerith – ensuring a steady flow of income during times of recession.

The importance of marketing was recognized above all by John Patterson, the founder of National Cash Register. By 1890 this firm had become the dominant force in the American cash register market, with 16,400 machines in operation. Besides its mechanical simplicity, which reduced manufacturing costs, the product was constantly improved to enhance its appeal to the consumer and marketed by an integrated and highly motivated sales team that was paid on commission. Patterson was something of a pioneer in modern salesmanship and marketing methods: he founded one of America's first company sales schools in 1894 to teach the principles of 'scientific salesmanship' to young, fit, white Protestant males with plenty of ambition. He motivated them by catchy slogans, high commissions, guaranteed territories, paid vacations and frequent bonuses and backed them with massive advertising and promotional campaigns. Patterson spent almost as much on advertising as on production. He was also not above using illegal tactics – such as underselling legitimate dealers until they went bankrupt – to capture market share.

Patterson was a direct link with the twentieth century's most successful computer manufacturer – IBM – since one of his executives was Thomas J Watson. The latter's sales-oriented business outlook was shaped at NCR, even to the extent that Watson was sentenced to a year in jail for alleged violations of the Sherman Antitrust Act (a sentence that was never served because of a technicality). By 1914 Watson had joined the Computing-Tabulating-Recording Corporation (CTR), an amalgam of four firms which included Hollerith's Tabulating Machine Co. Watson recognized the potential of the tabulating machine wing of CTR and his development of it secured his own future and that of the company. Although Watson had pushed at the earliest opportunity for a development department at CTR (with the expiry of Hollerith's patents, competition was soon to be expected), his major emphasis was on sales. At IBM (a name that was adopted after Watson became head of CTR in 1924) Watson concentrated on making the salesman the king, using the same motivational techniques learned from Patterson: high commissions, guaranteed territories, excellent fringe benefits and the full apparatus of paternalism. Drinking, smoking and fornication were frowned upon and salesmen were expected to dress conservatively. Company sing-songs, the Hundred Percent Club for star performers and the famous 'THINK' motto completed the picture (Rodgers 1970).

Though it had its ridiculous aspects, Watson forged a highly effective salesforce. Its importance can perhaps be seen by looking at what happened when the US punched-card machine industry was transferred across the Atlantic to the UK. Hollerith had founded a British subsidiary, the British Tabulating Machine Co. Ltd (BTM), in 1907. By 1915 it was joined by a subsidiary of the Powers Co. (a rival of Hollerith in the US market), which was known as the Accounting & Tabulating Corporation of Great Britain Ltd (or 'Acc & Tab'). Together these firms dominated the British market for punched-card machines in the inter-war period, yet they consistently under-performed their American counterparts. (BTM had by the 1920s become a subsidiary of IBM; Acc & Tab later found itself in 1927 under the wing of Remington Rand, which had bought out Powers.) One study has concluded that 'probably the single most important factor that accounts for the relative disparities in BTM's and IBM's growth rates between the Two World Wars was the competence of their sales operations' (Campbell-Kelly 1989: 52). Both BTM and Acc & Tab lacked an aggressive and highly motivated salesforce, partly a reflection of the generally amateurish level of British marketing. In both companies salesmen tended to have a technical rather than sales-oriented outlook. Sales commissions, for example, were considered too ungentlemanly to use at BTM, and were only introduced at Acc & Tab after 1930. Certainly, IBM's view was that its subsidiary's poor performance – selling, it must be said, exactly the same machines – was due to managerial failures and the lack of an efficient salesforce.

IBM itself flourished in the 1920s on the sales of its punched-card machines (which were still leased rather than sold outright), with Watson making the most of economic developments in the American economy which hastened the development of a mass market, white-collar community that relied upon IBM's sorters and tabulators. With a lion's share of the lucrative tabulator market, IBM at the end of the 1920s was among the top five office machine manufacturers in the USA (the others being Remington Rand, NCR, Burroughs and Underwood). It was well-placed to weather the depression (rentals continued to accrue and the growth of government agencies under the New Deal ensured at least some new business) and was well-positioned in the market when the next technological leap occurred with the arrival of the modern computer.

ELECTRONIC DIGITAL COMPUTERS

Punched-card machines had become an indispensable feature in offices in both the UK and America by the outbreak of World War II. So too had desk machines such as the Brunsviga for various accounting and mathematical calculations. However, though these machines had penetrated the business market, and could also be found in many scientific laboratories, they were still too bulky, expensive and specialized to find a true mass market. 'Computing' prior to 1940 still meant only one thing – a clerk equipped with a hand-calculating machine, who could 'compute' the standard calculations required for wages, actuary tables and ballistics. Only after 1945 was this to change.

It was World War II which gave the impetus to the development of general-purpose devices. The war boosted the demand for machines and scientists to perform the calculations for weaponry and code-breaking; it brought together experts in unrelated fields in mathematics and electronic engineering; and it provided massive funding which was to be the catalyst for the technological revolution behind the modern computer. In Britain and America wartime challenges spurred two major developments: the Colossus, a code-breaking machine constructed for the British government at Bletchley Park; and the ENIAC (Electronic Numerical Integrator and Computer) which was commissioned late in 1945 for the US Army Ordnance Department for ballistics' calculations. From these twin poles by the end of the conflict the theoretical design (and much of the engineering work) of the electronic digital computer was in place. It was to be a major leap forward, since until that time data and instructions for various calculating and computer devices had always been stored outside the machine. Now a new idea had emerged – the stored program concept – in which programs and data could be held *inside* the machine, making it immensely more powerful and faster. The computer was to be universal, capable of solving any mathematical problem (capable of solution) once an appropriate program had been inserted (Hodges 1983; Aspray 1990).

US developments were highly influential at this stage, but British electronics expertise and mathematical theory were equal to the Americans in 1945. Thus it was that for a brief period in the 1950s the UK led the way in the commercial development of the computer (Lavington 1980). The first commercial version of a stored program computer was delivered by Ferranti Ltd in 1951 to Manchester University (where the development work had been done). Other

British firms – English Electric, LEO Computers Ltd, Elliott Bros, Marconi, and eventually BTM and Powers Samas – also took up the challenge. They were provided with a measure of Government support, which was channeled through the National Research Development Corporation (NRDC) (Hendry 1989).

The 1950s was very much a pioneering period for the digital computer, both in terms of technology and marketing. It is clear from contemporary accounts that technological differentiation was the most important element in competition, with computer technology rapidly passing from valve-based to transistor-based circuitry, and with rapid advances (at least in America) in peripheral devices such as discs and printers. It is also apparent that in marketing terms the niche of the computer was by no means apparent. Advertisements for computers in the mid-1950s show that the computer was perceived only as a sophisticated calculator, an electronic 'brain'. An index in *Fortune* at this time advised readers searching for computers to 'see calculators' (Aspray and Beaver 1986).

As the pioneer in the field, Ferranti met these difficulties first. Amongst the most intractable were: computers were new, expensive (at current prices about £1 million per machine) and relatively unreliable; they were ill-adapted for use by any but the most experienced programmers and mathematicians; and no attempt had been made to use them for business calculations. 'Would there be a market?', asked Ferranti's sales manager, and then added: 'There was a need for computers in universities, but both here and in the USA there was doubt that enough would be needed' (Swann 1975: 13). Expert opinion was that a few, large scientific computers would be all that would be required to serve the needs of the computer community nationwide. Douglas Hartree, one of the country's leading mathematical and computer experts, told Ferranti: 'We have a computer in Cambridge, there is one in Manchester and one at the NPL [National Physical Laboratory]. I suppose there ought to be one in Scotland, but that's about all' (Swann 1975: 13). Most mathematicians, the brilliant John von Neumann included, regarded computers as mathematical machines quite exclusively (Aspray 1990).

A marketing strategy was therefore slow to emerge at Ferranti. Much effort went into the R & D effort, with Ferranti working in close conjunction with Manchester University to register a series of technical landmarks: the first stored-program machine; the first commercially available computer; and the first transistor-based design. There were also advances in programming techniques and by

1956 experience in commercial work included wages calculations, inventory control investigation and airline seat reservation problems. But a study of Ferranti's marketing has shown that the firm remained essentially conservative in outlook, a reflection of the fact that it was a family firm with the computer as only one of its products. The defence market was particularly congenial to the firm and, though it did make a successful attempt to break into the expanding commercial market with its Pegasus machine, it was happiest designing and producing large-scale scientific computers. Ferranti's business was technologically driven, heavily influenced by its links with the design team at Manchester University (Tweedale 1992a).

Selling was clearly not a priority amongst other British computer manufacturers. At Elliott Bros the early impetus was primarily military; while at English Electric the first customer for its DEUCE computer in 1955 was the National Physical Laboratory. At LEO Computers Ltd it was said that little attention was paid to marketing; there too technological considerations fostered by a link with Cambridge University proved all-absorbing (Hendry 1987).

Computers for business were therefore slow to emerge in the UK and the lead over America had largely been squandered by the late 1950s. At that date the electrical engineering firms – Ferranti, Elliott and English Electric – were building computers aimed at scientific and defence applications. Available government support went to this group. Meanwhile, the office machine manufacturers were slow to realize the importance of the technological change taking place, remained wedded to the declining punched-card industry, and received little official support. In the UK in particular there was also a failure to realize that the manufacture of peripheral devices and software was at least as important as the design of the computers themselves. Magnetic storage discs, computer programs and printers were to become an important area of product differentiation in the emerging industry.

The apotheosis of the UK's technologically driven computer effort was reached in the design of the Atlas, a 'supercomputer' built as a joint effort between Ferranti and Manchester University with a modicum of support from the NRDC. Though a brilliant technical triumph, and one of the most influential computers ever built, the Atlas found no market. With a price tag of over £1 million each, marketing had become an irrelevance, and only three were ever sold in the early 1960s.

In the USA, after a brief early loss of leadership, expansion of the computer industry was rapid. In 1951 the first data processing computer, the UNIVAC (Universal Automatic Calculator), was delivered to the Census Bureau by Remington Rand. By the end of the decade 5,400 electronic digital computers were in use in the USA (the total in the UK being 217); by 1965 the respective figures were 24,700 and 1,582. Besides this difference in scale, American computers were by this time generally in advance of anything Europe could offer in the three main areas: processors, software and peripherals. By 1960 almost all American computers had second-generation transistorized processors. Software was certainly in advance of that in the UK: the programming languages FORTRAN and COBOL were widely available, and operating systems and real-time applications were far in advance of any software products offered in the UK. Magnetic tape and disc storage facilities were increasingly available in the US, while British manufacturers had virtually no capability in these areas, leaving computer operators to grapple with paper tape and punched cards.

A consensus view is that this wide technology and commercial gap was due to a number of reasons. First, and above all, was the massive government sponsorship of the American computer industry. The US military establishment guaranteed support to the industry for the sake of national security. Even a partial list of computer projects funded during the 1940s and early 1950s is impressive for the number, diversity and cost of the projects included. By 1950 the US was already directly funding computer R & D at roughly $15–20 million (current) a year (Flamm 1988: 78; Cohen 1988). The development of magnetic core memories in the early 1950s, for example, grew from a US Navy flight simulator program. IBM, for one, owed its launch into the digital era to a large government contract which allowed it to build its 701 computer (named aptly the 'Defense Calculator') during the Korean War. The second factor affecting the size of the US industry was the scale of its computer market, evident in the figures already cited. Here the US was at least two or three years ahead of Europe in its per capita installation of computers. There is also some evidence that US businesses and their leaders were far readier to accept the new technology.

The extent to which superior marketing was responsible for American success is difficult to quantify, especially since the industry was being driven by military needs. Once this began to slacken and commercial opportunities presented themselves, however, those firms best placed to market the machines effectively succeeded best. In the early days there was apparently much to learn. The background to the development of the UNIVAC before 1950 by two of

America's pioneers, John Mauchly and Presper Eckert, shows the team making mistakes in marketing that were not too dissimilar from Ferranti: development costs were drastically underestimated; technical staff were allowed to develop business policy; and too much effort was spent in perfecting devices at the expense of failing to complete them (Stern 1981). But once IBM entered the field and the commercial business in America took off, its sales-driven philosophy brought huge dividends. As its chairman remarked:

> technology turned out to be less important than sales and distribution methods . . . [and] . . . we consistently outsold people who had better technology because we knew how to put the story before the customer, how to install the machines successfully, and how to hang on to customers once we had them.
>
> (Watson and Petre 1990: 242)

By 1961 over 70 per cent of America's $1.8 billion in computers had been built by IBM. UNIVAC was a distant second, with about 10 per cent market share, followed by Burroughs and then finally by Honeywell, RCA, Philco, NCR, General Electric and Control Data. By 1964, when integrated circuits in computers made their appearance, IBM's share of the $5.3 billion installed computers had reached over three-quarters.

By now the market had split into segments as technical differentiation of computers into application-oriented categories proceeded. UNIVAC (with fast input/output of data rather than computational power) was aimed at business; John von Neumann at the Institute of Advanced Study, Princeton, designed a machine for scientific users; at the MIT the Whirlwind was oriented to real-time command and control situations, which were to spin off into process control in industry; while smaller companies focused on building compact but affordable computers, using lower performance components that made serious computing available to users on a budget.

IBM gradually aimed its business increasingly towards the commercial mainframe market (rather than the top-end supercomputer field), which it increasingly came to dominate with its ruthless pricing policies (Englebourg 1976; Sobel 1981; Delamarter 1986). It also had a share of the university market, fostered by its policy of giving 60 per cent discounts for educational customers. But by the early 1960s, it was producing six different, and incompatible computer product lines, and successful competitors for several IBM machines had appeared. RCA was challenging in the large-scale business market; Burroughs was attacking the high end; Control Data was increasingly competitive in scientific applications (Lundstrom 1987); and Honeywell was working on a low-cost machine. IBM's dominant position was far from assured (Fisher et al. 1983).

IBM's fragmented and incompatible product line caused concern, especially in view of the increasing importance of software at this time. Its response was to introduce a 'compatible' family of third-generation computers – the System/360 – which was intended to replace at a stroke all IBM's current computers, except the smallest and largest. The idea of compatibility was not IBM's invention, but no company had ever implemented the concept before and to such ruthless effect. The launch of the System in 1964 sent shock waves through the industry and is generally recognized as one of its great watersheds. For IBM it was a gamble that paid off: after reported development costs of some $5 billion and herculean research efforts, the System/360 (and its successor, the 370) became an industry standard, so much so that computers based on its architecture still account for more than 25 per cent of all computer sales (Pugh et al. 1991).

For the first time in the industry IBM had created a unified market that greatly stimulated the commercial use of computers – a market moreover now circumscribed by IBM with a proprietary, internally controlled standard. So attractive was the idea of compatibility in reducing processing costs and broadening applications, that others chose to develop 360-compatible lines. The first such offering was RCA's Spectra 70 series, announced only eight months after System/360. The Amdahl Corporation was perhaps the most successful at supplying 360-compatible processors. Even more rapidly, an entire industry was created to supply plug-compatible peripheral products. Led by Telex with tape drives in 1967 and Memorex with disc storage units in 1968, this industry enjoyed dramatic early growth.

THE PERSONAL COMPUTER

By the mid-1970s well over 150,000 electronic digital computers were at work in the USA; the figure for Europe was over 70,000. This was an astonishing advance since 1950 when America had only two computers and Britain three. Punched-card machines were now a thing of the past (though they could still be seen in many offices and universities). The business office was now becoming highly automated, with the mechanization of white-collar labour. Advertisements in the mid-1970s reflected attempts by advertising agencies to create new sales opportunities, in part through diminishing costs of hardware and increasing miniaturization. The computer promised to place at your fingertips answers to questions you needed to ask, simply and easily, and to transport information anywhere, instantly (Aspray and Beaver 1986).

But the computer was still seen as a child of the office or educational establishment. The creation of the mass market for computers – the concept of a machine for every desk, home or even pocket – depended on a number of factors: in the first place decreasing costs and miniaturization, and second new marketing approaches.

The first move in this direction was the minicomputer. Although low-cost, high-performance machines had their roots in the 1950s, the crucial event was the launch in 1963 of the PDP-8, the first successful minicomputer (about the size of a fridge). This was made by the Massachusetts-based firm, Digital Equipment Corporation, which was founded by an ex-IBM engineer, Kenneth Olsen. It exploited a niche market – sophisticated industrial and academic users – and had a completely different marketing philosophy to IBM. Olsen believed in bringing computing to the individual, whereas IBM saw the world in terms of large number crunchers. He also refused to give his salesmen commissions, believing that DEC should work with customers not at them. The novelty of his ideas can be seen by the fact that initially business did not understand the message of the PDP-8. The *Wall Street Journal* did not think an editor would want to sit in front of a computer terminal all day. The minicomputer market, however, rapidly expanded, with other firms such as Control Data (founded by ex-DEC engineers) entering the sector (Kidder 1981).

However, even Olsen 'insisted that personal computing had no basis in need or reality. No one, he believed, seriously required a computer at home. He viewed early PCs as toys, metal boxes that were bought so children could play video games at home rather than in games rooms' (Rifkin and Harrar 1989: 199). This belief was proved erroneous on the West Coast of America. In 1975 a company in New Mexico, Micro Instrumentation and Telemetry Systems (MITS), marketed by mail the Altair 8800 computer both in assembled and kit form. The Altair inspired many American hobbyists to design their own machines, amongst them two Californian enthusiasts, Stephen Wozniack and Steven Jobs. They set up a partnership, the Apple Computer Co., and in 1977 introduced the Apple II, a machine that became the archetype of personal computers. Its success enabled Apple to become the fastest growing company in history and the story of how Jobs and Wozniack had sold a car to buy parts and then built the computers in their parents' garage became part of American business folklore. They showed how the computer market could be further exploited through demographic and lifestyle segments by a new marketing philosophy. The Apple motto was: 'one person – one computer'; and not only computers were being sold. There was also a new vision of society: utopian, liberating, with a message of democratization that it was hoped would alter the balance between the individual and institutions (Butcher 1988; Young 1988; Rose 1989).

Ironically, after its initial success, Apple became too absorbed in its myths and technology, and it was John Sculley – a marketing executive at Pepsi-Cola, credited with reviving the 'Pepsi generation' campaign – who usurped Jobs as head of the company and made it much more market-oriented (Sculley 1989). Even more ironic, Apple's high prices and refusal to allow the manufacture of 'clones' militated against the kind of mass market the company had envisaged and it was Apple's hated rival, IBM, that produced the most popular and influential personal computer. The success of the IBM PC, launched in 1981, owed little to technological novelty (80 per cent of the machine was built by outside suppliers and the operating system, MS-DOS, was bought from Microsoft, a West Coast company whose fortunes the IBM PC was to make), but everything to marketing and distribution. The strategy was to expand the market with the IBM operating system as standard. To do this IBM turned to a New York advertising agency to create the 'Tramp' image 'to dispel a fear of computers in general and a certain revulsion towards IBM in particular' (Chposky and Leonsis 1989: 77). It also used retail outlets, such as Computerland and Sears Business Centres, instead of IBM dealers. By 1983 sales of the machine were 800,000. Within months the famous 'clones' of the IBM PC had appeared, while software, such as the advanced Lotus 1–2–3, was also proliferating.

IBM clones in the UK were marketed with the greatest success by Amstrad. Here the market had initially grown out of the demand for computer games and pocket calculators, with Sir Clive Sinclair cleverly marketing a series of machines that had price and size as their chief selling points (Dale 1985). By the end of 1983 a million Sinclair Spectrums had been sold, but this market had already peaked. Instead, Amstrad recognized and created the move up-market, by launching a 'peoples' computer' that was cheap enough to be within the range of every small business and self-employed professional. Its great success was the PCW 8256, which was marketed with dramatic effect by the advertising agency Delaney Fletcher Delaney. Its advertisements showed scenes of trucks dumping piles of old typewriters into a scrapyard full of similar dead machines, with the slogan: 'It's more than a word-processor for less than most typewriters'. There was also an exclusive link with Dixons, the electronics retailer, whose chairman, Stanley Kalms, found the Amstrad computers exactly what he wanted: 'The dream of a business like ours was that computers should cease to be exclusive, magic products. They would become *consumer* electronics. That was the breakthrough' (Thomas 1990: 182). Amstrad was a classic market-driven company, with its founder Alan Sugar carefully cultivating an East End barrow-boy image with pronouncements such as: 'We're in the mass merchandising of anything. If there was a market in mass produced nuclear weapons, we'd market them too' (Thomas 1990: 187). The success of his strategy saw the eclipse in the UK of the more technologically inclined Sinclair Research and Apricot Computers. While Amstrad regularly topped the league tables of best performing companies (absorbing Sinclair in the process), Apricot moved out of computer manufacture entirely and into software by selling its interest to Mitsubishi of Japan (Harvey-Jones 1990: 71–98).

CONCLUSION

Dividing the history of computing into marketing phases, as has been done so cogently for other American mass-market consumer products (Tedlow 1990), is difficult. As this brief survey has shown, computers have never been a single product, like soft drinks or soap: a history of computers encompasses calculators, punched-card machines, scientific machines (both digital and analogue), mainframe business computers, PCs and supercomputers. A product that was initially mostly subsidized by the government for military use (even though that linkage is not so important now) is also clearly unlike any other consumer durable. Complicating matters further are several 'generations' of technical development (valves, transistors, chips), and now talk of another 'fifth generation' of 'intelligent' machines. In recent years, the focus has been shifting away from the hardware to software developments, whose importance has rarely been examined in detail by historians. Computers are also now seen less in their own right than as part of an 'information society', interacting with telecommunications and a myriad of other professional services. In short, the era of a machine on every desk has appeared, but defining the nature of that mass market is problematic.

Nevertheless, there have been identifiable phases during these decades of intense battle in the computer marketplace. Technological differentiation was the key factor in the 1950s, with pricing and market segmentation being relatively unimportant. By the 1960s the winning formula was the internal company standard – the concept of compatibility within a firm's entire product line – so successfully pursued by IBM. The 1970s and 1980s saw the emergence of the minicomputer and PC and the dethronement of the mainframe as the mainstay of computer sales (it now accounts for under half the market). By the mid-1980s two other basic themes had emerged in the computer industry. First, the uncertainties of rapid technological change were proving formidable even for a company with great resources like IBM, and unexpected shifts could still upset the established balance and make a nonsense of sales forecasts. Second, experienced competitors now understood the economies of scale and scope and saw the potential gains that could be increasingly realized by new business strategies.

Those new strategies revolved, as before, around standards and the challenge of 'connectivity'.

> By banding together and setting industrywide standards for interfaces between processors and peripherals, and communications between computers, and by settling on a standard operating system permitting a software application to run on many different types of computers, other computer vendors would have access to a market with at least approximately the volume of IBM's sales.
> (Flamm 1988: 243).

Today companies have joined together in an unprecedented way to develop hardware, software and communications standards. In the USA there are several cooperative industrial undertakings and the Electronics Industry Association and the Institute of Electrical and Electronics Engineers (IEEE) are also involved. Government-backed efforts to define new standards have also emerged, notably the organizations in Europe, Japan and the USA to develop the so-called Open-System Interconnection (OSI) standard. In the important area of software compatibility, AT & T's UNIX operating system is at the centre of most effort outside IBM – a coordinated attempt to challenge the latter's enormous advantage in installed computer base.

These new strategies are increasingly multinational in scope, an aspect of computer technology that was apparent from the pioneering Anglo-American roots (Tweedale 1992b), but has been gaining strength recently. A 1984 study of technology-oriented joint ventures involving European electronics firms counted eleven new agreements in 1980, twenty-eight in 1981, thirty-five in 1982, and forty in 1983. ICL's link-up with Fujitsu, which resulted in a complete Japanese takeover by 1990, is perhaps the best UK example.

What marketing consequences may result from these developments? In other consumer products, it has been said that companies are now facing a crucial strategic decision: should they further segment the markets they serve, or should they return to mass market strategies before market segmentation becomes excessive? Or should they synthesize these first two options into a strategy of mass 'customization'?

Given the nature of the product, questions about the marketing of computers can probably not be put in quite the same terms. What is certain is that non-proprietary standards – whether official, industrial or marketed-generated – are a dominating influence. It has been suggested that this will reinforce a split in the industry: on the one hand a high-technology segment, dominated by the economics of R & D investment; on the other, a low-technology end, with more modest requirements for technological resources (Flamm 1988: 248). Whatever happens, competition for markets looks likely to increase and cross national boundaries. In high technology, the spread of software and communications standards will make it easier to build large systems, computer users will be less locked in to a single manufacturer's products, and the traditional problems of matching different supplier's equipment and services will diminish. Small performance differentials will become important; competition and the pace of technological change will increase. In the low-end market, the development of open standards and the availability of cheap components has already increased the ease of entry of firms into the industry, as demonstrated with IBM PC clones. Further segmentation in the commodity computer market is therefore inevitable: indeed it is already occurring with the rapid increase in portable computers, for example, an intense area of PC activity at present, a development partly fostered by the enormous stock of useful software already in the consumer domain. In short, today's computer marketeers are now fighting a many-sided battle, wielding not only the old weapons of price and performance, but also standards, abilities in special applications, and the strength of their international ties.

REFERENCES

Aspray, William (1990) *John von Neumann and the Origins of Modern Computing*, Cambridge, Mass.: MIT Press.

Aspray, W. and Beaver, D. (1986) 'Marketing the monster: advertising computer technology', *Annals of the History of Computing* 8: 127–43.

Augarten, Stan (1984) *Bit by Bit: An Illustrated History of Computers*, New York: Ticknor & Fields.

Austrian, Geoffrey D. (1982) *Herman Hollerith: Forgotten Giant of Information Processing*, New York: Columbia University Press.

Bashe, Charles J., Johnson Lyle R., Palmer, John H., Pugh, Emerson W. (1986) *IBM's Early Computers: A Technical History*, Cambridge, Mass.: MIT Press.

Bowden, B.V. (1953) *Faster than Thought: A Symposium on Digital Computing Machines*, London: Pitman & Sons.

Butcher, Lee (1988) *The Rise and Fall of Steve Jobs at Apple Computers*, New York: Paragon.

Campbell-Kelly, Martin (1989) *ICL: A Business and Technical History*, Oxford: Oxford University Press.

Chandler, Alfred D. (1977) *The Visible Hand: The Managerial Revolution in American Business*, Cambridge, Mass.: Harvard University Press.

Chposky, James and Leonsis, Ted (1989) *The People, The Power and the Politics Behind the IBM Personal Computer*, London: Grafton.

Cohen, I. Bernard (1988) 'The computer: a case study of the support by government, especially the military, of a new science and technology', in Everett Mendelsohn *et al.* (eds) *Science, Technology and the Military*, Boston: Kluwer Academic.

Dale, Rodney (1985) *The Sinclair Story*, London: Duckworth.

Davenport-Hines, Richard (1986) *Markets and Bagmen: Studies in the History of Marketing and British Industrial Performance, 1830–1939*, Aldershot: Gower.

Delamarter, Richard T. (1986) *Big Blue: IBM's Use and Abuse of Power*, New York: Dodd, Mead & Co.

Englebourg, Saul (1976) *International Business Machines: A Business History*, New York: Arno Press.

Fisher, F.M., McKie, J.W. and Mancke, R.B. (1983) *IBM and the US Data Processing Industry*, New York: Praeger.

Flamm, Kenneth (1987) *Targeting the Computer: Government Support and International Competition*, Washington, D.C.: Brookings Institution.

—— (1988) *Creating the Computer: Government, Industry and High Technology*, Washington, D.C.: Brookings Institution.

Harvey-Jones, John (with Masey, A.) (1990) *Troubleshooter*, London: BBC Books.

Hendry, John (1987) 'The teashop computer manufacturer; J Lyons, LEO and the potential and limits of high-tech diversification', *Business History* 29: 73–102.

—— (1989) *Innovating for Failure: Government Policy and the Early British Computer Industry*, Cambridge, Mass.: MIT Press.

Hodges, Andrew (1983) *Alan Turing: The Enigma of Intelligence*, London: Burnett Books and Hutchinson.

Kidder, Tracy (1981) *The Soul of a New Machine*, New York: Avon Books.
Lavington, Simon (1980) *Early British Computers*, Manchester: Manchester University Press.
Lundstrom, David E. (1987) *A Few Good Men from UNIVAC*, Cambridge, Mass.: MIT Press.
Pugh, Emerson W., Johnson, Lyle R. and Palmer, John H. (1991) *IBM's 360 and Early 370 Systems*, Cambridge, Mass.: MIT Press.
Rifkin, Glenn and Harrar, George (1989) *The Ultimate Entrepreneur: The Story of Ken Olsen and Digital Equipment Corporation*, Chicago: Contemporary Books.
Rodgers, William (1970) *THINK: A Biography of the Watsons and IBM*, London: Weidenfeld & Nicolson.
Rose, Frank (1989) *West of Eden: The End of Innocence at Apple Computer*, London: Hutchinson Business Books.
Sculley, John (with Byrne, John A.) (1989) *Odyssey: Pepsi to Apple*, London: Fontana.
Sobel, Robert (1981) *IBM: Colossus in Transition*, New York: Times Books.
Stern, Nancy (1981) *From ENIAC to UNIVAC; An Appraisal of the Eckert-Mauchly Computers*, Bedford, Mass.: Digital Press.
Swann, Bernard (1975) 'The Ferranti computer department', unpublished typescript, National Archive for the History of Computing, Manchester University.
Tedlow, Richard (1990) *New and Improved: The Story of Mass Marketing in America*, Oxford: Heinemann.
Thomas, David (1990) *Alan Sugar: The Amstrad Story*, London: Century.
Tweedale, Geoffrey (1992a) 'Marketing in the second industry revolution: a case study of the Ferranti computer group, 1949–63', *Business History* 34: 272–303.
—— (1992b) 'Aspects of the Anglo-American transfer of computer technology: the formative years, ca 1930s to 1960s', in David J. Jeremy (ed.) *Studies in Technology Transfer*, Aldershot: Gower.
Watson Jr, Thomas J. and Petre, Peter (1990) *Father Son & Co: My Life at IBM and Beyond*, London: Bantam Press.
Williams, Michael R. (1985) *A History of Computing Technology*, Englewood Cliffs, NJ: Prentice-Hall.
Young, Jeffrey S. (1988) *Steve Jobs: The Journey is the Reward*, Barnet, Herts: Glentop Press.

8 Marketing in British banking, 1945–80

Margaret Ackrill

There is no agreement on a definition of marketing. A shelf-full of textbooks on the subject produces a shelf-full of differences. Some authors attempt a definition of the term, others avoid it, presuming that readers will be enlightened about its meaning as they proceed. Nevertheless there are ideas which are common to most volumes. They are that marketing has as its end-product purchases of goods and/or services, or at least a greater awareness of their existence, by an identified range of customers or consumers. Such sales and awareness are created largely through advertising in the media, and possibly also on bill-boards and in other public places, and through personal contacts made by purveyors of the goods and services, or people acting on their behalf. Market research builds up profiles of the finances, interests, wants, needs, and likes and dislikes of cross-sections of the population: from these surveys possible customers and consumers of the product or service in question are identified, and advertising calculated to appeal to their large or small numbers is created. The correct placement of marketing departments within corporations is of crucial importance to those corporations.

British banks in 1945, if judged by this description of marketing, did no marketing whatever. None had marketing departments: such advertising as they placed in the press was often arranged behind doors labelled 'press office' or 'information'. The advertising itself was very low key. Lloyds Bank, one of the five large London clearing banks (the others were Barclays Bank, the Midland Bank, National Provincial Bank and the Westminster Bank), in its newspaper advertisements to recruit new staff from among school-leavers, had neat line-drawings of attractive teenagers, interested in the idea of working for Lloyds (Winton 1982: 156), but no eulogy of the bank's services. Other banks, often in local newspapers, mentioned the advantages which they could offer staff, but rarely those which they

Marketing in British banking 151

could offer customers. Yet the larger banks had millions of customers and nationwide networks of branches, though with greater representation in some counties than in others. Why did they not market or even advertise their services, and how had they recruited and retained customers? The answers to these questions were embedded in the history of banking in Britain.

British banks had always attempted to cultivate an image of stability, sobriety and dependability. Failures of small country partnership banks in the nineteenth century had brought much misery to their local customers: the development of joint stock banking, the amalgamation of smaller bankers to form larger, stronger units (not all as yet with head offices in London or Edinburgh), and the monitoring eye and preventative actions of the Bank of England all but eliminated such failures by 1914. The aim of British banks was to appear uninfluenced by tides of fashion or fortune, and a good deal of their image was conveyed by their ornate head offices, spacious branches, and the aloof demeanour of bank managers. By the 1920s, after the control over bank activities exercised by the government during the 1914–18 war was loosened, and bank failures seemed part of a past era, a bolder, more competitive atmosphere might have been expected in banking. But the depression of 1920–1 did not encourage banks to open their purse-strings, or appear avid for business.[1]

Britain's return to the gold standard in 1925 required coordination between the major banks and the Bank of England, and the effect of the economic depression of 1929–33 was to draw the connecting ropes between the banks tighter. Bank of England pressure induced the major banks to help in the financial restructuring of ailing industries and firms; banks themselves, with outstanding loans to loss-making firms, had no wish to poach each others' more risky business – and no great urge to extend their number of customers, unless such customers already had a good record. In such a case, customers were likely to have a bank already, and as later surveys showed, firms rarely changed their banks. The exception was for incoming foreign firms, often American, which set up or extended their operations in Britain. At least some banks made efforts to attract the business of individual newcomers.

In 1931, as the depression deepened, Britain retreated from the gold standard; there was a run on major banks in Austria and Germany, and over 600 lesser banks in the USA collapsed under pressure. The great virtue of British banks was that they did not collapse, nor did they readily foreclose on defaulting customers. If they did not recruit many new customers, they retained those which they had, because of their reliability. In the personal sector, customers were largely people in upper income groups; in the corporate sector, they ranged from small business accounts (often virtually indistinguishable from personal ones) to surviving manufacturing giants. To reduce the interest on government borrowing, and to make money affordable, the Bank of England set Bank Rate at 2 per cent in 1932. (The external value of the pound was to be controlled by means other than the interest rate.) British banks, to give themselves some profit against which to offset bad debts, agreed between themselves to charge borrowers a minimum of 5 per cent interest, with the exception of a lower rate for favoured customers – mainly large, virtually risk-free corporate borrowers. They also agreed to pay 2 per cent below Bank Rate, with a minimum of $\frac{1}{2}$ per cent, as interest on all deposit accounts left with them, which usually required seven days' notice of withdrawal. Current accounts yielded no interest to their owners, though within the banks' book-keeping systems they were credited with 'notional interest' which served to reduce the charges made for services performed. These charges therefore varied between customers; the Bank of England gave grudging assent to these agreements (Sayers 1972: vol. II, 557) by which dog did not eat dog. The Bank held Bank Rate at 2 per cent until 1951.

British banks, unlike all other British firms, did not publish their true reserves until the financial year 1969; the increase in the number of their branches between the wars, and the continued solid presence of existing branches reaffirmed the strength of the banks' hidden reserves. Newspaper advertisements largely took the form of publication of chairmen's annual addresses; there were few new services to publicize, and most press notices were simple reminders of their existence. Marketing had still not arrived.

With World War II (1939–45) government controls, extended over much of the economy, put limitations on what proportion of bank assets could be lent, and to whom, and reinforced the understated approach to business by now typical of British banks. Much of their finance during the war went into a variety of Treasury bills, Treasury Deposit Receipts and longer term government securities: demand for their typically short-term advances fell as firms were paid directly by the government for goods made to its order. The clearing banks in 1941 established the Banking Information Service to handle press releases (Newman 1984: 293), but wartime government restrictions on the use of paper limited press advertising, and of course all radio in Britain was run through the British Broadcasting Corporation, which had 'no advertising' as part of its charter. Television, experimented with before the war, was suspended. Where bank business expanded, this was due to localized demand from the construction and operation of new airfields, British and American, and of munitions factories. Such wartime activities had great impact on the number of banking transactions – as well as on the overall economy.

When the war ended, the business climate was one of restriction and repair, not of vigorous renewal. Through Bank of England pressure, banks were restrained in the proportion of their deposits which they could lend to the public. Continued restrictions on the use of paper (largely imported, and hence detrimental to the precarious balance of payments) meant that annual reports were not promotional material. Barclays' was a small sheet of paper which folded into an ordinary envelope, carrying a brief address from the bank's chairman and an even briefer statement of accounts. In 1948, worried by an increase in general advertising which was deemed an extravagant use of money and likely to lead to wasteful competition in a market still restricted by rationing and controls, the government proposed making half of all advertising expenditure non-allowable against tax (Dow 1970: 35). Alarmed, the Federation of British Industries hammered out a voluntary code of restraint from advertising to which the banks and other members agreed (National Westminster Bank archives 1948/49:a).[2] In fact, the best commercial reason for *not* advertising was that advertising, meant to reinforce a brand image, tended to create annoyance in a public which found the actual products unavailable. Banks' basic services of receiving, transmitting and lending money, and their ancillary services in trustee work and insurance of course *were* available, so their self-denial was the greater (NWA 1948/49:b). In 1949 the ban eased: but by now banks had made a virtue of more-or-less necessity. 'Touting for custom' was deprecated among bankers. While bomb damage to bank branches could be made good, building controls did not readily allow the construction of new commercial buildings or of extension to existing ones (Dow 1970: 149–50) until 1954. Until that year, in spite of attempts at refurbishment, branches became somewhat dingier and less compelling as witnesses of financial strength, and certainly forbidding to people who were not accustomed to their solemn atmosphere. Nor did renewed agreements between the banks, this time limiting interest charged on advances to 'blue chip' companies to $\frac{1}{2}$ per cent above Bank Rate, promote new initiatives in lending.

However, as physical controls eased and the economy expanded, banks began to compete with each other for customers by building new branches and improving their existing ones, although their siting relied on rule of thumb and observation rather than market survey. A few 'prestige' bank advertisements appeared in the 1950s: Lloyds offered a series on British coins (Winton 1982: 156) but at first there were no new services to promote. In any case, from 1951 the clearing banks were required by the Bank of England to hold 30 per cent (later reduced to 28 per cent) of their deposits in cash, money at call with the discount market, Treasury bills, and government or government-approved securities. They had built up large government holdings during the war, and only slowly reduced them, so that they did not lend even the permitted 70 per cent for some years. From 1958, as guidelines were temporarily relaxed, they nevertheless had to make 'special deposits' with the Bank of England if their advances exceeded Bank of England criteria. None of this was conducive to vigorous advertisement of current services. So far, they had provided personal advances, sometimes in the form of agreed short-term loans, but more often as un-negotiated overdrafts, and advances to businesses, which were divided into loans and overdrafts. Whether security was taken on such advances depended to a large degree on the individual bank manager's assessment of the character of a person or a business, and default was, in fact, low – well under a fraction of 1 per cent for most banks. Advances could be 'rolled over' so that they in effect formed longer term loans, but there was no publicity for this. Banks' insurance, stock-broking, and trustee services were promoted by discreet notices in branches; these services were often loss-making in themselves, provided as an adjunct to the retention of accounts, and not widely advertised. However, the finance houses which supplied money to firms which sold their goods through hire-purchase were not so reticent: they freely advertised their longer term (and higher priced) facilities, borrowing money from the wholesale money markets to lend to their customers. Banks began to take note of the business done by the finance houses and the hire-purchase firms themselves. But they did not offer comparable facilities until the late 1950s, and then through special subsidiaries bought or set-up during the 1958–60 credit relaxation.

Television broadcasts had resumed post-war and commercial television was added to BBC output; in 1955 the Midland Bank broke ranks, and provided the first television advertisements for a bank's products. The advertisements promoted embellished 'gift cheques' as birthday, wedding, or Christmas presents (Holmes and Green 1986: 224). Most purchasers of the cheques proved to be Midland customers already, and thus the project was scarcely worthwhile. Nevertheless from 1957 to 1958 the Midland Bank spent 37 per cent of the total advertising bill of the big five clearing banks. When the Bank of England loosened restraints on lending in 1958, the Midland broke new ground again, providing a well-advertised personal loan scheme for sums between £50 and £500 at 5 per cent, repayable over two years (the true rate of interest was actually 10 per cent). It also offered personal cheque accounts which did not provide overdrafts, and for which customers were charged five shillings (25p) for every cheque used (Holmes and Green 1986: 224). Before launching the accounts with suitable advertisements, the Midland had not done market research in Britain, but it had investigated similar personal accounts in both the United States and Australia. In just two months, 45,000 personal loan accounts were opened, over half of them for car or motorbike purchase (Holmes and Green 1986: 225). The Midland had, as prime minister Harold Macmillan remarked, 'set the cat among the pigeons'. A.D. Chesterfield, chief general manager of the Westminster Bank, was convinced that the personal loan accounts would prove unremunerative to the Midland: considerable discussion took place between the chief executives of the clearers, who did not want the loss of customers which might result, and yet did not want to establish rival schemes (NWA 1958:c). Nevertheless, some banks followed suit with rival accounts. They were in any case becoming more adventurous in their general advertising; while they argued that advertisements on television and on 'pirate' radio would produce only an upward spiral of costs for them all, and agreed among themselves not to use such promotion, they were developing advertisements for the still-popular cinema. In 1960 they promised each other not to use television or cinema advertisements without six months' notice (NWA 1960:d).

Then in the 1960s a number of considerations affected the attitude of British banks to marketing in general and to advertising in particular. More foreign banks of every size opened up in Britain, most usually in London, taking advantage of the ease of registration offered by the Bank of England or Board of Trade (Reid 1982: 23–30). The Eurodollar money market, fed by funds spent abroad by the United States and not repatriated, grew. New small British banks also mushroomed, and they and the foreign banks were not bound by the same restrictions on lending, or by the mutual agreements on interest rates, which tied the major British banks to the Bank of England and to each other more strongly than ever in 1967 and 1968. These secondary banks raised their funds on wholesale money markets, prepared to pay more for them, and to charge more to borrowers. It was said with some truth in established British banks that the incoming banks were attracting a good deal of riskier business which the banking establishment did not want; but the same could not be said of the largest of the newcomers.

These were major American banks: the three largest banks in the world (measured by deposits) in the 1960s were American. All of them advertised their image and their services. Particularly impressive was the Chase Manhattan Bank. Its slogan 'You have a friend/ In Chase Manhattan' was familiar to the ears of East Coast Americans and appeared on stylish advertisements in the *New Yorker*, the monthly journal for English-speaking sophisticates on both sides of the Atlantic. Its appeal was to a wider audience than expatriate Americans. Restricted by United States legislation from expanding across state boundaries, US banks followed their domestic customers abroad as the latter acquired new subsidiaries, opened new plants and offices, and increased investment in Europe as an integral part of their activities. These banks had a growing presence in London, and did not confine themselves to American companies. They began small, but to British eyes significant, inroads into the business of domestic corporate borrowers.

Meanwhile the growth of British building societies, with interest rates on savings higher than the banks offered in less-accessible seven-day bank deposit accounts, with their expanding branch network, and their longer hours of opening than the banks, were presenting a major challenge to the banks' collection of deposits from personal customers. The Post Office Savings Bank, founded with Gladstone's blessing in the middle of the nineteenth century, was losing ground somewhat, but was presenting a glossier identity: Harold Wilson's Labour government created the National Giro Bank in 1968, also accessible through hundreds of post offices throughout Britain, and offering a wider range of services than the Post Office Savings Bank. Additionally, various types of national savings bonds and certificates competed for the longer term savings of personal customers. In fact, the share of government-sponsored deposit takers fell, but the share of total deposits in Britain held by the major clearers also fell from 34.8 to 27.4 per cent between 1961 and 1967 (NWA 1967:e) while that of foreign and overseas banks rose from 7.2 to 19.7 per cent, and building societies from 14.8 to 19.3 per cent.

At the same time a new range of customers began to have its attractions for British banks. The socio-economic category C4, which applied largely to weekly-paid manual workers, had not formerly seemed attractive to the banks, because it was presumed that C4 deposits would be small, and C4 transactions would be numerous and therefore costly. But, pioneered by ICI, large firms began paying their manual workers by cheque, rather than by cash. Until 1960, the Truck Act (1831–1960) forbade, *inter alia*, payment of wages in tokens, which expression was held to cover cheques. With the increase of robberies, firms pressed for the repeal of the act, effected in 1960, and so here was a phalanx of new customers, waving cheques, and at very least needing somewhere to cash them. To attract these cheques – and especially to persuade their owners not to draw out all the money – banks not only opened new branches near or in places of work, sometimes sending a mobile branch on pay day, but also, with experience, looked harder at the characteristics and requirements of C4 customers, and gave special advice to staff about an appropriately friendly manner. They found in them a propensity to save which was almost equal to that of C3 (white-collar) workers. Further off-setting the cost of managing these accounts was the decline in the need for and risk of a bank sending large quantities of money to places of work at a time when robbery was on the increase. There was also the thought that even if such accounts were not profitable today, they might become so in future, as wages pursued their upward trend in real purchasing power (NWA 1973:f).

Thus both at the level of corporate lending, and at the level of payment into branches by personal customers, British banks reconsidered their strategies – and their attitude towards marketing. The introduction of central computing and branch terminals into British banks held out the promise of cheapening transactions, and also of facilitating sophistications such as calculations of interest on a daily basis. It was but a step to the creation of special types of account based on better market knowledge, and promoted by wider advertising, even though the government and the Bank of England continued to restrict clearing bank lending and to discourage advances to certain sections of the economy. Clearing banks, given an example by the Midland with its Samuel Montague merchant bank subsidiary, also developed merchant bank offshoots, through which large loans, often medium term rather than the traditional short-term ones, could be lent at higher rates to large companies, and this entailed discrete advertisement.

A new departure which more nearly approached the full marketing concept was made by Barclays in 1966, when it first issued Barclaycard. It utilized the US technique of the direct mail shot to recruit holders for this card, intended to effect payments for retail goods and services. Its introduction and the method employed 'was a contentious action regarded by some as provocative' (Barclays Report 1966: 19), and outraged recipients wrote complaining that they were somehow being 'forced' to hold the card. Successful as this launch proved to be, it did show the hazards of moving ahead of prevalent views of how banks should behave. But driving the banks forward in the late 1960s and early 1970s were the far freer approaches to advertising of the incoming banks. Some such organizations had been far too free, prompting the 1963 Protection of Depositors Act, which required more information from firms which were not banks, but nevertheless offered financial services (Reid 1982: 24).

Further, led by Barclays' chairman, John Thomson, the clearers reviewed their mutual agreements on interest rates, although no change was made until 1970 (when rates to 'blue chip' borrowers were raised to 1 per cent above Bank Rate), in spite of recommendations from the 1967 report of the National Board for Prices and Incomes on bank charges (NBPI 1967: Cmnd. 3293). Within the banks there was more attention to style and general presentation in an attempt to dispel the pervading, somewhat formidable, image. Most resistant to change were the remote branches of the National Provincial Bank. The National Provincial and Westminster Banks merged to form the National Westminster Bank in 1968. When Westminster head office executives paid visits to National Provincial branches, in order to see how the merger should best be managed, they were privately appalled by the threadbare carpets and creaking lifts of some of the branch managers' offices (NWA 1968: g). (To traditional National Provincial men, this austerity was intended as a reassurance to customers and shareholders that profits were not made at their expense, but were passed on in reasonable terms and good dividends.) In 1961 Lloyds Bank appointed a public relations officer with a department of his own to handle advertising and relations with the press (Winton 1982: 181). The National Provincial in 1965 appointed INFOPLAN, the public relations firm, to make recommendations. Its major conclusion was that public relations alone

> could not achieve a change for the better in the overall image of your bank. [What] has to be changed is the attitude of your own people towards their jobs, the customers, and the public . . . we would say that you are considered nice people but old-fashioned.
> (NWA 1966: h)

National Provincial nevertheless went ahead with well-received cinema advertisements. Barclays Bank also gave cinema animation to its spreadeagle sign. The Midland had its stationery, lettering, and house-style redesigned in 1964, emerging with brown and yellow colours and the griffin as its sole symbol (Holmes and Green 1986: 232–3). J Walter Thompson devised an advertising campaign used by the National Westminster Bank. With the slogan 'our roots are our branches', cheerful bill-boards and animated cinema cartoons appeared. Other cinema advertisements produced jointly by the clearing banks depicted bank managers as comic figures, to the consternation of bank employees (NWA 1972: i). The old order was changing.

Advertising expenditure by banks grew, though with renewed agreements between them not to use television, which, it was thought, would simply provide an upward spiral of costs to all banks. This taboo was broken by National Westminster in 1972, and indeed an upward spiral followed. By 1980, the expenditure of Barclays, Lloyds, Midland and National Westminster on television advertising had risen from nothing in 1970 to £880,000, £673,000, £3,232,000 and £1,373,000 respectively, surpassing their press expenditure which totalled £6,033,000, and had been £1,839,000 in 1971 (MEAL 1980).

The publication of true profits and reserves in 1970 and the ending of the existing set of lending controls by the Bank of England in 1971 (they were replaced by a less restrictive regime) had led to a great expansion of bank credit, the creation of new types of accounts which had to be publicized, and a reappraisal of the approach to personal customers. For instance, university students had hitherto been a target for new accounts, since although such accounts were not profitable, experience taught that their holders would ultimately become of the rewarding A and B status – and that people still changed their banks infrequently. Now the general age-group 18–35 became a target as young people's wages were higher proportionately to those of older people than they had been. The 1968 merger of the National Provincial and Westminster Banks, and of the smaller Martins Bank with Barclays Bank in 1969, brought the opportunity and the occasion for reappraisal of general style and intended appeal in both new entities, and a uniform house style was commissioned and created for each bank, with a readily identifiable symbol, and a distinctive set of lettering and colouring.

Bank premises in the later 1960s and 1970s were redesigned to be less forbidding, more user-friendly and more cheerful, annual reports became glossier, with colourful illustrations. In the National Westminster Bank, traditional expenditure on recruitment advertising and press versions of chairmen's statements was separated from more directly promotional advertisement (NWA 1968: k). While the clearers had largely used their branches to create investors as they entered the competitive unit trust business in the 1960s (Newman 1984: 153), when they entered the home mortgage market in the late 1970s, initially offering larger sums on mortgage than the building societies, they made wide use of television and other media. There was more change in the years 1970–80 in the approach to publicity than in the previous four decades.

But was this really marketing? Had the banks carefully chosen the appropriate target customers, and correctly appealed to them? They certainly had set up marketing departments in the late 1960s: Deryk Weyer, at Barclays, was the first manager to have 'marketing' incorporated into his title. The place of the marketing departments within head offices and the work assigned to them varied, but undoubtedly in the 1970s more and more use was made of market research, commissioned or supplied from outside the banks, and added to by information generated within them. The sheer bulk of information supplied by their own computer records of customers was a barrier to some types of analysis even beyond 1980: before that time some use was made of it for specified purposes, but much more use was made of outside agencies and experts.

Most of what was done in the media related to personal customers. In 1970 51 per cent of the adult population of Britain had no bank account, but the percentage was down to 26 per cent by 1981 (Newman 1984: 314). In terms of numbers therefore, the marketing efforts of the 1970s can be judged very successful. The profitability of some of the new accounts was another matter; pricing of services depended on a mixture of extrapolation and forecasting, and could not always be accurate. For smaller business customers, banks set up special advisory centres within major branches and regional offices, and these too were well-publicized; as with personal customers, these accounts had some of their commercial justification in the future growth of the business, rather than present profit to the bank.

For large corporate customers, a different approach to marketing was taken. Advertising in the mass media was inappropriate: financial journals at home and abroad, and personal contacts, were used instead. National Westminster's new international division in the 1970s instituted a programme of personal calling on international businesses – and calling again.

Thus banks sought to tailor both product and publicity to more carefully identified customers. But was this enough? To thorough-going believers in a market-driven strategy for firms, it was necessary first to identify a need or want, and then create the appropriate service or product. In this sense, British banks were not market-led. They saw others providing something which they wished to emulate, whether to create or retain customers. Market share was important for some scale economies if the existence of branches and 1970s assumption of no redundancies were taken as given, as British banks did so take them in the 1970s, and so market share was sought through marketing. Profitability did not always follow: nevertheless there had been a transformation in the attitude of head offices to marketing – even if some branch managers found it hard to accept that they were now required actively to sell products (the very words were still distasteful) instead of passively to provide services. Marketing had become part of the banks' perception of themselves.

NOTES

1 For the general history of the major British banks see Committee of London Clearing bankers, The London Clearing Banks: *Evidence by the Committee of London Clearing Bankers to the Committee to Review the Functioning of Financial Institutions*, London, CLCB, 1978 and M. Collins *Money and Banking in the UK: a History*, London: Croom Helm, 1988.
2 I wish to thank the National Westminster Bank plc for permission to make use of material collected for an internal report, hereafter referred to as NWA. The material includes papers from the bank's two major constituents, National Provincial Bank and Westminster Bank, which merged to form the National Westminster Bank Ltd in 1968. These papers are not part of the accessible archive.

REFERENCES

Barclays Bank annual reports.
Dow, J.C.R. (1970) *The Management of the British Economy, 1945–60* (student edition), Cambridge: Cambridge University Press.
Holmes A.R. and Green, E. (1986) *Midland, 150 Years of Banking Business*, London: B.T. Batsford.
MEAL (Media Expenditure Analysis).
National Board for Prices and Incomes (1967) *Report no. 34 on Bank Charges*, Cmnd. 3293, London: HMSO.
National Westminster Bank plc archives, Lothbury, London.
Newman, K. (1984) *Financial Marketing and Communications*, London: Holt Rinehart & Winston.
Reid, M. (1982) *The Secondary Banking Crisis, 1973–75, its Causes and Course*, London: Macmillan.
Sayers, R.S. (1972) *The Bank of England, 1891–1944*, Cambridge: Cambridge University Press.
Winton, J.R. (1982) *Lloyds Bank 1918–1969*, Oxford: Oxford University Press.

9 International wheat marketing in the post-war period
An Australian perspective on the era of discriminating buyers

Greg Whitwell

Investigate international wheat marketing in the post-war period and you immediately enter the world of political economy where the outstanding feature seems to be the use of tactics designed to 'buy' customers. The casual observer can be forgiven for thinking that wheat sales have nothing to do with marketing skills and everything to do with the willingness of governments to provide both sufficient funds to ensure that prices are competitive and the means (credit) by which customers can pay for grain. There is, nevertheless, as this chapter seeks to show, another, more subtle, side to wheat marketing. Its importance derives from the fact that, notwithstanding the critical role of price and credit considerations, a great many wheat buyers are quality-conscious. They want cheap wheat, certainly, but they also want wheat which will meet their quality requirements. The quality characteristic upon which most attention has focused – whether the purchasers be bakers, noodle makers or biscuit manufacturers – is the protein content of wheat, for this has a greater influence on processing quality than any other single factor. That buyers have become more discriminating can be seen most readily in increasingly tighter specifications with respect to protein content and in the ever-growing proportion of total sales based on specific protein requirements. Buyers have also been insistent that suppliers be able to deliver wheat with particular quality attributes on a regular basis. The argument here is that in this world of increasingly quality-conscious wheat buyers, true marketing skills, and not just the budgetary largesse of an exporting country's government, have been and remain important in determining a wheat exporter's ability to enter new markets and to maintain and increase market share in existing ones.

MARKETING VERSUS SELLING

The reference just above to 'true marketing skills' raises some definitional questions. A useful definition, one provided by William Stanton in his popular general text, *Fundamentals of Marketing*, is to consider marketing (agricultural or otherwise) as 'a total system of interacting business activities designed to plan, price, promote and distribute want-satisfying products to present and potential customers' (Stanton 1975: 5). Stanton contrasts marketing, which is a process or course of business action, with the 'marketing concept', which is a philosophy, an attitude or a way of business thinking. He points out that the marketing concept highlights the distinction between selling and marketing: terms which in common parlance are often seen as being synonymous. In selling, the emphasis is on the product whereas in marketing it is on customers' wants. In selling, the company first makes the product and then tries to determine how to sell it profitably, whereas in marketing the company first determines what the customers want, and then the firm tries to determine how it can profitably make and deliver a product to satisfy those wants. There is an internal, company orientation in selling whereas there is an external, market orientation in marketing. Finally, selling emphasizes company (sellers') needs whereas marketing emphasizes market (buyers') needs (Stanton 1975: 13).

Much of the discussion in this chapter is about the monopoly organization responsible for exporting Australian wheat, the Australian Wheat Board (AWB), established in 1939. Part of the aim here is to show that the AWB changed in the post-war period from a mere seller of wheat to one which marketed it.[1]

THE INTERNATIONAL WHEAT TRADE

As a starting point, to put the discussion in context, we need a brief outline of changes in the international wheat trade and markets. International trade in wheat expanded greatly, if erratically, in the post-war period. In the late 1940s it averaged about 25 million tonnes a year. By the early 1960s it had doubled and by the early 1980s it had doubled again. For most of the post-war period four major suppliers accounted for some 75–85 per cent of world wheat exports. The United States has consistently been easily the most important wheat- and flour-exporting nation, its market share averaging about 40 per cent. Before the late 1970s Canada was almost invariably second to the United States, Australia third and Argentina fourth.

From the late 1970s the European Community (notably France) suddenly emerged as an exporter of major importance. Its market share accelerated greatly during the 1980s (Roberts *et al.* 1989: 35).

Whereas the exporting side of the international wheat trade has been dominated by only a handful of countries, there are a large number of countries which fall into the category of major wheat importers. In the 1980s they included the USSR, China, Egypt, Japan, the Republic of Korea, Iran, Algeria, Iraq, the European Community (EC-12, much of whose imports are intra-community), Poland, Brazil and Morocco. Historical data on world wheat imports by destination reveal a dramatic change after World War II. In the 1930s Western Europe accounted for almost three-quarters of world wheat imports. Britain alone was responsible for about one-third. The post-war period saw a rapid increase in the demand for wheat by developing countries. Accompanying this, the geographical focus of the international wheat trade shifted from Western Europe to Africa, Latin America, the Middle East and Asia (Roberts *et al.* 1989: 35–7).

The institutional arrangements for both exporting and importing wheat vary considerably.[2] Canada, like Australia, has a monopoly statutory authority responsible for marketing wheat abroad, namely the Canadian Wheat Board (CWB).[3] The United States has a more decentralized and privatized system. It relies on private traders – dominated by the 'great grain companies' such as Continental, Cargill, Bunge and Louis Dreyfus – who are aided and abetted, as some would put it, by the immense bureaucracy making up the United States Department of Agriculture (USDA).[4] The USDA is responsible for a great variety of things, including the administration of government programmes, policy development and the provision of market intelligence services on customers, actual and potential, and on competitors. The job of promoting United States wheat, and more generally of export market development and analysis, is entrusted to US Wheat Associates (US Wheat). US Wheat is a non-profit organization funded by wheat producers in sixteen states through their respective state organizations. It also receives funds by virtue of agreements with the Foreign Agricultural Service of the USDA. By the late 1980s it had, in addition to its United States offices, some fourteen overseas offices.[5]

A SEGMENTED MARKET

The international wheat market is highly segmented. End uses and hence wheat requirements vary from country to country. Thus from the seller's perspective segmentation can occur in the first instance at the national level: one country's requirements may be high-volume bread, another's flat bread, yet another's chappatis or noodles, and so on. There may also be market segmentation within countries, perhaps along regional lines. In Iraq, for example, the bread preferred in the north is quite different to that in the south. Segmentation can also occur, of course, within a single country in the range of wheat flour: an individual country may divide its use of wheat between the manufacture of bread and noodles. In many countries consumer tastes have changed over time, leading to greater market segmentation. Wheaten products have increased in popularity in many countries previously heavily reliant on rice as a staple food. In Japan, for example, bread consumption per capita increased rapidly in the 1950s and 1960s. As well there have been marked changes in Japan in the popularity of different sorts of (wheat) noodles. From the early 1960s, for example, Chinese-style noodles grew in popularity at the expense of Japanese-style noodles. The same period saw instant noodles consumed in greatly increased quantities.

The wheat marketer has faced, in short, a situation in which quality requirements vary between and within countries and over time.[6] In responding to this, some exporters, notably Canada, persisted for a long time with the strategy of concentrating on supplying as many countries as possible with superior quality, high-protein wheats ideally suited to making breads. This was a strategy of what could be called concentrated marketing. In this case the marketer focuses on one or a limited number of market segments within individual countries with the objective of trying to achieve a larger share of them. The marketer can offer greater knowledge and try to capitalize on the reputation it has acquired for providing particular sorts of wheats. Even with this approach, however, the strategies required to win and maintain customers within a single market segment will vary depending on an importing country's income, geographical location, buying attitudes and practices, consumer tastes, the degree of mechanization of local processing industries, baking practices, and so on.

Other exporters sought to broaden the range of wheats they produced and/or make it clearer to buyers the true extent of product differentiation by altering the national wheat classification system. The aim here was to broaden the range of actual and potential customer countries and to supply a variety of market segments within individual countries. This essentially was the strategy adopted by

Australia. The AWB's aim was to dispel the popular notion that it produced only one kind of wheat. The United States, by contrast, had no alternative but to engage in differentiated marketing. It was unique among the major exporters in not being heavily reliant upon a single major class of wheat and having instead a large exportable surplus of wheat classes ranging from hard to soft.

MECHANIZATION AND TECHNOLOGICAL CHANGE

Why have wheat importers become more quality-conscious? And why does wheat uniformity matter to them so much? To a large extent the answer lies with the spread of mechanization in the milling and processing industries of importing countries, and ongoing technological improvements in the sorts of machinery employed in these industries. Since the adoption of the gradual reduction system and the introduction of the basic milling machines – the rollermill, purifier and plansifter – which began some 130 years ago, the major changes in the milling industry have been in the continual improvement in the operation of the basic machinery rather than in the adoption of new sorts of machines.[7] The division and subdivision of grain as it passed through the mill increased greatly the need for separate conveying of mill stocks. The use of automation accelerated rapidly. Compared to the milling industry, the technological changes which occurred in the baking industry in the post-war period were much more profound. A feature of the period was the steady replacement of manual production in small-scale bakeries by semi- and fully-automated bakeries in large plants. In those countries, such as Britain and the United States, which already possessed highly mechanized baking industries, changes in production practices such as the introduction of 'no-time' and 'continuous dough' techniques required additional investment and changes in the scale and layout of plants. Here, as in the milling industry, the result was a greater emphasis on uniformity and consistency and increasingly more rigid specifications.

MARKETING TACTICS IN A WORLD OF DISCRIMINATING BUYERS

Wheat marketers, faced with increasingly discriminating buyers, have had open to them a range of options to try to meet customer requirements. In the remainder of this chapter I want to consider some of these options under two broad headings. Each is followed by a summary of the Australian experience.

Segregation, varietal control and payment for quality

To begin, wheat marketers can impose (or in some countries seek to have the government impose) a wider set of, and stricter, receival or grading standards.[8] This refers to the criteria which determine, at the delivery point, the grade into which the farmer's wheat will be placed. The criteria might include test weight, moisture content, degree of unmillable and foreign material, grain vitreousness or hardness, degree of weather damage, protein content and so on. Tightening receival standards would require that each criterion be capable of accurate (objective) measurement, rather than be determined simply by visual inspection. The use of this 'tactic' is therefore dependent on the availability, accuracy and relative cost of devices capable of measuring these characteristics. It depends too on scientific developments (for example, the development of techniques able to reduce grain contaminants such as insects and pesticide residues) and on changes in agronomic practices (for example, the adoption of ley farming and other practices designed to increase soil nitrogen levels and thereby protein content).

Next, one can attempt to improve the inherited quality characteristics of the grain. The efforts of the wheat breeder are critical in this respect. So too are the rules governing the release and use of new varieties. In addition one has to try to encourage the farmer to use existing varieties which are known to have superior processing qualities and to discard those known to be inferior. Here the introduction and refinement of some form of varietal control is critical.

Both of these 'tactics' are intertwined with, and to a degree are dependent on, the way in which a country's wheat is classified. The question of responding to the quality demands of buyers has been intimately linked with debate on the need for radical change in, or sometimes simply modification of, existing classification systems. The argumentation on classification has been about the extent to which wheat should be segregated into different classes and grades, the criteria to be used, the rewards and disincentives a classification system might provide to growers, and the ability or otherwise of the handling and transportation system to cope with an increasingly segregated crop. This in turn has led to questions about promotion, customer education and after-sales service and, more generally, the best ways to inform existing and potential buyers of the range of quality characteristics found in a country's wheats.

One function of classification systems is that they provide a basis for differential payments to growers. Whether growers are actually paid the premiums and discounts paid by the market for different classes and grades of wheat is another matter. In Canada and Australia pooling systems operate which can and have distorted price signals to growers. Likewise in the United States the officially administered loan rate and reserve price schemes have served to distort price signals. The point is, then, that a wheat exporter's ability to compete on quality terms depends in part on whether there are adequate incentives for growers to improve quality and – a closely related point – the extent to which payments to growers reflect the market valuation of their wheat. There are potentially a number of complications in trying to ensure this. In Australia, for example, a long-standing problem, from the AWB's point of view anyway, was a deeply entrenched adherence to the principle of egalitarianism among growers and hence a resistance to suggestions that the industry accept a more disaggregated pooling arrangement.

With these generalizations in mind, we can now turn to the Australian story. Before 1974 Australian wheat marketing was based on the fair average quality (FAQ) standard, a grading system employed in Australia from the late nineteenth century. The United States and Canada, by contrast, exported their wheat on the basis of a 'certificate final with respect to quality', the certificate being issued under federal inspection at the point of loading, using a numerical standard based on quantitative measurement. In these two countries wheat was classified into types, classes and grades. Each grade had a specified minimum bushel weight, minimum percentage of vitreous kernels, maximum limit of foreign materials and a specified degree of soundness. These standards applied year after year. Under the Australian FAQ system, by contrast, the standard for each of the wheat-growing states was fixed annually, usually near the completion of the harvest. It was determined using a systematic and well-organized sampling technique. Once determined, samples would be sent to customers as representative of the quality they would (or should) receive. The FAQ standard provided no guide to baking value. Some idea of milling value, however, was indicated by the declaration of the FAQ's bushel weight. To be accepted as FAQ, wheat had to meet certain minimum receival standards. Those that did not were designated 'off-grade'. Traditionally the receival standards consisted of simple physical tests which could be carried out at the country receival point by a relatively unskilled operator. They involved a sieving test to check for the presence of live insects and any foreign or unmillable material, a moisture test (with a strict maximum of 12 per cent) to ensure that the grain would not deteriorate with prolonged storage, a visible check for sprouted and/

or weather affected grains and, finally, a grain density measurement to determine whether the grain was suitable or otherwise for flour milling purposes. The individual deliveries would then be received into the bulk handling system, composite samples prepared for subsequent testing, and sales made on the basis of these results. All growers ultimately received the same average return per bushel.

There were two major problems with the FAQ system, both of which became more obvious during the 1950s. The first was the marked heterogeneity of samples. Especially in New South Wales and South Australia, where more and more farmers had grown high-protein hard wheats, there was a tendency for each state's FAQ to become nondescript. The second, a related problem, was the marked inconsistency in the standard from one year to the next. The question was: how to deal with these problems? For twenty years from the mid-1950s onwards attention focused on altering the classification system by segregating the annual harvest. After an intense and highly emotional debate, segregations began to be introduced in the late 1950s when hard wheats grown in certain states began to be received and sold separately from what were predominantly soft wheats. The 1960s saw further changes to the classification system. By 1971 the AWB could offer its export customers twenty-eight different classes of wheat, though more than 80 per cent of the crop still fell into the FAQ category. Despite these changes the AWB's chairman could point to continuing problems in marketing FAQ wheat. The idea still persisted among some buyers, he said in 1972, that Australia sold only FAQ wheat and that it was all of similar quality. Furthermore,

> Foreign buyers, traditionally unfamiliar with the Australian FAQ are, more frequently than not, confused by the term, especially as the so-called 'quality' is 'fair' and 'average' yet, in point of fact, in no way relates to quality. In some countries 'quality' products are distinguished from 'average' ones. No amount of explanation completely banishes the prejudice arising from such confusion in the minds of overseas buyers, unfamiliar with this class of Australian wheat.

In short it was hard to imagine a more self-effacing and more confusing description of wheat. FAQ was, in fact, a misnomer, for it was simply a fair average sample. It should be said, however, that FAQ was by no means an exclusively Australian term. It was the standard term used in the grain trade for wheat sold on sample rather than by a certified quality grade.

The FAQ standard was eventually abandoned in 1974 and a new

classification system adopted. This was achieved with a minimum of fuss for the simple reason that nothing radical was done. In part, the change simply involved new names. Australian Standard White was substituted for FAQ. (One of the great advantages of this name, it was thought, was that it would reinforce the point that Australia was unique in that only white wheats were grown.) 'Off-grade' was henceforth to be handled under two new classifications, Australian General Purpose and Australian Feed. The other classes were Australian Prime Hard (sold at three different guaranteed minimum protein levels), Australian Hard (which was also sold at different guaranteed minimum protein levels), Australian Soft (which had a maximum protein level) and Australian Durum (a very high protein pasta wheat grown in extremely limited quantities in Australia).

There have been only minor changes to the classification system since 1974. In Australia the classification of all receivals are assessed using the same basic set of receival standards. These standards are extremely strict and have been used in part for promotional reasons, that is for building and exploiting a reputation as a supplier of wheat which is dry, clean, insect-free and uniform. An additional rationale for having stringent receival standards at the first point of sale is that it helps to mitigate a great many quality problems which are likely to emerge further downstream in the marketing system. Faced with rigid standards on the degree of unmillable material, for example, farmers have had an incentive to modify their harvesting techniques to ensure delivery of clean wheat. In Canada, by contrast, a charge has to be imposed on all growers to cover the cost of post-delivery cleaning, an operation usually undertaken at terminal elevators.

ASW wheat, like its predecessor, suffered from being an extremely large class. At least 70 per cent of deliveries were classed as ASW. It had to satisfy a wide range of end-use requirements (alone or in combination grist). By definition it was a compromise of quality characteristics and it was marketed as a multi-purpose wheat with protein content in the range of 9–11.5 per cent. The definition was left deliberately vague. ASW, again like its predecessor, was a residual class. It continued to be the case too that a new standard was set each year.

The AWB acknowledged that the problem of heterogeneity, though less serious, had not been overcome simply by these changes to the classification system. Something more was required. Attention focused increasingly on a topic which had been much discussed, then curiously abandoned, in the late 1950s: the use of varietal control. This can be effected in different ways. It might involve control (statutory or otherwise) over the release of varieties, so that only officially approved or recommended varieties are released. Alternatively or in addition it might involve the imposition of penalties (discounts) for the continuing use of varieties judged to be unsuitable for certain areas or having inferior milling and baking qualities. The Australian system involved both of these.

A system of varietal control, coupled with stringent receival standards covering the physical and chemical characteristics (including a measure of protein content) of wheat, has the potential to provide buyers with a highly reliable prediction of the processing quality of the wheat they are ordering. Indeed a feature of French wheat sales is the inclusion of stated varieties in the contract. Varietal control gives the wheat marketer the opportunity to improve the homogeneity (or at least reduce the heterogeneity) of each class by limiting the total number of varieties and by listing varieties by region, that is by nominating annually the varieties which will be accepted without a discount at groups of silos in certain geographical areas. Both of these help in turn to provide the marketer with the means to ensure – to mention the two extremes – that hard-grained, high dough strength bread wheats are grown only in areas conducive to producing high protein levels and that soft-grained, weak biscuit wheats are grown only in areas suitable for producing low-protein wheats. The end result should be greater uniformity and consistency. Through the encouragement and discouragement of particular varieties it is also possible to shift the quality characteristics of a class or grade of wheat to suit market requirements more closely.

There is, unfortunately, a major problem in implementing varietal control in a large and amorphous wheat class such as ASW. It is simply that it is extremely difficult to determine variety by visual inspection in a situation in which a very large number of varieties exist. In Canada the approach had been simply to insist that new varieties be visually distinguishable, a requirement which created difficulties for wheat breeders and greatly lengthened the breeding process, but one which much facilitated grading. The Canadian varietal release scheme was extremely rigid and statutorily controlled and the first such scheme to be introduced. In addition to the requirement that kernels be readily identifiable, the release of a new variety was permitted only if, after several years of testing, it could be shown to match or surpass the baking and milling performance of a prescribed variety. The end result was that the total number of Canadian varieties, by the standards of its competitors, was very limited. The Canadian approach was obviously not an option, however, for the AWB. Nor was the French system whereby local cooperatives sold seeds to farmers and thereby controlled the varieties available. With so many varieties making up the ASW class this approach was simply not possible. It was decided eventually to use an affidavit system, in which growers would be asked to declare the varieties they were delivering. This was coupled with the threat of random checks conducted after delivery. Routine sampling and subsequent laboratory testing has shown consistently that false declarations are rare. After a trial run, the scheme was eventually introduced in 1980.

What has been recognized more recently is the usefulness not only of varietal discounts but of varietal bonuses. Again the driving force in their introduction was the need to satisfy customers whose requirements have become more precise. It became necessary to encourage growers to sow particular varieties within the ASW category. This was achieved by paying varietal bonuses which partially reflected the market value for wheat but in some cases also compensated the grower for the yield disadvantage associated with the desired variety. This approach was used for the first time in the 1989–90 season to establish a 'noodle zone' in Western Australia where two varieties, highly prized by the Japanese for the colour and texture of the noodles they produced, were encouraged through the use of varietal bonuses.

In the late 1980s the AWB began considering the possibility of using another tactic to improve the quality of the ASW grade. In 1989 it introduced a 'payment for quality' scheme. The scheme was effectively an assault on the egalitarian principle at the heart of the Australian pooling system. For it was a move away from the practice of paying a single average price to those farmers who delivered ASW. Instead they were now to receive $A3 a tonne extra for each percentage increase in protein above 9.5 per cent and up to 11.5 per cent. This gradient was deemed comparable with market differentials.

The decision to introduce the scheme was motivated by a variety of factors. One was the simple fact that the 1980s had seen a rapid increase in buyer demands for ASW with specified minimum protein levels. In 1982 only 19 per cent of ASW was marketed on a protein requirement basis. By 1985–6 the proportion of sales of ASW with specific or implied protein requirements had risen to 56 per cent. What had also happened was that buyers were now seeking protein levels well above those of only five years earlier. Coinciding with this there had been an apparent trend toward lower protein levels of

ASW. Both developments had made the marketing of a broad banded category such as ASW (in which protein levels could be anywhere between 9 and 12 per cent) increasingly difficult. The inability to meet protein requirements had seen the AWB either lose business or face significant problems with buyers.

When the chairman of the AWB foreshadowed in 1978 the introduction of the varietal discount scheme he explained, in language that was then uncharacteristic of Australian wheat industry leaders, that it was intended to expose growers to market signals, to provide them with a better understanding of how the market valued the varieties they grew. The payment for quality scheme was a necessary complement to varietal discounting. The board announced that growers 'should be given financial incentives to produce and deliver higher quality, higher protein ASW wheat'. The industry needed 'to embrace the concept of varying the payment to growers within the ASW grade according to quality of wheat delivered by the wheat-grower'. This seemed obvious enough but even in the era of economic rationalism it smacked of heresy to some wheat industry leaders.

Market research, technical training and customer loyalty

Another tactic in dealing with an increasingly quality-conscious market is not simply to respond submissively to buyers' demands but to convince them that there are alternative and perhaps more efficient means to achieve a desired end. (This admittedly is to revert to the seller's approach rather than the marketer's.) If, for example, buyers demand high-protein wheat because they believe that that is what is necessary for the production of high-quality, high-volume bread, and if Australia can only produce a relatively small amount of high-protein wheat, one possible response is to develop new methods of making such bread with lower protein wheat. Then one can try to convince buyers not to seek higher protein wheat and to adopt instead new baking practices which save the customer money (in part because the higher the protein the higher the premium to be paid). This in turn will increase the demand for the sorts of wheat more readily available in Australia.

Alternatively it may be that buyers feel that Australian wheat has failed to meet certain quality specifications because of some inherent defect when in fact the fault lies with the techniques they are using in processing the wheat, such as improper conditioning prior to milling. One way to overcome this problem is to arrange training seminars, on-shore and/or off-shore, to instruct bakers and millers on the best ways to process Australian wheat so as to use it to its greatest advantage. These seminars can be used in turn to meet broader promotional goals and to establish and consolidate goodwill and loyalty. One can also try to anticipate the nature of tighter quality specifications. This might be done by undertaking ongoing technical missions designed to gather information on end uses. Furthermore one might commission in depth scientific analyses of the factors which make for, say, high-quality noodles. (This might seem all too obvious but it was something neglected for a remarkably long time by all the major exporters.)

What was the Australian record in this respect? For all its stress on responding to customer requirements, the fact is that the AWB long ignored the all-important area of market research. Throughout the 1950s and 1960s the AWB's marketing strategy had concentrated on trying to provide customers with a much clearer guide to the different categories of Australian wheats and their qualities and on encouraging steps which would lead to an improvement in quality. Where it had failed was in trying to discover exactly what customers wanted. As I have just noted, the latter could only be determined through an investment in the provision of in-depth and regularly updated technical information on the current and potential quality requirements of the board's overseas markets.

In 1971 the AWB decided to create a market servicing and research section. Its objectives were to identify the long-term market requirements for Australian wheat, interpret these requirements in terms of the board's ability to fulfil them on a national basis, and pass on this information in a readily usable form to the various wheat-breeding organizations in the different states. As part of this new initiative the board established the position of wheat quality adviser. In March 1974 the appointee, Bob Cracknell, reflected on what he had achieved since then. His report exposed the great gaps in the board's market intelligence and was testimony to the fact that the board had yet to make a complete transition from a seller of wheat to a marketer of it. He pointed out, for example, that the board's knowledge of China's quality requirements was understandably limited, 'and it has been argued that as quality has not been a major factor in negotiations to date, it is of little consequence'. Nevertheless 'the fact that the Chinese authorities have indicated the quality of Australian FAQ wheat to be ideal for their purposes is sufficient to cause alarm, bearing in mind the marked quality changes taking place in FAQ'. The Middle East, including Egypt, was another important market area 'about which we know very little'. 'Trade practices range from the most sophisticated to the most primitive, and quality requirements, particularly for the latter, are not well understood.' The Indian subcontinent was admittedly 'not one of great importance technologically' but 'a better understanding of the basic quality requirements for unleavened products such as chappatis and parathas would be of value for routine marketing purposes'. Japan had 'probably the most sophisticated milling industry in the world' and certainly was one of the board's most discriminating markets. The board urgently needed a deeper understanding of the quality requirements for Japanese noodle manufacture. And so it went on. The paper finished on a note of despair (and understatement): 'It is a little worrying that large portions of our crop are going to markets about which we know so very little.'

If this seemed a sorry state of affairs, it needs to be said that Australia was probably not very far behind its major competitors in its efforts to determine the exact nature of user requirements. Where Australia was most certainly lacking was in what might be called after-sales service. The AWB's experience in the Middle East provides a useful illustration. An AWB mission learnt in October 1977, when visiting Saudi Arabia, that no less than twenty-one employees of the Grain Silos and Flour Mills Organisation (GSFMO) had just returned from a Canadian International Grains Institute course and that some of them had also spent twelve months in the United States working in commercial flour mills and studying at Kansas State University. Perhaps not surprisingly the director general of GSFMO pointed out that, because of their training, the technicians had a 'sentimental preference' for United States and Canadian wheat. The GSFMO was in the process of building a mill just outside of Riyadh and had employed as consultants Pillsbury Holdings (Canada) Ltd (whose head office was in Minneapolis). This link had also helped to consolidate a preference for North American wheats.

The AWB mission reported that a host of other developments were occurring in Saudi Arabia. A mill was also under construction in Dammam and one was about to be built in Jeddah. A new bakery was under construction in Riyadh and another in Dammam, while still others were being planned. The situation there was typical of the Middle East as a whole. A mill had been established in Kuwait in 1965 and one in Bahrain in 1971. Another was opened in Qatar in 1973, one in Dubai in December 1976 and three months later one in Oman. Mills had also been established in Yemen and Abu Dhabi. Many of these countries bought all or nearly all of their wheat from

Australia, being impressed in part by the price (Australia enjoyed a freight advantage) and by the quality. Developments in Saudi Arabia, so it seemed, offered another major opportunity for Australia. Indeed GSFMO officials maintained that they were anxious to import Australian wheat to take advantage of competition between the major exporters and to ensure continuity of supply.

It was nevertheless clear that the Australians faced major obstacles in entering the Saudi Arabian market and more particularly expanding their share of the market:

> The GSFMO stressed that the flour milled [for the new bakeries] must be acceptable and it would reflect on both the Government and GSFMO if such flour was rejected by the bakeries. In order to minimise the risk of such event, the mill is adhering to American wheat in their grist hoping it will match the American flour presently mainly imported through Dammam. Whilst one can only be sympathetic to their aims it could lead to dependence upon U.S.A. wheats with bakeries being constructed accordingly rather than in a fashion more acceptable to baking Australian flour.

Saudi Arabia, the Australians noted, was an influential Arab country, both economically and politically, in a region where Australian wheat had gained a high degree of acceptance. The risk was that this acceptance could be prejudiced should Saudi Arabia continue to show a preference for United States wheat.

One of the lessons of the Saudi Arabian experience was, or should have been, that the AWB had tended to rest on its laurels. The Saudi Arabian minister for commerce had stressed the need for the board to visit the market regularly to obtain the widest possible understanding of their end user requirements, a statement which should have caused the board some embarrassment.

The AWB was deficient in another respect. From the early 1950s the CWB organized missions to bring existing and potential buyers of Canadian grain to Canada while the Canadian Grain Commission (CGC) began inviting foreign scientists and technical staff to Canada for training at the Grain Research Laboratory. In 1971 the CWB and CGC successfully recommended to the federal government that these programmes be broadened and formalized by creating a Canadian International Grains Institute. The idea was that the institute would be an educational and training facility offering courses, of a generalist and specialist nature, for Canadian and foreign participants. The institute was incorporated in 1972 on a non-profit basis. One of its first initiatives was to launch a regular series of what it called international grain industry courses. The promotional body of the United States wheat industry, US Wheat, had long been active in the use of training seminars. Unlike the Canadians, who concentrated on bringing people to Winnipeg, US Wheat arranged such seminars both in the United States and abroad. It had used them, for example, in Japan in the late 1950s. It had made much use of them too, from the late 1960s, after the establishment of a baking school in Manila. The school offered extensive training in baking technology. Participants from a range of South East Asian countries were invited to attend the courses. Likewise seminars were held in Penang, the aim being to teach modern milling and baking techniques. In Indonesia US Wheat sponsored and ran courses for master bakers, who in turn experimented with the new methods in their own bakeries. One of the direct results of US Wheat's efforts was the widespread use in Indonesia of no-time dough procedures, methods which suited United States wheat.

The success of US Wheat in changing baking practices in Indonesia and elsewhere suggested that the AWB should try to do something similar. It also revealed, as the board was later to comment, that 'it is most important that a strong effort is made by Australia if the thinking of the Indonesian baking industry is to be broadened and persuaded to adopt practices which best suit Australian wheat'. Similar sentiments were expressed again and again.

Perhaps not surprisingly, then, the AWB decided in 1977 to launch a series of off-shore baking and milling seminars in conjunction with the Sydney-based Bread Research Institute (BRI). Initially it concentrated on South East Asia. Simultaneously a range of other initiatives were begun or expanded: milling and baking personnel from customer countries were invited to join training courses at the central Grain Research Laboratory in Sydney, scholarships were provided, technicians from customer countries were invited to undertake research and to attend courses.

One of the most important benefits of the AWB's milling and baking seminars was their ability to change the demand pattern for bread flour. Up until the end of the 1970s, the fact was that in Malaysia, Thailand, Indonesia and Singapore the bread flour demanded by bakers and recommended by mills had been high-quality flour with a protein level of 13 per cent or more. In nearly every case this had been made entirely from United States Dark Northern Spring wheat. Use of this flour had been coupled with the use of long-fermentation systems of dough making learned from United States instructors and reinforced by teachers at US Wheat's baking school in the Philippines. The AWB/BRI seminars were able to show how bread of equal quality could be made from a flour of around 11 per cent protein, milled perhaps from a 100 per cent blend of Australian wheat.

To do this required the adoption of a new method of baking bread: not the Chorleywood process developed by the British Baking Industries Research Association in the late 1950s and 1960s, but a rapid dough method developed by the BRI. The AWB made much of the fact that the Australian rapid dough method, like the Chorleywood process, would save customers money because it permitted the use of lower protein flour than those currently used and recommended. Furthermore, it considerably reduced the time taken for breadmaking by eliminating bulk fermentation. In many developing countries old equipment and inadequate temperature and time control during processing meant that high-protein, hard wheats had to be used if bread of acceptable quality was to be consistently produced. The Australian method gave a greater degree of control because doughs could finish within a reasonably large temperature range without adverse results. Also it produced more loaves of bread per bag of flour and reduced the area of bakery floor space. Importantly the Australian method could be easily used in conventional slow-speed dough mixers, whereas the Chorleywood process required a heavy investment in specially designed high-speed mixers. The secret was the use of oxidizing agents to improve the dough (improvers included ascorbic acid and potassium bromate) and reducing agents such as cysteine or sodium metabisulphite to reduce mixing time.

After the success of the South East Asian technical seminars the board's attention turned toward the Middle East. An AWB delegation to the area in September and October 1979 reported that

> Technical training will . . . prove a strong marketing tool in resisting competitive pressure from U.S.A. wheats. All markets visited are seeking assistance in this direction and it is in the Board's long term interests to initiate appropriate technical training programmes and seminars tailored to each country's particular needs.

Apart from annual visits to the region the board had done very little promotional work: at the end of the 1970s it was only just beginning to think about having literature on the Australian wheat industry translated into Arabic.

The board's senior wheat quality adviser visited the Middle East in November 1979. Visiting Kuwait he found that the general manager of the largely government-run Kuwait Bakeries Company was having difficulty deciding what baking procedure and equipment to employ in a planned large, loaf-bread plant. He had visited the United States and the United Kingdom studying plant and equipment and was very much in favour of the American 'sponge and dough' method. 'From an Australian point of view,' Cracknell later reported to the board, 'such a move would be disastrous as the current bakers' flour being produced by the Kuwait Mill [which purchased all of its wheat from Australia] would almost certainly perform poorly using this method.' The sponge and dough method, Cracknell said, 'always shows Australian wheats in a bad light'. Accordingly he strongly argued against the general manager's move, citing high equipment costs, length of procedure and low bread yield. Not surprisingly he suggested that the Australian rapid dough procedure was much more appropriate. The point is that the use of the sponge and dough baking method in Japan had been a factor in limiting the growth of Australian wheat exports to that market. In Kuwait the adoption of the method threatened Australia's monopoly on the market. Here too there was a need for the Australians to promote their own baking and milling practices.

If Australia seemed slow in this respect, the fact remains that when the board began a series of technical seminars in Bahrain and Baghdad in March 1980, attended by delegates from flour mills in Abu Dhabi, Bahrain, Dubai, Iraq, Kuwait, Oman, Qatar, Saudi Arabia and the Yemen Arab Republic, these were the first such seminars to be presented in the region by any of the wheat exporters. They were a great success. They followed the pattern of those given previously in South East Asia, highlighting the Australian rapid dough system in breadmaking and emphasizing the causes of common faults in bread (the latter were generally not well understood). There were both discussions and practical demonstrations. Not only did the seminars provide an excellent vehicle for presenting much needed technical background on Australian milling and baking technology, they won the board much goodwill and provided contacts and a great deal of publicity.

It was clear not only that seminars would have to be held in the region on a regular basis but that a range of other things needed to be done. The AWB's assistant general manager reported in April 1980, after a tour of eight Middle Eastern countries, that

> With only a brief history of flour milling and with some mills already looking at expansion programmes the subject of training

was a topic with all mills visited. The mills in a number of markets have been constructed with northern hemisphere wheats in mind, and mill technicians have received their basic training in either Europe, U.S.A. or Canada. In some cases their experience with Australian wheat has been self taught. It would seem that some form of training on Australian wheat at the milling, laboratory and storage level will be necessary to follow on from the Bahrain seminar.

These were all duly instituted. Eventually too it was decided to base technical personnel (bakers, millers, storage experts) in the Middle East to service clients.

In summary, although it was disappointingly slow in adopting such techniques, the AWB has used these forms of after-sales service to great effect, in promoting goodwill, showing the best ways to use and condition Australian wheat, and by revealing how baking techniques can be adapted to save customers money by using lower protein Australian wheats. It has also done much to improve basic bread-making skills. The irony is that, in doing so, it has also made its customers more quality-conscious than ever and has raised their expectations of what they require from Australian grains.

CONCLUSION

The point should now be clear that whatever tactic might be used to respond to the growing importance of quality considerations, the problem facing wheat marketers is that invariably there are a great many technical difficulties which need to be overcome before any tactic can become effective. Another point, an obvious one but worth emphasizing, is that wheat marketing, unlike the marketing of manufactured goods, is made all the more problematic because of the difficulties of exercising control and coordination over all those individuals, organizations and state bodies who determine the availability or otherwise of wheats which satisfy the demands of the marketplace. There are problems too in that the wheat marketer is dealing in raw materials. The acceptability of the final product depends in part on how the raw material is subsequently processed by millers and then bakers and other manufacturers. Yet another problem, a critical one, is of course the weather. What matters to buyers is not just that wheat meet certain specifications but that there be a continuous and regular supply of the wheat they have requested. The fickleness of the weather may undo the hard work put into improving quality characteristics by giving a country a reputation for being an unreliable supplier. Over and above this there are, as I said at the start, all the problems emanating from the mingling of economic and diplomatic considerations. The wheat marketer's job is a decidedly difficult one.

NOTES

1 The discussion is based almost entirely on AWB archives, located at their head office in Melbourne. Unfortunately the archives have not been professionally catalogued, making proper citation impossible. For a fuller account of the AWB's activities, see Whitwell and Sydenham (1991) especially chapters 12 and 13.
2 Gilmore (1982: chapter 10) provides an overview of both exporting and importing arrangements. An excellent guide to the major exporters in US Congress, Office of Technology Assessment (1989b). See also US Congress. Office of Technology Assessment (1989a: chapter 10).
3 On Canadian wheat marketing, see Morriss (1987); Wilson (1979); and Canadian International Grains Institute (1982: sections A and C).
4 Two excellent studies of the USDA and the great grain companies are Morgan (1979) and Gilmore (1982). For a penetrating analysis of US grain policies, see Roberts et al. (1989). On the great grain companies see also Chalmin (1987: 181–211); Davies (1986).
5 Surprisingly there is, as far as the author is aware, no history of US Wheat.
6 A particularly important analysis of the growing importance of quality considerations and what has been and could be done in response to this development is US Congress, Office of Technology Assessment (1989a,b).
7 We should qualify this by noting that a number of developments, notably the use of 'sizing' rolls, enabled millers to eliminate purifiers from the mill flow. Other important post-war developments include the incorporation of the high-speed impact mill, 'entoleters' and other forms of flake-disrupting equipment, bran finishers and vibrating sifters. All of these facilitated a phenomenal increase in extraction rates. The ability of the miller to control water absorption was increased too. Another important development was the introduction of air classification, something which was used mainly for the production of speciality flours of high- or low-protein content.
8 A useful introduction to this complex topic is Hill (1983). See also US Congress, Office of Technology Assessment (1989a: chapter 8).

REFERENCES

Canadian International Grains Institute (1982) *Grains and Oilseeds: Handling, Marketing, Processing*, Winnipeg: Canadian International Grains Institute.

Chalmin, Philippe (1987) *Traders and Merchants: Panorama of International Commodity Trading*, London: Harwood Academic Publishers.

Davies, Susanna (1986) 'The grain trading companies', in Nick Butler *The*

International Grain Trade: Problems and Prospects, London and Sydney: Croom Helm.
Gilmore, Richard (1982) *A Poor Harvest: The Clash of Policies and Interests in the Grain Trade*, New York and London: Longman.
Hill, Lowell D. (1983) 'Grain grades and standards', in Gail L. Cramer and Walter G. Heid (eds) *Grain Marketing Economics*, New York: John Wiley & Sons.
Morgan, Dan (1979) *Merchants of Grain*, New York: Viking Press.
Morriss, William E. (1987) *Chosen Instrument: A History of the Canadian Wheat Board: The McIvor Years*, Edmonton: Canadian Wheat Board.
Roberts, Ivan, Love, Graham, Field, Heather, and Klijn, Nico (1989) *U.S. Grain Policies and the World Market*, Bureau of Agricultural and Resource Economics Policy Monograph No. 4, Canberra: Australian Government Publishing Service.
Stanton, William J. (1975) *Fundamentals of Marketing*, Tokyo: McGraw-Hill, Kogakusha.
US Congress, Office of Technology Assessment (1989a) *Enhancing the Quality of U.S. Grain for International Trade*, Washington, DC: US Government Printing Office.
—— (1989b) *Grain Quality in International Trade: A Comparison of Major U.S. Competitors*, Washington, DC: US Government Printing Office.
Whitwell, Greg and Sydenham, Diane (1991) *A Shared Harvest: The Australian Wheat Industry, 1939–89*, Melbourne: Macmillan.
Wilson, Charles F. (1979) *Canadian Grain Marketing*, Winnipeg: Canadian International Grains Institute.

10 An economic theory of marketing

Mark Casson

Economic theory provides an important tool for understanding the evolution of marketing. The theory presented in this chapter emphasizes the entrepreneurial nature of marketing, and in particular the link between marketing and innovation. It highlights the role of marketers in manipulating preferences, and in reducing transaction costs. The theory builds on existing literature by emphasizing some of the points which are only implicit in previous work.

BASIC CONCEPTS

The concept of marketing is not easy to define. To begin with, marketing embraces a number of quite distinct, though related, activities. Furthermore, these activities interact with other activities of an entrepreneurial nature, such as research and development. Marketing is therefore a system of interdependent activities which is itself a sub system of a larger set of activities. Because this larger set of activities is concerned with innovation, it may generate changes which feed back to alter the structure of the marketing system over time.

Entrepreneurship may be viewed as specialized problem-solving (Casson 1991), and marketing as the presentation and delivery of the solution to the customers. Entrepreneurs address problems that regularly afflict other people and embody solutions in the form of goods and services which they sell to these people. Some problems – such as subsistence – are very basic, and create a demand for necessities, such as food, whilst others – such as finding entertainment – are solved by luxury products. Because the perception of some problems is subjective – and influenced by social aspirations – entrepreneurs may strive to create a perception that there is a problem simply so that they can sell a solution to it. This is where manipulation comes in.

An entrepreneur can, in principle, license his solution for others to deliver, but the limited coverage of the patent system discourages this. Entrepreneurs therefore become involved in the delivery of their solutions. As such, they act as middlemen, linking the solution-seeking customers with the resource suppliers.

On this view, four main aspects of marketing may be distinguished (see Table 10.1), each of which is examined separately below. Market research is concerned with identifying new opportunities and evaluating trial products; promotion is mainly concerned with the manipulation of customers' preferences for the product; transactions management is concerned with making contracts; whilst distribution is concerned with the logistics of physical delivery of the product. When delivered, the product must meet the claims advanced for it during promotion, and comply with the detailed specifications contained in the contract too.

Table 10.1 Four key aspects of marketing

Market research
    Analysis of income and population trends
    Monitoring competitors' strategies on price and quality
    Panel studies of buying behaviour
    Test marketing

Promotion
    Familiarize potential customers with the problem
    Explain the solution, and give it cultural legitimacy
    Choose the appropriate media
    Name the product and specify the exact claims

Transactions management
    Make contact with the individual customer
    Negotiate the price
    Control quality and organize warranty work
    Collect and validate payments

Distribution
    Plan the logistics of transport and warehousing
    Design point-of-sale display
    Provision of after-sales service

Strategic complexity is involved in every aspect of marketing, and it is therefore sometimes difficult to see how these different aspects fit together. The second part of this chapter therefore examines a number of issues – such as internalization and internationalization – which serve to integrate these different aspects. The chapter concludes by considering the welfare implications of marketing and identifying issues for future historical research.

MARKET RESEARCH

Market research is used to discover what problems other people have. In the context of mass marketing, it aims to discover whether there are certain common types of problem that affect an identifiable subgroup of the population, who can be targeted with a standardized solution to the problem.

In a well-functioning economic system, *normal* levels of *existing* needs will tend to be well-catered for. Entrepreneurial opportunities therefore relate mainly to increasing needs in existing areas and, above all, to newly emerging needs. No system is perfectly efficient, however, and so there will always be some areas where existing needs have still not been recognized or properly catered for (Leibenstein 1979).

Popular discussions of entrepreneurship tend to emphasize informal and intuitive ways of discovering new opportunities. A more analytical approach, however, suggests that the recognition of opportunities involves systematic scanning of the environment and synthesis of the information gathered. Accumulated experience of this cognitive process may allow certain aspects of discovery to be rendered routine. Thus Schumpeter (1942) argued that the process of innovation, which was once the prerogative of an entrepreneurial elite with a distinctive psychology might, in the post-war period, be rendered routine within a bureaucratic system. Although Schumpeter had in mind a socialist planning bureau, his prediction has more validity if applied to the managerial hierarchy of a modern multinational corporation.

In the modern mass market economy, the discovery of new mass markets involves a mixture of routine and improvization. The routine element has two main aspects: the analysis of market trends to identify where new product experiments are worthwhile, and the pragmatic process of trial marketing in which information from test markets is fed back to determine whether an opportunity really exists and, if so, what modifications to the product are required.

Conventional economic theories of consumer demand (Deaton and Muellbauer 1980) indicate the main kinds of market trends to be considered. The most important concern income levels. Aggregate income governs aggregate consumer purchasing power, but the proportion of purchasing power devoted to mass products depends upon how aggregate income resolves into total population and income per head. It also depends upon the distribution of income per head across the population. For a given level of aggregate income the conditions most favourable to mass markets are a large population with average income per head well above subsistence levels, but a small dispersion of income – for example, a large and relatively affluent working class, and a relatively small wealthy landed class.

With a given pattern of tastes, an increase in personal income will cause the proportion of an individual's income spent on different categories of goods to change. In a progressive economy, market growth will be concentrated on goods which have a high income-elasticity of demand. In the post-war period high income elasticities have been associated with consumer durables, travel and tourism, and luxury food and clothing, and low (or negative) income elasticities with basic foodstuffs and low-quality items. Historically, the high income elasticity of demand for superior quality food and household utility items – packaged teas and coffees, soaps, general purpose medicines, etc. – provided an early impetus to mass marketing.

Demographic factors are an important influence on consumer demand, not only because they affect the overall size of population but because consumption patterns are age-dependent: toys for children, household furnishings for the newly-married, large family cars for parents, hospital care for the aged, and so on. When past birth rates are combined with actuarial data on age-dependent mortality rates it is easy to obtain accurate predictions of the age distribution of the population, so that in general there is no excuse for entrepreneurs to be caught unawares by demographic trends. The main uncertainties concern future birth rates – which can be affected by earlier or later marriages, changes in family planning practices, etc. – and future net migration.

Price is, of course, an important consideration in any assessment of demand. The prices of both substitutes (butter for margarine) and complements (petrol for motor cars) are relevant. In an established market the cross-price elasticity of demand with other variants of the same product is crucial. Cross-price elasticities are highest in mature industries producing relatively standardized products – sometimes referred to as 'commodities' – and lowest in new industries, and industries producing differentiated products, where a supplier may occupy a monopolistic 'niche'.

Anthropological studies indicate that different social and cultural groups have different tastes. Mass markets depend on similarity of tastes, which implies a high level of social integration and cultural homogeneity within the population. In this context it is interesting to contrast the United States, where immigrants from different parts of Eastern Europe were assimilated quickly into a materialistic culture, with Eastern Europe itself, where the groups they left behind have remained culturally distinct. It is evident that the cultural conditions for the rise of the mass market were more favourable in the US.

Culture-specific tastes manifest themselves in occupational choices as well as consumption patterns, and this means that occupation is often a good indicator of tastes. For this reason contemporary marketing analysis makes heavy use of a socio-economic typology of the population which attaches as much weight to occupation as it does to income level.

On the practical side of market research, the development of statistical sampling theory early this century made it possible to infer conclusions about the population as a whole from a small, but representative, sample of members. This technique has gradually evolved to support longitudinal panel studies which chart the buying behaviour of randomly selected groups of people. Such studies also provide evidence on the popularity of various media amongst people who purchase particular kinds of product, allowing promotion to be accurately targeted by an appropriate choice of medium. They also allow the results of test-marketing to be more accurately interpreted, since panel members can be invited to try out new products on an experimental basis.

PROMOTION

The first objective of promotion is to ensure that the customers, as well as the entrepreneur, perceive that there really is a problem. The existence of a problem presupposes a norm, because a problem only exists if a norm fails to be satisfied. If a norm is sufficiently low then a problem will disappear. If a society has low norms for cleanliness, for example, then dirt is not a problem and soap may be difficult to sell. But if norms are very high, so that even a speck of dirt can precipitate a crisis, then not only soap but all kinds of cleaning fluid can be sold as well. Entrepreneurs, therefore, have a vested interest in promoting high norms. More accurately, it pays them to promote high norms in respect of the particular problem that their product solves, but to encourage laxity in respect of problems which the side-effects of their products make worse. Thus it pays motor manufacturers to encourage high standards of travel comfort, but low standards of atmospheric pollution.

The more subtle a problem, the less obvious are the means of solution. Everyone knows that food solves a hunger problem, for example, but not everyone knows that some new chemical product will clean up a particular kind of spillage. The second function of promotion is therefore to explain the connection between the problem and the recommended means of solution. This is easier the simpler and more familiar the solution, and the fewer are the alternatives with which a particular solution needs to be compared.

The converse of this is that novel and complex solutions require a great deal of explanation, and that customers are particularly interested in these explanations when they have a wide choice. These conditions normally prevail in advanced economies where sustained innovation has generated a wide variety of goods designed to solve a particular problem in different ways. It is compounded by the fact that in an advanced economy customers are far more concerned about quality and convenience than in a poor economy, and correspondingly less concerned with the single dimension of price. Consumer durables, in particular, involve a wide range of quality dimensions that are important to the customer. Motor cars, for example, vary in fuel consumption, acceleration, turning circle, durability, safety, and so on. Customers need to be informed about all these characteristics because they have a choice between different variants, which in turn reflects the fact that the solutions have been specially designed and engineered, and do not merely represent variants found in nature.

The norms that are used to identify problems are derived not from scientific evidence but from moral values. Norms are part of the culture of a society, and can be of great emotional significance to its members. People who violate cultural norms lose status and may be ostracized or physically punished. In most societies, for example, cleanliness is not just a matter of hygiene but of respectability. It may also be the subject of ritual religious observance. These attitudes can be harnessed in the promotion of cleaning products by suggesting, for example, that those who really care about cleanliness will choose a particular kind of soap. Promotion of culturally significant products needs to be sensitive, however. Customers may be reluctant to be seen buying large quantities of a powerful cleaning agent in case people believe they have a cleanliness problem, and so packaging and point-of-sale display may have to be very discreet.

The social dimension of consumption is also apparent in the way that certain products are purchased mainly for display. Style of dress, for example, can be used to suggest a prestigious occupation (smart suit), great wealth (expensive fabrics), elitist leisure pursuits (casual wear) and up-to-date knowledge of trends (high fashion clothes). Status-enhancing products have been called 'positional goods' (Hirsch

1977); much of their value to the customer derives from the fact that other people cannot afford them. Up to a certain point, such products may have a demand that increases rather than falls with price, and their promotion will emphasize their exclusive nature.

Status expresses relative position within a social group. Products can also be used to indicate to which group the purchaser belongs. Young people use T-shirts and jeans as badges of affiliation to their own generation, for example, whilst other groups identify themselves by possession of 'cult' objects such as 'classic' records, cars, etc.

The complications created by the social significance of products are nowhere more apparent than in gift-giving. The donor (who is the purchaser) seeks to win the approval of the recipient. There may be a specific favour that the customer wants, and the gift is intended to initiate reciprocation. On the other hand, the objective may be merely to renew an existing relationship for a further period – as in the giving of birthday and seasonal presents. Whatever the occasion, the donor must choose a gift that is well-packaged, to emphasize the esteem in which the recipient is held. The gift must not be too cheap, but not too expensive either, in case the recipient should resent being placed under obligation to reciprocate with something more valuable than he wants to. Finally, the gift must be differentiated or customized to express how special the recipient is supposed to be. In a traditional society such a gift would be produced by the donor himself, whereas in a market economy the gift is more likely to be selected with care from a widely differentiated range.

A good deal of the seasonal fluctuation in consumer sales is attributable to gift-giving at festival times, and the promotion of suitable gifts is a prominent feature of media activity around such times. Such promotion has to convey to potential customers an impression of the effect the gift will have on the recipient, and so dramatic portrayals of the recipient's response to the gift figure prominently in media activity.

This leads on to the more general issue of media strategy. All explanations of product qualities require the customer to cooperate by listening for an appropriate time. But time as well as money is a scarce resource so far as customers are concerned. There is therefore likely to be intense competition between entrepreneurs for the customer's attention.

The opportunity cost of a customer's time (Becker 1964) is lowest when he has few alternative things to do – for example, when travelling. Hoardings therefore appeal to the pedestrian and motorist, whilst magazine advertisements are aimed at rail and air travellers.

Since travellers often take the opportunity to relax from work, promotional messages must not be too demanding. They can therefore only supply a fairly small amount of information – often just sufficient to arouse interest – thereby leaving retailers to supply information of a more detailed kind.

Customers' preferences will determine which messages they decide to attend to. This reflects not only their preferences for different types of product, but also their preferences for messages presented in different ways. Some people are naturally more curious than others and will therefore concentrate their attention on presentations involving jokes and puzzles. People who value aesthetics more than curiosity will focus their attention on visually stimulating presentations instead. It is therefore important for entrepreneurs to know not only their customers' travelling and reading habits, but also the kinds of things that arouse their curiosity or hold aesthetic appeal. In many cases there is a fairly obvious connection with the product. Cars can usefully be advertised from hoardings because most car-buyers already own a car which they regularly drive. Quality newspapers can usefully be advertised using jokes and puzzles because people who read such newspapers desire stimulation from the written word. A media strategy that exploits such associations is likely to be particularly successful in winning the attention of potential customers.

The final consideration in promotion is that the message must be memorable, since the customer must retain it between seeing the advertisement and reaching the point of sale. This suggests that a product must carry a simple name. Furthermore, the claims made for the product must combine simplicity with honesty – a difficult task, since an honest claim often requires a number of important qualifications. Music and rhymes can help in this respect – people can often remember a simple 'jingle' long after the product has become obsolete. It is in this field of populist artistic creativity that some of the scarcest – and most highly rewarded – talent is to be found.

The importance of the name, and the aesthetic quality associated with it, explains the remarkable significance of branding – especially where consumer goods are concerned. Much of the reputation of the product is intimately associated with its name, and so the exclusive right to use the name can become a major barrier to entry discouraging imitation.

TRANSACTIONS MANAGEMENT

The main role of transactions management is the reduction of overall transactions costs. Transaction costs are the costs incurred in bringing transactors together, negotiating a price, monitoring delivery and payment, and enforcing penalties on defaulters. In the absence of an intermediary, transaction costs are shared between the parties. When an intermediary is used, he typically incurs most of the transaction costs – thereby making life easier for the other parties (Casson 1982). Intermediation provides efficiency gains because the intermediator is a specialist. He may be someone with a personal comparative advantage in intermediation, and this initial comparative advantage may be reinforced by the experience he gains on the job. The intermediator covers his costs by setting a margin between buying price and selling price.

An entrepreneur engaged in promoting a particular product will normally function as an intermediator too. As an intermediator, though, he faces a strategic difficulty. Many of the costs he seeks to cover in any one transaction are sunk costs. They are either the costs of investments made in special infrastructure – for example, retail premises – or costs incurred in making contact between the parties before price negotiations begin – advertising costs, for example. If his customers and suppliers realize this, they may attempt to bargain for prices that do not provide sufficient margin to cover the sunk costs. The intermediator can, however, credibly claim that, as he is continually involved in trading, any weakness in conceding to such demands would undermine his position in all future trades and cause him to go out of business. Individual customers and suppliers are not so vulnerable in this respect as they only enter the market intermittently – although occasionally customers or suppliers may be sufficiently large that they can insist on negotiating a special discount or premium. Thus the intermediator adopts a 'hard line' negotiating strategy – quoting firm prices and refusing to make concessions. In this way he covers his transaction costs successfully.

Transactions management involves a number of other strategic issues, such as the way in which contact is made with the individual customer. Potential customers who read advertisements can be directed to retail premises, or given phone numbers they can call to request further information. Advertisements themselves can be personally addressed using mailing lists or displayed impersonally on hoardings or in magazines. The choice of appropriate strategy depends very much on the type of product. Very specialized products benefit from accurately targeted contacts, whereas other products have to be handled more indiscriminately. Complex products require personal service at retail premises, or even special demonstration in the office or in the home. This applies both to complex physical products, such as computers, and complex financial products such as insurance and wills. Where the total number of contacts required is expected to be high, it may pay to formalize the presentation, providing glossy brochures, training manuals for salesmen, and so on. This incurs fixed costs in order to reduce the marginal cost of each contact. Such an approach is not warranted, however, when the anticipated number of contacts is small.

Quality control and payment validation are also important aspects of transactions management. Quality control ensures that the product supplied to the customer corresponds to the specification, as indicated in advertisements and on the packaging, and as detailed in the written contract (if there is one). Quality control is easier for 'inspection' goods, where faults are normally either superficial or create visible symptoms in the product's appearance, than for 'experience' goods where faults normally only come to light through use. Quality problems in experience goods cannot usually be avoided altogether (despite the enthusiastic claims of modern advocates of 'total quality management') and so part of quality assurance is to provide good warranty terms and an effective network of after-sales support (the 'network' element being very important for vehicles).

The converse of quality control is payment validation, which ensures that what the customer offers in return is legal tender and, where cheques or credit cards are involved, will be honoured by the bank. It is also necessary to determine what credit terms (if any) are to be offered to the customer.

The product-specific nature of transaction costs emphasized above suggests that a product could usefully be designed specifically with low transactions costs in mind. There is one particular strategy which merits close attention in this respect, and that is the bundling of different products into a single composite product so that one transaction replaces many. There are several relatively trivial variants of this.

The new product could be simply a collection of existing product units put together – in other words, a pre-packaged bulk purchase. Bulk purchasing reduces the frequency of transactions and hence the number of separate purchases. Another example is where the regular supply of a service is replaced by the once-for-all sale of a durable good – for example, the user of a photocopying bureau buys their own desk-top photocopier. In this context the durable good can be thought of as an embodiment of a bundle of future services to be delivered at different times over the life of the good.

The most significant case, however, concerns the versatile

multi-component good, such as a music centre or, indeed, the modern family motor car. These goods can replace a variety of existing specialized goods. Thus the music centre replaces stand-alone tape-recorders, record players, compact disk-players, and so on. In a more modest way the modern family motor car, with its fold-down rear seats, can replace a light van, whilst, with its high-performance engine and aerodynamic styling, it can be used as a substitute for a sports car as well.

Versatile goods are of particular value to consumers who have a variety of intermittent needs and hence do not normally need the product for two simultaneous uses. Producers are in a rather different situation, because they normally require to utilize their assets continuously, and cannot afford the compromise in quality which is normally associated with the versatile good. Nevertheless, the growing adoption of flexible manufacturing systems, and the increasing exploitation of robotics in factories, testify to the increasing impact of versatility on production as well.

The benefits of versatility to consumers have important implications for promotional activity, because of the difficulty of explaining all of the ways in which a versatile good can be used. Thus while transactions costs may be reduced, promotion costs are likely to increase; it therefore requires considerable entrepreneurial judgement to determine whether the innovation of a versatile good will be worthwhile.

DISTRIBUTION

Distribution is concerned with the physical delivery of the good or service. It is the reverse of the procurement activity involved in assembling inputs for production. The strategic issues which dominate distribution relate to transportation and storage, and if it were not for the fact that retailing combines storage with product display, the issues would be almost entirely independent of the issues that dominate promotion. Similarly, if it were not for the fact that retail units not only arrange local delivery but also help to make contact with the customer and collect his payment, there would be little interaction with transactions management either.

Of the four aspects of marketing, distribution is concerned much more with physical movements than with the communication of information. In the modern economy, distance is a greater obstacle to transport than to communication, and so the spatial dimension of the economy assumes particular significance where physical distribution is concerned.

The spatial pattern of distribution is best understood in terms of the well-known trade-off between transport costs and economies of scale. Large warehouses and retail units are more efficient than small ones because their heating and maintenance costs are related to surface area, whilst their value-added is related to volume. But large units are viable only if they serve a large area, and the larger the area the greater is the average distance from the customer and hence the higher the average transport cost involved. If heating and maintenance costs rise relative to transport costs then large units are preferred, whilst if heating and maintenance costs fall relative to transport costs then small units are preferred. Both heating and transport require energy, so that the rise in energy costs since 1973 has probably been fairly neutral. But motorway investments and advances in vehicle design have reduced transport costs, and so encouraged larger units to emerge.

The interaction between transport and communication costs is significant mainly in the context of retailing. Retail units typically agglomerate in towns and cities. This allows customers to spread the fixed costs of their journey time across several different kinds of purchase, and also to make comparisons between different variants of the same product at one and the same time. Retailing of bulky and perishable generic items such as food is dispersed into towns and villages, whereas retailing of portable, durable and specialized items such as jewellery and fashion goods tends to be concentrated in major cities only. This is because bulky items are difficult for customers to transport over long distances, perishable items have to be bought frequently, and generic items require only limited comparison shopping because there are few different variants to compare. Retailing of the most highly specialized, complex, customized products tends to occur only at the major metropolitan centres because an agglomeration of related specialists is needed to advise on solutions, and these specialists need a very wide market area to keep their indivisible assets fully employed. A major change in the configuration of retailing has recently occurred because households have acquired more cars and other consumer durables (such as refrigerators), and so it has become easier for them to buy generic items in bulk. This has encouraged retailing to shift from villages to larger towns whose suburban malls provide easy vehicular access.

INTERNALIZATION

The analysis of transactions management emphasized the role of intermediation in reducing transactions costs. Intermediation is not, however, the only strategy of this kind. Internalization too can be used to reduce transaction costs. Internalization is, however, a strategy confined mainly to intermediate product markets rather than final product markets, whereas intermediation is suitable for either. Internalization involves bringing the activities related by the market under common ownership and control. Examples of internalization include designing advertisements in-house instead of hiring an agency to do it, and integrating forward into distribution to avoid relying on independent wholesalers.

According to Williamson (1985), the main advantage of internalization arises when investments in related activities involved large sunk costs. Following Klein *et al.* (1978), he argues that independent owners will find it difficult to trust each other not to renegotiate their arm's length contract once sunk costs have been incurred. This is a refinement of the well-known proposition in the theory of vertical integration (Casson 1984) that bilateral monopoly encourages integration. When each party makes a commitment whose value depends crucially on a reciprocal commitment by the other party, both parties become locked into a bilateral monopoly. Thus if a wholesaler has to invest in special equipment in order to store a highly perishable branded product, while the producer has to invest in special equipment to produce it in the first place, then after the investments have been made, each acquires monopoly power over the other. If the producer withholds supplies then the wholesaler's investment is worthless, because his special equipment cannot handle other goods. Conversely, if the wholesaler refuses to handle the product then the producer's investment is rendered worthless because another wholesaler cannot be found at short notice. The problem could, in principle, be solved by a long-term contract negotiated before the sunk costs were incurred, but in practice such contracts are difficult to enforce in law. Merging the two firms to integrate production and wholesaling obviates the difficulty. Bargaining becomes merely notional, as it does not affect the overall profit of the integrated firm, and if there are any remaining disagreements these can be settled using the administrative procedures of the firm rather than more costly legal mechanisms.

Williamson's approach to internalization is much narrower than that adopted by writers on international business issues. They emphasize quality control as well. Quality control issues arise with respect to both the product itself, and the information used to identify the market for it.

So far as the product is concerned, the quality achieved on delivery to the final customer reflects the effort applied at various stages of production, transportation, warehousing, retailing, and so on. Yet overall responsibility for customer satisfaction typically rests with just one (or at most two) of the parties. The party that carries responsibility therefore has a strong incentive to manage the overall distribution channel in an efficient manner. He can devise incentives to manage each stage in accordance with observed performance at that stage, but frequently what can be observed from the outside is very limited indeed. Thus to fine-tune incentives it is necessary to gain greater rights of observation, and this in turn may require ownership of the activity. The more sensitive is the quality of the delivered product to individual efforts at intermediate stages, and the greater the difficulty of monitoring performance at these stages, the higher will be the degree of integration. This explains, for example, why integration tends to be higher where refrigeration is used throughout the distribution channel, for failures at any one stage can be fatal to the entire operation. Moreover, the quality of refrigeration is expensive to monitor because of the heat loss involved in opening up cold stores for inspection.

It is, of course, possible that an independent operator would permit external supervision, but this is only likely if he has no valuable trade secrets to protect. This introduces the information issue alluded to above. Because of the 'public good' nature of information it is more difficult to exclude people from the use of information than it is to exclude them from the use of ordinary goods. This in turn makes it difficult to charge for the use of information unless there is a special legal right of exclusion (such as a patent). In the absence of such a legal right, secrecy is the main exclusionary device issued. Secrecy over production technology is a major reason why firms will not freely submit to monitoring by their customers, and hence why internalization is necessary to achieve quality control.

The wider the scope of information, the more important it is to protect its secrecy. A solution to a widespread problem is enormously valuable to the entrepreneur who discovers it, and so to protect its secrecy he integrates forward into marketing (as explained earlier). On the other hand, a retailer's knowledge of a local market for the product is of more limited value to other people, and it is therefore more reasonable for him to submit to external supervision. This is one reason why franchising can flourish – it concentrates powers of inspection on those who have the most valuable secrets to protect.

The public good nature of information makes it inefficient to replicate its production. In other words, information affords major economies of scale and scope. All writers on internalization are agreed that economies of scale and scope are a major reason why external markets persist even where internalization economies are available. For example, an advertising agency may have knowledge of the purchasing habits of households analysed by region and income group. Such information is of potential value to entrepreneurs in a wide range of different product markets. It is more effective for them to buy access to this information than to replicate its acquisition themselves. But information, like other products, suffers from problems of quality control. It may be either true or false and, because convincing evidence of truth is often difficult to obtain, while erroneous information is cheap to produce, the problem of quality control is actually very acute. Thus while it is advantageous to buy information from an independent agency if it can be trusted, it is better to generate the information in-house if it cannot. The reputation of the agency is therefore crucial in determining the procurement strategy used.

Economies of scale and scope do not, of course, apply only to information. They also apply to warehousing and retailing, as noted above. The larger the optimal size of warehouse, the greater the number of different lines it is necessary to carry, and hence the wider the diversity of production technologies and final markets involved. It is unlikely that a single management team would have sufficient skill to integrate upstream into production and downstream into retailing in all of these activities. Thus as the optimal size of warehouse increases, integration within the distribution channel is likely to decline.

Historically, the growth of mass markets appears to have so increased the volumes associated with individual product lines that specialized warehousing has become more viable. It is no longer necessary to combine many different product lines in order to achieve significant economies of scale. Thus the economies of scale foregone by integration have declined because a general warehouse handling many lines is not much cheaper than a specialized warehouse handling just a few. At the same time advances in protective product packaging, and the containerization of transport, have reduced the need for special handling skills. Thus the costs of integrating warehousing with production have declined, and independent warehouses have become less important in the economy (Porter and Livesay 1971).

THE INTERNATIONAL DIMENSION

It is a truism of modern marketing that markets are becoming more global, although the present extent of globalization is much greater in some sectors – such as consumer durables – than others – such as equipment sold to public utilities. To the extent that globalization is a response to political and social changes that are dismantling barriers between nations, this means that international marketing raises fewer special issues than it did before. There may be little difference, for example, in selling to a distant region of the home country rather than a small neighbouring state. Moreover, to the extent that large multinationals are now very experienced in selling in most of the world's major markets, they may be just as familiar with foreign markets as they are with domestic ones, so that even if cultural differences persist, the expertise now exists to deal with them.

Historically, though, circumstances of this kind have prevailed only within the major trading empires, and certainly not between them. Moreover, learning about foreign markets seems to have been an important influence on ownership strategies, with many firms exhibiting a lower degree of internalization in their foreign operations than in their domestic ones (Nicholas 1983). The lower level of internalization allows first-time foreign investors to buy in expert advice on the local market from local sales agents, and also to subcontract production (where local sourcing is important) to indigenous producers with a good knowledge of local resource conditions. Limited internalization also reduces the down-side risks associated with the sunk cost of creating an independent distribution channel. Once successfully established in the market, however, the relatively weak information feedback from agents and subcontractors anxious to protect their own expertise through secrecy handicaps further growth. It then becomes advantageous to buy this information, and in order to encourage truthfulness it helps to buy out the collaborating firms rather than just license the information from them. Thus international expansion typically involves an incremental internalization process which reflects the growing information needs of a company seeking to capitalize on initial success in the market (Johanson and Vahlne 1977). The fact that firms in different source countries have different levels of accumulated experience in foreign markets may well help to explain why, at any one time, firms from different countries often use different strategies when sourcing foreign markets.

MANIPULATION

It was suggested above that a key aspect of marketing is the manipulation of customer preferences. It was also suggested that marketing is best regarded as one aspect of general entrepreneurial activity. The connection between these two observations is that marketing is not the only form of manipulation that a successful entrepreneur will practice. The manipulation of employees, financiers and business partners may also be an important factor.

Highly motivated employees can be effectively self-monitoring. If they believe in the social value of the product they are selling, for example, salesmen are likely to be far more committed than if they are doing their job simply to earn the commissions involved. Committed salesmen are also more likely to be loyal, and hence less likely to take short-term advantage of the commission system by, for example, getting customers to place extra-large orders which the salesman knows will never be fulfilled on time. Manipulation of the customer can, therefore, be usefully complemented by manipulation of salesmen as well.

Similarly with quality control: unless quality control is fully mechanized, it depends crucially on the care and attention exercised by employees. There is a limit to the extent to which management control can be applied to the quality controllers themselves, and so they must be self-motivated too. A strong belief in the social value of the product, and an altruistic concern for customers placed at risk by defective items, can therefore usefully be instilled by the entrepreneur.

Manipulation can also be useful in obtaining finance for start-up or expansion. Those who come forward with entrepreneurial ideas are likely to be more optimistic about the success of their idea than are other people. Indeed, other people's pessimism about the idea may be regarded as a natural barrier to entry which allows the successful innovator to make temporary monopoly profits. But this story presupposes that the entrepreneur can finance the launch of his product from his own resources. If he has to rely on external finance then he will have to convince other people – notably hard-headed bankers – to invest in the enterprise, often on rather poor security. The ability to persuade such people of the social value of the enterprise may at least encourage them not to dismiss the proposal out of hand. Having gained their attention, manipulative skills may then be used to present optimistic sales forecasts in a plausible way.

Manipulation can be useful in engineering trust in joint venture partners or franchisees. The costs of monitoring and enforcing contracts with such parties are considerably reduced by an atmosphere of trust. An entrepreneur who can encourage consumers to trust in the quality of his product may also be able to induce business partners to put their trust in his own integrity. Finally, manipulative skills are of obvious value in public relations and in lobbying – especially in highly regulated industries such as utilities or those, like defence, where government is a major customer.

WELFARE IMPLICATIONS

There are three distinct sets of welfare issues raised by the preceding analysis: the effect of manipulation on the intensity of individual demand, the impact of transaction costs on the efficiency of market intermediation, and the effects of market structure. The first is the most difficult and needs to be disposed of at the outset, since the answers to the other two are predicated on a given intensity of demand.

If manipulation deceives customers into believing that the product has qualities it does not really possess then they are likely to be disappointed. With the benefit of hindsight, therefore, consumption of the product will have been excessive. Moreover, the fact that expectations have been raised and dashed may mean that the consumer feels much worse off than if he had simply been forced to make the purchases when he already knew that he did not really want them.

If the product really does have the qualities claimed for it then the customer's welfare will be improved, in the sense that he feels better off than if he had had only the other products to choose from. He certainly cannot be any worse off, given that he could have chosen the other products had he preferred them instead. This argument is independent of whether the qualities are objective (such as the fuel economy of a car) or subjective (for example, peer group respect earned by the choice of a stylish car).

The only difficult area is where the consumer is deceived but never realizes it. The welfare implications of this cannot be deduced without a decision on the ethics of successful deception. If deception is deemed legitimate, on the ground that the end justifies the means, then welfare evaluation must be logically made with respect to these ends, and not those of the customer himself.

Assuming that the manipulation is honest, the effect of high transaction costs is simply to reduce the welfare gains that are realized from trade. The welfare loss has two components. The first is the transaction costs themselves – the value of the resources used up in managing the transactions which could have been put to an alternative use. The second – and less well-known – component is the loss associated with the trade that would otherwise have taken place but now does not, because the gains do not outweigh the marginal transaction costs involved. This is the same kind of welfare loss that arises with a tariff, and is directly attributable to the reduction in the overall volume of trade.

If the manipulation is dishonest then high transaction costs may actually improve welfare, if substantially fewer people are deceived into buying the product.

The final consideration is market structure. If the entrepreneur enjoys a temporary monopoly then he will exploit it by further reducing the volume of trade. This is because it pays him to widen his margin by pushing up selling price and also pulling down his buying price (provided that he also enjoys some monopsony power). The high selling price discourages demand and so reduces the volume of trade.

If the entrepreneur can charge discriminatory prices, however, then the reduction in trade will be less, and in the limiting case where a separate price is set for every unit sold, there will be no reduction at all. In general, however, such a strategy would require each customer to be confronted with an individually-tailored two-part pricing scheme. Schemes of this kind are difficult to implement, not only because of the lack of detailed information on the intensity of individual customer demands, but also because discrimination creates profitable opportunities for arbitrage between customers which undermine the strategy.

In the long run most successful entrepreneurs face a threat of competitive entry, and in this case they will have to reduce the margin they set. There are, of course, certain marketing strategies – such as building brand loyalty through coupon schemes – which can act as entry deterrents, but even here some reduction in net margin is usually involved. As the margin narrows, trade will expand, and some of the welfare losses associated with short run monopoly will be eliminated.

It does not follow, of course, that short run monopoly itself should be eliminated because of the need for entrepreneurs to cover the sunk costs of product development out of subsequent profits. Short run monopoly rents are normally much less than the total value of the welfare improvement – partly because a non-discriminatory pricing structure allows buyers to appropriate some of the rents, and partly because of the limited duration of the monopoly. Thus entrepreneurs normally appropriate only a small proportion of the rents created by a successful product innovation. As a result, there tends to be too little, rather than too much innovation, and reducing short run monopoly profits further would only make the distortion of incentives worse.

HISTORICAL APPLICATIONS

The economic theory presented above is, in fact, a collection of sub theories which share a common set of fundamental assumptions. Generally these sub theories complement one another, but occasionally they suggest alternative explanations of the same phenomenon. There is, for example, more than one way of explaining the connection between refrigeration and vertical integration. In such cases detailed historical work may be able to provide the evidence which makes it possible to discriminate between alternative explanations.

The application of economic theory to business history works best when a comparative approach is used. Economic theory assumes that people adapt to changing circumstances in a rational way, so that differences in the environment induce differences in behaviour. These differences can be observed in cross-section, at a given point in time, because of differences in local environments. They can also be observed over time, before and after environmental change has occurred.

Product characteristics have played an important role in the preceding analysis. Different products exhibit different degrees of novelty, complexity and specialization/versatility; these characteristics affect the nature of promotional activity and in particular the importance of presentation at point of sale. Some goods are naturally variable in quality, and some variations can be discerned by inspection and others not. This has important implications for the motivation of employees and for the degree of vertical integration in distribution. At a more mundane level, products differ in their perishability/durability and portability. At one extreme of perishability is the manual labour service – such as hairdressing – and at the other the durable consumer or producer good. These physical characteristics are significant for the organization of the distribution channel, as reflected in the location and internalization structures used.

A well-known phenomenon that can usefully be studied in this way is the change in the distribution of grocery items during the early twentieth century, which meant that fewer items were traded through organized produce markets where samples are displayed to buyers and spot sales made. This can, in principle, be explained by changes in food preservation technology, transport costs and market size interacting with fairly stable economies of scale in storage facilities. Whilst the broad picture is fairly well-understood, however, many of the details still remain to be worked out.

The emergence of the advertising agency is another phenomenon that can usefully be studied from a theoretical perspective. The agency sells specialized expertise which affords economies of scope, but also incurs problems of quality control. The agent's list of regular clients is used as a guide to quality by potential new customers, so much of the agency's reputation hinges on retaining key customers' goodwill. This means that agencies must exert their manipulative skills not only in the service of their clients but in manipulating loyalty in the clients themselves. The emergence of advertising agencies can therefore be usefully studied in terms of the interaction of economics of internalization and manipulation.

Manipulation is sometimes regarded as one of the skills of preachers. It has been remarked that some of the most successful US pioneers of mass marketing were the sons of church ministers (Tedlow 1990). The connection between the two probably goes much deeper than this, however. The temple economy of Sumer appears to have relied, in part, on the manipulative power of priests, who obtained tribute in kind from peasants, which they used not only to provision their temple but to pay skilled craftsmen in the city. In the Middle Ages a large tourist business developed around pilgrimages to shrines, in which the marketing of relics, and the exploitation of legends, played a major role. This should not be surprising, for in a hierarchical society where the major rewards are to be earned in the offices of the church, the most entrepreneurial individuals are likely to be attracted to careers in the church, and the most manipulative will find their way to the top. In a more individualistic and materialistic society, the same type of person builds their career by marketing consumer products instead.

Rather similar remarks can be made about political and military leaders (Redlich 1956). Both need manipulative powers to maintain the illusion amongst their followers that they are really in control of events. Military leaders in particular also require logistical skills to provision the army and plan the movement of troops. Such skills are highly relevant to the organization of product flow through distribution channels. Research into the family background, military experience and political ambitions of successful entrepreneurs should therefore shed light on their acquisition of marketing skills.

It should be clear, therefore, that the economic theory of marketing provides an extensive research agenda which calls for both the reinterpretation of existing secondary sources, and for new primary sources to be investigated. Such work will be useful not only for its intrinsic interest, but also as a valuable means of testing and refining the theory itself.

ACKNOWLEDGEMENTS

I am grateful to Tony Corley, Geoffrey Jones and Richard Tedlow for comments on an earlier version of this paper.

REFERENCES

Becker, G.S. (1964) *Human Capital*, New York: Columbia University Press.
Casson, M.C. (1982) *The Entrepreneur: An Economic Theory*, Oxford: Martin Robertson (reprinted by Avebury, Farnborough, 1991).
—— (1984) 'The theory of vertical integration: a survey and synthesis', *Journal of Economic Studies* 11(2): 3–43.
—— (1991) 'Introduction', in M.C. Casson (ed.) *Entrepreneurship*, Aldershot: Edward Elgar, pp. xiii–xxvi.
Deaton, A. and Muellbauer, J. (1980) *Economics and Consumer Behaviour*, Cambridge: Cambridge University Press.
Hirsch, F. (1977) *Social Limits to Growth*, London: Routledge & Kegan Paul.
Johanson, J. and Vahlne, J.E. (1977) 'The internationalisation process of the firm – a model of knowledge development and increasing market commitments', *Journal of International Business Studies* 8: 23–32.
Klein, B., Crawford, R.G. and Alchian, A.A. (1978) 'Vertical integration, appropriable rents and the competitive contracting process', *Journal of Law and Economics* 21: 297–326.
Leibenstein, H. (1979) 'The general X-efficiency paradigm and the role of the entrepreneur', in M.J. Rizzo (ed.) *Time, Uncertainty and Disequilibrium*, Lexington, Mass.: D.C. Heath, pp. 127–39.
Nicholas, S.J. (1983) 'Agency contracts, institutional modes, and the transition to foreign direct investment by British manufacturing multinationals before 1939, *Journal of Economic History* 43: 675–86.
Porter, G. and Livesay, H.C. (1971) *Merchants and Manufacturers: Studies in the Changing Structure of Nineteenth-Century Marketing*, Baltimore: Johns Hopkins Press.
Redlich, F. (1956) 'The military enterpriser: a neglected area of research', *Explorations in Entrepreneurial History*, (Series 1) 8: 252–6.
Schumpeter, J.A. (1942) *Capitalism, Socialism and Democracy* (5th edn) T. Bottomore (ed.) London: Allen & Unwin, 1976.
Tedlow, R. (1990) *New and Improved: The Story of Mass Marketing in America*, Oxford: Heinemann.
Williamson, O.E. (1985) *Economic Institutions of Capitalism*, New York: Free Press.

11 Conceptualizing an adaptable marketing system
The end of mass marketing

Ken'ichi Yasumuro

INTRODUCTION

The purpose of this chapter is to analyse the forces in the market environment which have stimulated Japanese manufacturing enterprises to develop an adaptable marketing system (AMS), and to describe the developmental process as an aspect of contemporary history.[1] Throughout the analysis, the focus is on why mass marketing has been replaced. In connection with this, it is important to discuss the recent move in business from mass production to the flexible manufacturing system (FMS), also known as 'lean production' (Womack *et al.* 1990: 48–69).

To study adaptable marketing and flexible manufacturing (AM and FM) systems, many scholars have been attracted by the Toyota production systems, because the automobile is 'the industry of industries' (Drucker 1946). Because the automobile industry is on such a large scale, many writers have argued that lean production must involve complicated methods, and that it will be difficult to apply outside Japan. However, this is not true; lean production is not limited to the automobile industry and simple, effective applications can be found almost everywhere, especially in the production of electrical appliances and electronics.

This chapter will analyse how AM and FM systems have been developed in Japanese companies using case studies from refrigerator and washing machine manufacture. In the first section, there is an analysis of the nature of the drastic environmental change after the first oil crisis in 1973, which led to the collapse of the mass-production and mass-marketing system in Japan. The next section describes how Japanese manufacturing firms responded to this environmental upheaval through the development of AM and FM systems. Then a more detailed case study of Sharp Corporation's AM and FM system is provided.

Although AM and FM systems can succeed over mass production in the world market, their market share-oriented strategy and excessive product diversification can produce additional costs. The result can be, and has been in some cases, a deterioration of productivity. Japanese manufacturing firms, especially in consumer goods, began to realize the pitfalls of AM and FM systems in the late 1980s.

The conclusion offers a critique of the market-share strategies of Japanese firms. It is argued that coordination between marketing and manufacturing in the upstream, that is, at the product development and design stage, is needed to maintain an adequate balance between flexibility and productivity. In short, the AMS can integrate R & D function with FMS through the active role of the marketing manager.

THE CATASTROPHIC CHANGE OF ENVIRONMENT AFTER THE FIRST OIL CRISIS

Japanese awkward mass production

Contrary to received wisdom, Japanese manufacturing firms in the 1960s and early 1970s were awkward mass producers, at least in relation to their domestic market. The Japanese market is difficult to standardize, not only for foreigners but also for domestic firms. The Japanese market has been constructed from traditional markets which date from feudal days and from new Westernized markets which were introduced after the Meiji era (1868–1912). This dual character creates difficulties for standardized marketing in Japan. Other factors, such as the sharp change of the four climatic seasons, differences in regional markets, neurotic quality-conscious customers, and, at the extreme, inter-linked markets by '*Keiretsu*' (industrial groups linked by cross-holdings) all add to the complexities of Japanese market. As a result, the Japanese market is one of the most dynamic but confusing markets in the world, and difficult to approach.

Nevertheless, after World War II, especially in the 1950s and 1960s, the Japanese market was organized as a standardized mass market under the strong cultural influence of the American lifestyle. In retrospect, this period can be seen as exceptional in Japanese economic history.

The consumers' acceptance of standard goods and services was partly conditioned by the Japanese feeling of yearning for 'American life' (psychographic factor; Tedlow 1990), but mainly by the shortage of supply of most commodities. From the nature of the Japanese market, it was obvious that as consumers became richer, they might become dissatisfied with standardized goods and services, and, as a result, they would revert to their inherent natural 'diversity'. In the 1970s, when Japanese consumers reached a respectable income per capita, the market for mass products began to be eroded by degrees.

The Japanese market was still small in the late 1950s and 1960s. Competition was so fierce that newcomers were forced to abandon their domestic market, and pursue growth in foreign markets, especially in the United States. Typical examples included Sony in consumer electronics, Honda in motorcycles, Sanyo in colour televisions, Akai in tape recorders, and JVC in audio systems, etc. Those export-oriented manufacturers successfully established the ability to manage the mass-production system, and thus adapted well to the standardized markets of the West. However, their major competitive advantages depended on such country-specific factors as cheap labour costs, government support for exports, and an undervalued Yen. As a result, their business had an element of vulnerability.

The large Japanese firms which were primarily domestic-oriented were attracted by the success of the small export firms. They established export-specified factories on a large scale. Japanese large firms therefore differentiated markets between standardized (for export) and diversified (for domestic), and applied different types of production system: mass production versus small batch-diversified production, or what we can call 'hotchpotch' production. Consequently, the Japanese market remained less standardized and varied than that in the West. This was an important factor which prevented the entrance of foreign firms into the Japanese market.

Having failed to reorganize their domestic market into a homogenized and standardized market, Japanese firms were left with domestic production systems which were poorly designed, and sometimes clumsy and confused. The average productivity for domestic production was lower than export-specified mass production. When this irregular production system, differentiated between domestic and export production, had to be integrated, the idea of FMS emerged. But why did this happen, and in what manner?

A sudden great collapse

The Japanese economy achieved double-digit growth in the 1960s, but it was deeply rooted in vulnerable resource dependencies. The Japanese economy was inefficient and gluttonous, consuming a huge amount of energy and natural resources, but only producing low-added-value products, such as heavy industry products, and standardized consumer products for export. It continued to cause harmful pollution in the small Japanese islands. Japan's growth mechanism in the 1960s can be compared, at least in some respects, to that of the Eastern European economies in the era of communism. The result in Japan, as in Eastern Europe, was costly and inefficient.

In the early 1970s, the Japanese economy showed the symptoms of social disintegration: a high inflation rate, anti-pollution movements and law suits, and radical student riots, etc. In addition, the international environment was suddenly transformed. The escalating international monetary crisis was finally brought to an end in December 1971, and the floating currency system was introduced. This was the so-called 'Nixon-shock' (Uchino 1978: 186–7). In September 1972, prime minister K. Tanaka signed the Joint Communiqué on Sino-Japanese Friendship. Excess liquidity inflation started in 1973.

The revaluation of the Yen against the US dollar market meant that Japanese export firms began to lose their price competitiveness, and their businesses declined. Moreover, labour shortages resulted in soaring wages. The country-specific advantages of Japanese firms were diminished and the low-price exporters experienced difficulties.

To add to the problems of Japanese business, the first oil crisis hit the Japanese economy. Oil prices more than doubled in October 1973, and, as a result, in March 1974, wholesale prices increased 37 per cent and consumer prices rose 26 per cent over the same period a year earlier. Strong anti-inflationary measures continued through 1974 and 1975. As a result, the general level of wholesale prices finally declined in January 1975, but this was the first time in thirty-six months.

The result of these adverse environmental circumstances was the deepest and most prolonged recession in Japan's post-war history. In 1974, Japanese real GNP declined for the first time in the post-war period (Uchino 1983: 208). Until the end of summer 1974, Japanese firms continued to enjoy the inflationary profits that had been produced by shortages and crazy prices. However, they suddenly faced a sharp decline in prices, rapid increases in inventory, and the necessity for large cutbacks in production. As the result of hyper-inflation, large-scale wage increases were demanded in 1975, on top of the 33 per cent won by labour in 1974, resulting in a re-acceleration of the wage-price spiral (Uchino 1978: 210–11).

Figure 11.1 shows a hundred years of Japan's economic growth. The economic upheaval from 1973 to 1975 looks like a small 'blip', but when it is magnified in Fig. 11.2, a severe shock can be observed.

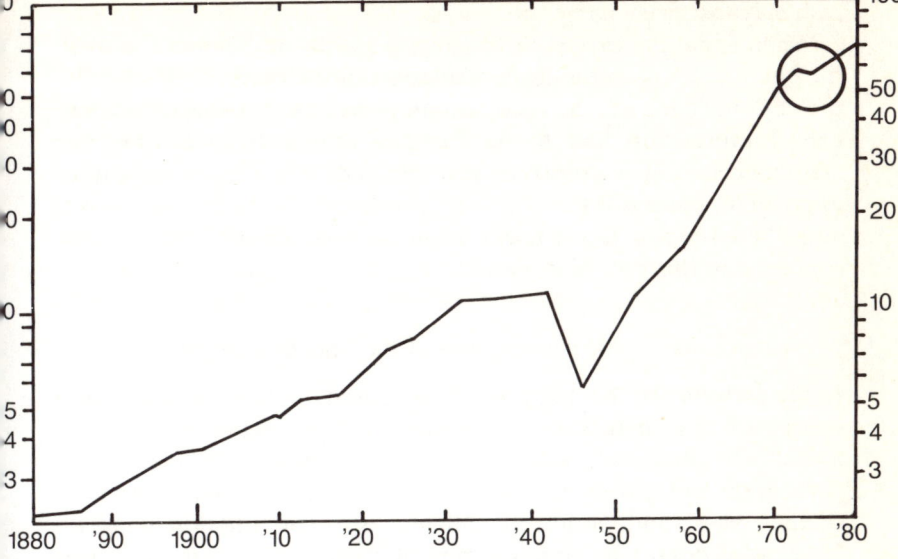

Figure 11.1 Japanese real per capita GNP, 1880–1980 (USA 1980=100). Adapted from Anzai *et al.* (1990: 11)

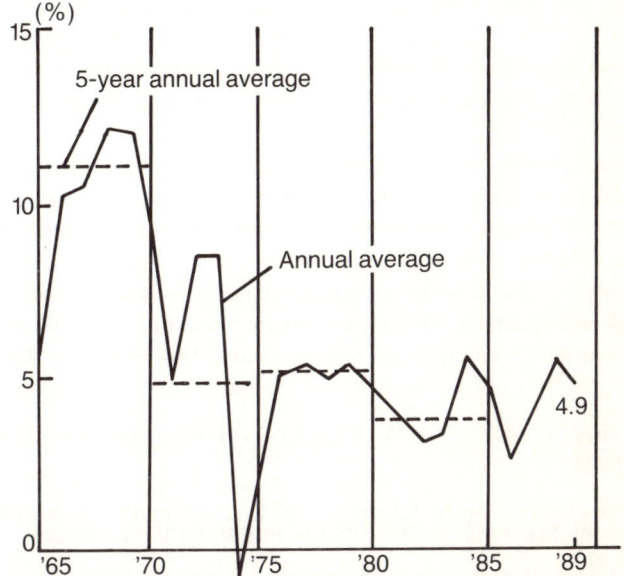

Figure 11.2 Trends in Japan's real GNP growth rate, 1965–89. Adapted from Anzai *et al.* (1990: 11)

The upheaval proved to be a fatal blow to the export firms, which suddenly lost price competitiveness.

When Japanese export firms came back to the domestic market, they had to adapt to the diversified units of the markets. To achieve the certain share which could sustain firms in the domestic market, export production had to be changed into a more flexible and adaptable system as quickly as possible. The transformation seemed impossible, but it was the only way to survive. The history of the AM and FM system in Japan began from the resolution of life or death problems in this recession period.

The baby boom and the emergence of the 'moody market'

In the early 1970s, the 'baby boom' appeared on the scene as a major driving force of demand. The mass-market generation in the 1950s and 1960s faded out, and the baby boom took their place. This generation had grown up under the improved economic conditions of the 1960s, and preferred individualistic consumption patterns. Most were double-income and typically nuclear families, and their lifestyle presented a new luxurious market in the mid-1970s.

Under severe recession, the baby boom market was the hope for consumer durable industries. They were less interested in mass-produced goods, however, and their buying behaviour was still unpredictable. The baby boomers made market conditions more unstable and moody and the mass producers began to pile up unsold products.

To adapt to market uncertainty, the product lifecycle needs to be shortened to minimize product exposure in the risky conditions, and lot size (production volume of each item) should be minimized to adjust to elastic demand. In short, there is a well-known law of cybernetics – the law of requisite variety – that if the market environment becomes diverse, production must be more flexible, and products must be more diversified (Ashby 1956; Pascale 1990: 14).

EMERGENCE OF A NEW PARADIGM OF MARKETING STRATEGY

Incremental approach to the flexible manufacturing system

Faced by this deterioration in economic conditions, Japanese industries attempted every possible means to save energy, materials and labour. For example, New Japanese Steel reduced the average quantity of petroleum required to process 1 ton of raw iron ore from 128,000 litres in 1973 to 86,000 litres in 1979. Similar energy conservation plans were introduced in the chemical, cement, petroleum refining, and paper pulp industries. However, in the automobile and home electric appliance industries, capital investment was aimed at producing new product lines that emphasized the conservation of energy and manpower (Uchino 1978: 225).

Through conservation efforts, Japanese executives realized that the mass-production system was not only uneconomical, but also that the use of mass-produced goods wasted energy and materials. They also found that if labour-saving machines and energy-saving equipment were introduced on the assembly line, costs and product defect ratios could be reduced drastically. When the assembly line was designed carefully and maintained, an automated assembly line could reduce process uncertainty, because it eliminated the assembler's trivial errors and whims.

However, when machinery became more precise and fragile, the production system needed highly sophisticated controls to avoid serious breakdowns. In-house training to improve the technical skills of operators and assemblers was indispensable to maintain the stable operation of a complicated production system. For this purpose, the 'self-management by team' concept was necessary, and group activities such as 'quality circles' arrived in the workshops.

The concept of the 'compound assembly line'

The structure of the problem was clear, but the solution was difficult to implement. Increased product diversity, reduced lot size and shortened product lifecycles increase the ability to adapt to changing market conditions, but when product diversity is increased without maintaining the inter-changeability of parts and equipment between products, production costs rapidly escalate.

The core of the problem was how to achieve product diversification without losing the benefits of scale economies. In general terms, the problem can be defined as follows: how can 'scope economies' be achieved without losing the merits of 'scale economies'?

As is generally known, Toyota Automobile Co. were first to come up with a solution. This was the so-called 'Toyota Production System', which evolved in the 1960s and 1970s. The 'Toyota' lean production system could achieve product diversification without losing the merits of mass-production (Womack *et al.* 1990: 52). Toyota developed 'compound assembly lines' which enabled diverse

212 *The rise and fall of mass marketing*

models, more than 2,000 different types of cars, to be assembled one after another on the same line.

The 'compound assembly line' was a kind of 'mutation' created by 'hybridization' of the export-oriented mass-production system and the diversified domestic production system. Consequently, it could share the merits of both parents, but it also had the potential disadvantages of its parents if it lacked appropriate management.

Surprisingly, Toyota developed the initial flexible production system without the use of information technology, applying a simple order-entry system like '*Kanban*' and human skills. Consequently, if information technologies could be substituted for '*Kanban*', the 'Toyota system' could be substantially improved. This was a challenge for information technologists and engineers, in Toyota and in other firms. Electrical appliance and electronics firms, which already possessed the information technology, could easily modify the 'Toyota system' with their own schemes. When the 'Toyota production system' was opened to Japanese firms in the late 1970s, many versions of 'our company FMS' quickly emerged.[2]

Market-share strategy and application of FMS

The purpose of marketing is to sell products as much as possible. In theory, to realize this goal, products should be diversified to cover all market segments. On the other hand, the purpose of production is to produce goods and services for the lowest costs. In theory, mass production is the best way to achieve this goal. As long as stable market conditions continue, the production department can choose this 'easy way', and marketing has to obey the logic of 'scale economy'.

However, even when market conditions become diverse, production managers still stick to the 'easy way', leaving the marketing managers to sell standardized products to a diversified market. In this case, the only way to attract reluctant customers is to offer lower prices.

The typical mass producer chooses the market positioning of the lowest price offerer, but this position was vulnerable in the 1970s because of the threats posed by the newly industrialized economies (NIEs). NIE firms prefer the same positioning (lowest cost and lowest price strategy), because the management of standardized mass production is relatively 'easy to learn'. Consequently, typical mass-production and mass-marketing firms in the advanced economies lose their markets when NIE firms enter through an export strategy. Such a strategy is very similar to that chosen by Japanese firms in the 1960s.

Throughout the recession period of the early 1970s, the Japanese market changed to a typical buyer's market. The 'easy way' of production was not an option. Production was forced to follow 'the logic of marketing' – diversification.

Japanese firms, which strive for growth, tend to choose a market-share maximization strategy. They have an inclination to neglect the profitability of the product lines when they choose an aggressive market share strategy which can justify unlimited product proliferation and diversification to plough marginal niche markets. To increase market share additional costs for marketing and production were allowed (or overlooked) for the sake of the wider strategic goals. As a result, the worldwide market share of Japanese manufacturing firms consistently increased in the 1980s, but their average ROI ratio began to decrease.

The logic of adaptable marketing

When the market is made up of one large segment and numerous small segments, the mass producer can focus on the largest segment, and give up the small segments for niche producers. To defend the largest segment from aggressive niche producers, the mass producer needs mass advertising devices. A peaceful coexistence between mass producers and niche producers can be achieved by a separation of territory by products. Domain governance is critical for survival.

On the other hand, when the largest segment is decomposed into many small segments, the mass producer suddenly loses the lion's share. Nevertheless, if a firm pursues growth and desires to keep the lion's share, marketing for small segments is essential.[3] Firms have to develop a full line of products to meet various market conditions.

The logical consequence of a growth strategy through full-line policy in the segmented market is FMS, which is characterized by the 'compound assembly line' and 'just-in-time'. In short, when markets become diverse, production systems also become diverse to adapt to market conditions – the law of requisite variety – and then adaptable marketing has a strategic importance.

The basic principle of AMS is quite simple. It is almost the opposite of mass marketing. Usually, the concept of mass marketing is as follows. New products are developed in the R & D centre and introduced into the production line without any consultation. Before starting mass production, the marketing manager estimates the volume of demand (possible sales volume) as accurately as possible. If demand estimation is inaccurate, excess or shortage of production will result, and profit will be lost by the disposal of unsold stocks or as an opportunity cost. Consequently, the merit of mass production depends on the accuracy of demand estimation.

To ensure the accuracy of demand estimation, sophisticated methods are widely applied, consumer behaviour researches are employed widely, and a huge amount of data are processed by mainframe computers. Even if the most sophisticated assessment methods and computers are applied, however, the results of estimation of demand and forecast of possible sales volume are always inaccurate because no simulation model can include all unforeseen contingencies. As market conditions are always threatened by uncertainty to a certain extent, estimated results are also uncertain in nature. To stabilize market conditions, an effort to control consumer behaviour is needed.

In addition, mass producers force workers to work in inhuman labour conditions, and mass marketers apply dangerous psychological methods like 'brainwashing' in advertising which can cause moral problems in society (Corrigan *et al*. 1991: 105–11). In short, statistical research for demand estimation and applied psychology for advertising are two basic factors of mass marketing.

In adaptable marketing thinking, those methods are regarded as less important. In adaptable marketing, the salesperson approaches the segmented markets rather like a waiter coming to the dinner table, and asking the customers: 'Are you being served, sirs?' 'We shall be happy if we can be of any service to you.' Showing a thick catalogue book, the salesperson continues: 'We can prepare this variety of products for you. You have a free choice between these alternatives. But what if you should not be satisfied and you will pay additional cost, we can prepare any order for you, Sir.' Thus adaptable marketing is able to make a customer believe that a quasi-custom-made product is better than a standardized mass product.

In adaptable marketing, advertising policy is not focused on the product or service itself. Rather the emphasis is on the corporate reputation, just as a high-grade hotel never advertises the price of the room charge. In adaptable marketing, the status of the company and the quality of the products are the major part of the advertisement, and the focus is on maximization of customer satisfaction.

The mass marketers often turn into impudent high-pressure salespersons when their products are in poor demand. In such a case, they ignore customers' requests, only emphasizing the low price, and push the unpopular goods down their throats. The impudent pushing salesperson is a common feature of mass marketing failure. On the other hand, the adaptable marketers appeal to the intelligence of their customers. They help the customer to shape an attractive lifestyle through consulting and preparing various products and services. On occasion, they modestly recommend a set of products and services for the particular lifestyle of the customer.

Adaptable marketing is only effective if goods and services are produced at a price competitive to those of the mass producer. In short, the success of adaptable marketing greatly depends on, not the marketing method itself, but the manufacturing technologies which can realize a variety of products.

Emergence of the new business paradigm

The AM and FM system can be regarded as very much like the innovation which McDonalds introduced into the fast food industry. Somewhat contrary to commonsense, the success factor of McDonalds' hamburgers is not their 'uniformity', but their 'variety'. McDonalds created variety through the combination of standardized materials. If it is possible to introduce McDonalds' production system into the consumer durables industry, simultaneous achievement of scale and scope economies can be realized. Although US mass producers never tried 'McDonald-ization' of production and service, Japanese manufacturers have applied it in a different form; the AM and FM system combined can be said to be a 'McDonalds-like' system.

When the AM and FM system appeared in Japan, market segmentation accelerated, and mass producers were driven away. American mass producers and some NIE firms suddenly realized they had failed to adapt to the Japanese market. Mass producers looked upon the Japanese market as a puzzle, and perhaps those who were educated by old paradigm – the 'absolutism of scale economy' and the mass marketing gospel – failed to comprehend the meaning of the revolution. They challenged the Japanese market again and again but never succeeded, because their methods could no longer adapt.

On the other hand, Japanese manufacturing firms were not only able to adapt to environmental change swiftly, but also fragmented the mass market into small pieces, each having some distinctive features. As FMS could assemble diversified products on the same line (the so-called 'compound assembly line'), domestic and export production was integrated, enabling Japanese manufacturing firms to become huge 'global suppliers' (Yasumuro 1988). FMS can respond to a variety of specifications, so global marketing became easier and more profitable. As a result of this production revolution, the Japanese trade surplus reached $100 billion in 1987.[4] More than 50 per cent of this trade surplus was obtained in the United States. How did this happen?

The basic character of American society is, perhaps, not uniformity but diversity. Many Japanese executives believed that diversified products would be adequate for the individualistic American customers. American customers needed a variety of products to satisfy their individual lifestyles and cultures. Japanese international marketing managers perceived the US consumer durable market as a 'diversified one', but the average American marketers recognized it as a 'single-standardized market'. The cognitive map of the US market on both sides of the Pacific was different.

The mass producers suffered from the disadvantage that flexible producers preferred to break the mass market into small segments, and then to re-adapt the conditions by applying the adaptable marketing concept. To defend their business from flexible producers, mass producers found themselves compelled to change themselves into the same business archetype, because as the mass-production line is only one special condition (a large lot size) of a 'compound assembly line' (small lot and variety of product on the same line), the viability of mass producers is quite limited. The Ford Motor Co. is one of the successful cases of this transformation (Womack *et al.* 1990: 92; Pascale 1990). The spread of the flexible manufacturing archetype is now pandemic rather than endemic.

FORMATIVE PERIOD OF THE COMPETITIVE EDGE

The extraordinary application of mediocre methods

When we look at a sophisticated machine system, we are impressed by its precise design and the integrated functions of the mechanisms. However, if one looks at the prototype, usually the mechanism is quite simple. The prototype of FMS in the early period of its development was also quite simple. The archetype of FMS was constituted by ordinary knowledge of production techniques and management know-how, though its objective was surely different.

Japanese firms thoroughly pursued cost reduction (C), shortening delivery term (D), and the improvement of quality (Q) in the early 1970s recession period. As C, D and Q are incompatible with each other, it is always important for manufacturers to keep a balance between them. Japanese engineers applied familiar methods, such as value engineering (VE), variable reduction (VR), industrial engineering (IE), and quality control (QC) to solve contradictory problems.[5] To look at the problem-solving process, we will look at Sharp Corporation's FMS in their refrigerator and washing machine factories. The company applied simple methods in effective ways.[6]

The large-size refrigerator factory in 1979

The space available in most Japanese houses is limited, so it is commonsense that home appliances should be of a compact size. However, this commonsense began to change as baby boomers entered the market and started to change consumer behaviour in the early 1970s.

When Sharp Corporation decided to build a new factory to produce large refrigerators (more than 240 litre capacity) in 1979, the expected sales volume was insufficient to allow mass production. In addition, when mass production was applied, a large amount of storage space for semi-finished and finished products was required, but the factory site was already full (Nikkei Business 1979: 45). When the plan of large refrigerator production was carried out, the only possible way to achieve it was automated production system which could realize a space saving and stockless manufacturing.

Before FMS was introduced, the refrigerator division produced five different types of large refrigerator without standardized designs, and each type had more than ten variations, e.g. three-door and four-door types, right-open and left-open door, and two different colours (green and white), etc.; total product variety was over sixty.

The division decided to simplify the variety into three basic models. In the process of simplification of the products, the design department applied VE and VR methods effectively. As the result of an investigation into Japanese housing, the marketing department found that the width and height of Japanese furniture varied, but the depth was almost standard. It would be convenient for customers if the depth of refrigerators was standardized in the same manner.

The product design department soon realized that if the depth of the frame was standardized, three different size of frames could easily be made using the same rolled steel sheet. That is, when a large-size box was made, the rolled steel could be cut into a long sheet and bent into a box, and when a smaller box was made the steel sheet could be cut into a shorter sheet and bent into a box, just like paper craft. By applying this simple idea, the time-consuming die change was eliminated.

The production technology department developed a new method to shape a frame by folding down the four sides of metal sheet, and putting it together by an inlay formula. By simplification, the welding process was eliminated, and assembly time was shortened drastically.

In the next stage, the design department standardized doors into two different sizes, large and small. The production technology department developed a flexible die system which quickly switched over from large to small, and vice versa. On the painting process, automatic shifting of pigments was introduced which could change colours in only 3 minutes. By allying those ideas, the lot size was drastically reduced from 1,000 to 50 units of refrigerators.

In the workshop, a free-flow line was introduced. On the free-flow line, products were assembled on the carriage, and assemblers could control the line speed to a certain extent. As a result, assemblers were responsible for their own jobs, and 'the next stage of work is my customer' thinking (built-in quality-consciousness) became established.

A distinctive feature of the carriage was the installation of a magnetic memory unit on the bottom. All the information concerning the specifications of the product, the course of assembling, type of parts and equipments, ordered colour, and delivery, etc., were memorized in it beforehand. When the parts and equipment were short, a computer-controlled automatic parts supply vehicle arrived just-in-time from the parts centre beside the workshop.

When a carriage arrived on the line, the micro-reader read the information, and the computer gave commands to each stage to prepare the parts to assemble. While the steel sheet was being cut, other assembly stages started to operate their own tasks. Instead of '*Kanban*', Sharp Corporation applied a self-made microcomputer network as shown in Fig. 11.3, that could implement just-in-time more simply and more effectively. Surprisingly, the factory was built as a six-storied building because, with the factory site already full, the refrigerator division was forced to build a high-rise structure as shown in Fig. 11.4.

On the first floor, rolled steel sheet was cut, shaped and painted and transferred to the frame-making stage on the same floor; it was then moved to the fifth floor by lift. On the second floor, internal frames and other interior components were assembled and polyurethane injection followed; they were then transferred to the fifth floor. Meanwhile, on the third floor, refrigerating cycle systems were assembled, and supplied to the fifth floor just-in-time.

On the fifth floor, the initial assembly stage, two different sizes of

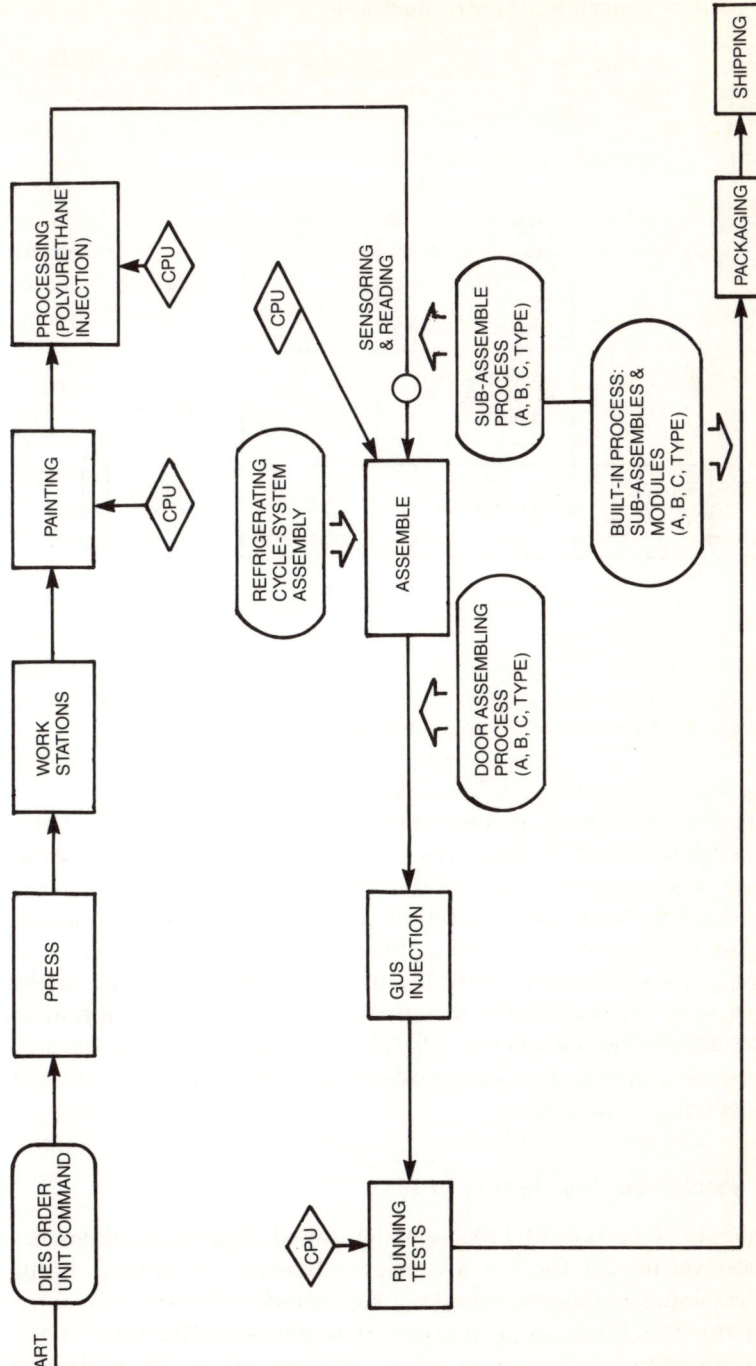

Figure 11.3 Flow chart of Sharp's refrigerator factory in 1979.
Source: Company document, *Sharp Corporation*

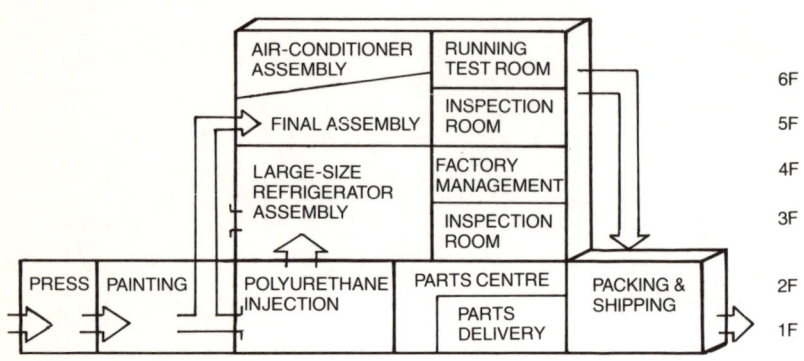

Figure 11.4 Elevation of Sharp's refrigerator factory.
Source: *Nikkei Mechanical*, 25 June 1979: 37

doors were presented, painted, assembled and fixed into the semi-finished frame, then freezing gas was injected into the cycle system, and the whole assembly process was finished. Finished products were sent to the sixth floor for inspection, and then transferred to the first floor by lift for packing and shipping.

The parts supply centre was located on the first floor, inspection rooms were on the third and sixth floor, and factory management centre was on the fourth floor. Sharp's 1979 version of FMS achieved full use of limited space and realized stock-less production, just as in automobile production.

The washing machine factory in 1983

As the 1979 version of FMS was developed further, an improved version was used in the new washing machine factory in 1983. In the new version, a mainframe computer was introduced as the core of the company-wide information network. Whole stages of the value chain, from accepting orders from users, placing orders of parts and

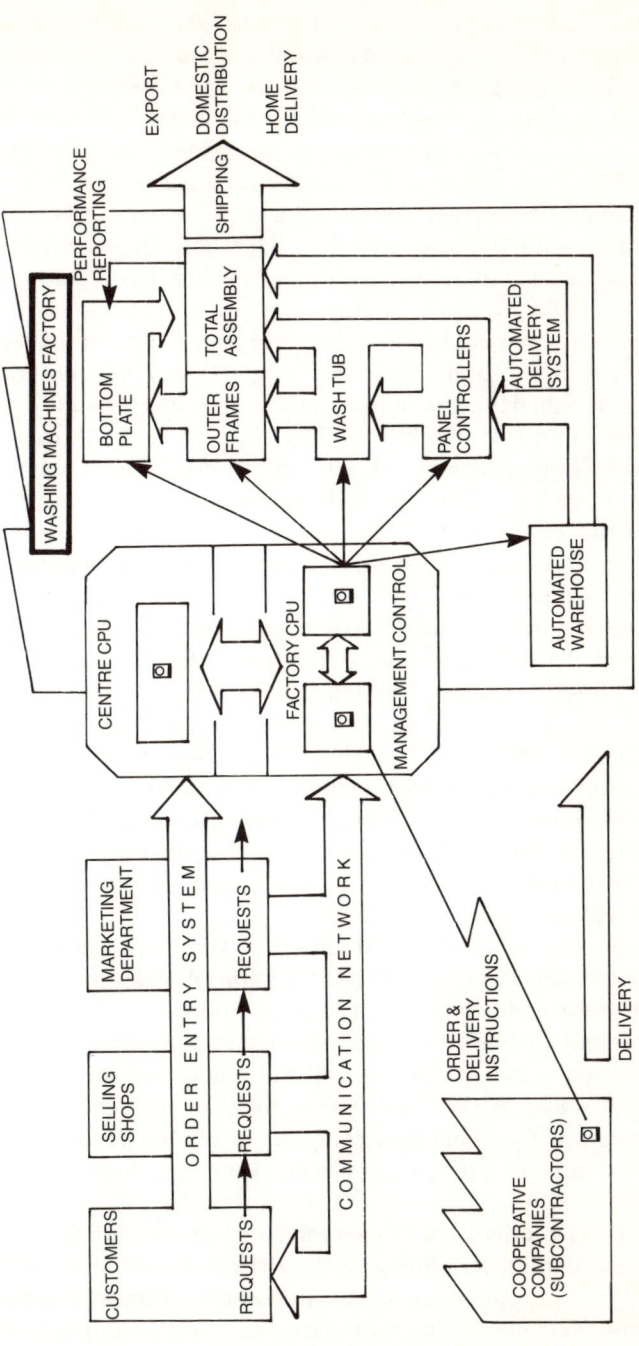

Figure 11.5 Concept of the new factory system: washing machines, 1983.
Source: Company document, *Sharp Corporation*

semi-assembled components to the subcontractors, assembling and shipping of the products, etc., were controlled by the network system shown in Fig 11.5. The main purpose of the new FMS was to respond to the various needs of customers as quickly as possible. The lifestyle of contemporary Japanese diversified in the 1980s, with the result that the needs for washing machines also diversified. A large family living in a normal-sized house demanded a large capacity, whereas a double-income family living in an urban flat where they sometimes used the machine at midnight, needed an automatic and low-noise type.

To develop the new FMS, the washing machine division exhaustively studied design simplification by using VE and VR methods. At first, the design department re-examined ordinary models and simplified them into two 'mother models' (Fig. 11.6). Each mother model could be equipped with one of two different sets of washtub and motor: a large high-power set and small normal-power set. Each model could use one of two different formulas of washing: regular swirl formula and new current formula. Added to this, three different types of control panel were prepared: dial type, push button type, and digital indication type. Finally, colour and pattern of outer frame could be selected from more than a hundred different samples. By combining different modules and colours, customers could choose the 'best' washing machine to fit their own lifestyle.

In spite of the variation, each module was simplified and standardized, and a large volume production of each module was secured. As a result, in comparison with ordinary mass-production methods, which produce different types of washing machines in a large lot base, the new FMS could increase productivity and reduce assembly defects drastically.

To operate the new FMS, far larger information processing capacity was needed than for the 1979 version of FMS (Fig. 11.7). The steps of information processing were as follows: at first, users' requests were memorized in the mainframe computer located in the headquarters. Then the specification of the request which indicates the capacity of washtub, function, type of panel, colour and pattern, etc., were issued by the mainframe computer to the branch computers in the automated warehouse, subcontractors, and production line in the factory.

Subcontractors produced semi-assembled products and delivered them to the automated warehouse at the right time, and in the right quality, but not so strictly as in the just-in-time system. Instead, the warehouse delivered parts, subassembles, and modules to the

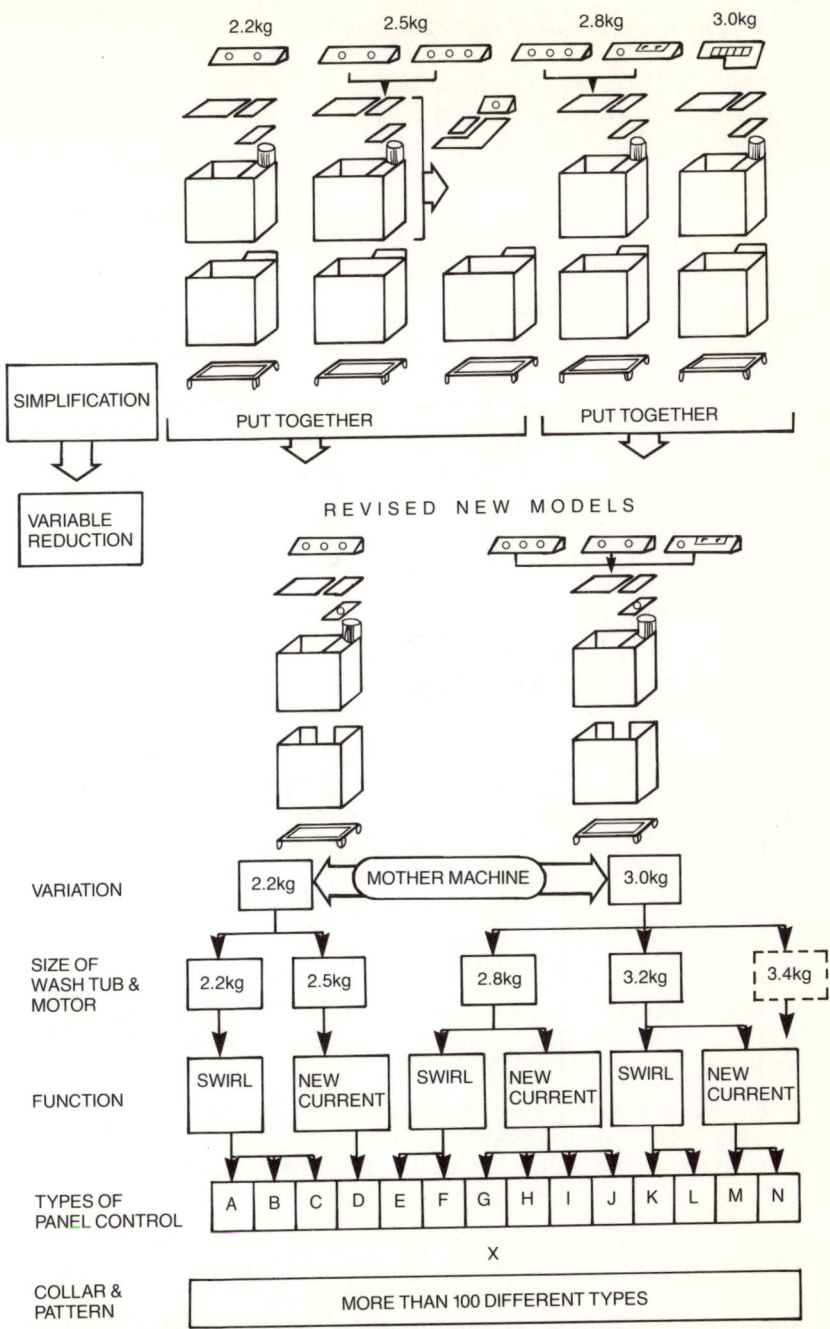

Figure 11.6 Simplification of design: washing machines.
Source: Company document, *Sharp Corporation*

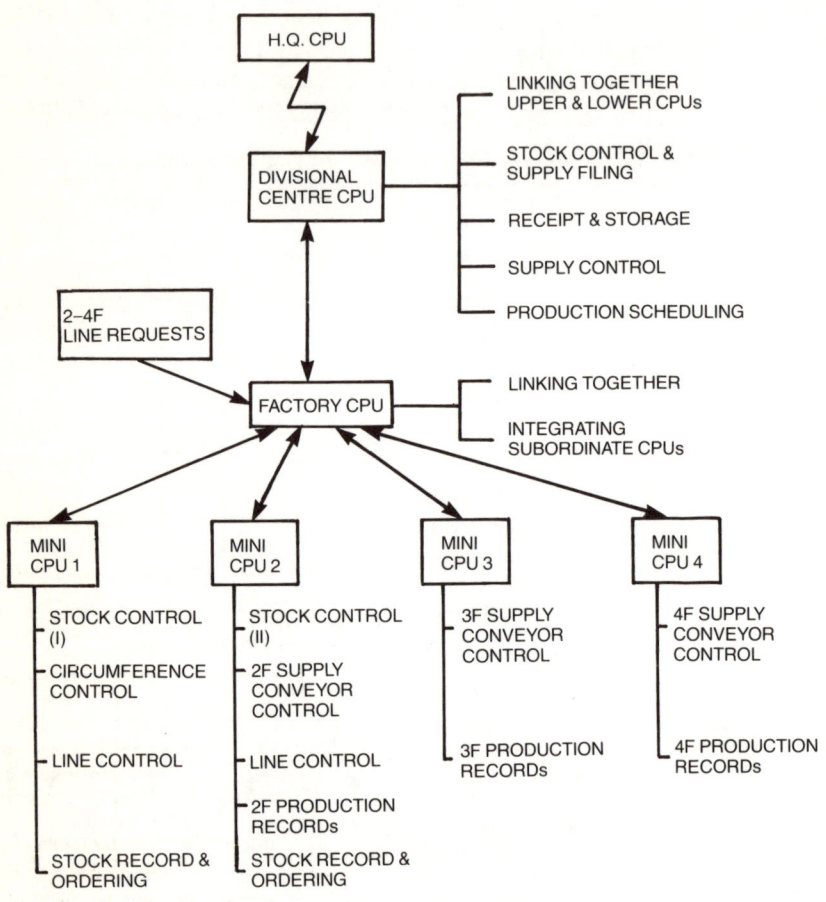

Figure 11.7 Computer network for marketing and production: washing machines.
Source: Company document, *Sharp Corporation*

production line on a just-in-time basis. The information concerning the line operations, distribution of parts, subassembles and modules, and automated warehouse, etc., was controlled by the mainframe computer. In short, Sharp's FMS introduced consumer durable industries to the McDonalds style: ultimate single-item order-made production. The 'McDonald-ization' of Japanese manufacturing firms can be achieved by a comprehensive use of information technologies. The FMS revolution gave a huge impact to marketing, thus the 'adaptable marketing' concept appeared in consumer durables.

Integrating marketing and production on the upstream

To bring out the latent advantages of the new FMS, marketing and production staffs gradually understood that to exchange ideas, teamwork was indispensable at the stage of new product development and design. If such cooperation was lacking, the production department could easily produce some useless product variation. The key factor was exhaustive studies of product simplification before launching production.

For successful FMS, production design and experimental manufacturing to eliminate waste, uselessness, and unevenness of operations is essential. To achieve sufficient investigation in a limited time allowance, computer-aided design (CAD) was an indispensable device. CAD system has the following advantages:

1 it can improve not only the productivity of drafting, but the quality of drafting also;
2 the system is able to use freely an extremely accurate design method, it can be linked with the other simulation methods and can even make experimental manufacturing by using numerically controlled (NC) machines which are linked with the system;
3 as the design function is the entrance gate to production activities, the system has to be integrated with the whole production system from design engineering to the shipping of finished products by using on-line computer system.

As a result of integrated manufacturing, the involvement of marketing managers in the upstream end at the design stage became essential. CAD, when linked with CAM (computer-aided manufacturing), can realize an integrative approach to the marketing and design in such a manner. Vague ideas which a marketing manager brings into the design department can be examined on a terminal

Table 11.1 Strategic integration of marketing and production through total planning procedure in the Sharp Corporation (1990)

Category	Stage title	Object and function	Major decision-making
St. 1	Conception & planning	Basic functions, merits, design, cost, needs, and targeted market (Strategic product planning committee)	Basic functions, features of product, level of quality, design, expected cost, targeted cost, rough schedule for launching
St. 2	Detailed design	Content of design, specification (parts, materials, circuits, mechanisms, methods of processing, etc.)	Everything concerning product development function, feature, quality,
St. 3	Zero stage design	Zero stage experimental manufacturing and checking (merits, quality, reliability, safety, maintenance, easiness) (Production arrangement meeting)	Reliability, safety, type, productivity, accountability, practicability, ease of operation, ease of assembly, indication devices
St. 4	First stage design	Assessment and test for first stage experimental product; whether or not it can satisfy the targeted specification (Technology assessment committee)	Reporting check points & measures, and follow-up Reconfirm of schedule and coordination
St. 5	Final Stage	Final assessment for a large quantity of experimental product ahead of full-scale production (Mass production assessment committee)	Total assessment for launching full-scale production

Source: Company document, *Sharp Corporation*

supported by design engineers, and modified in many ways before being manufactured by way of trial.

As shown in Table 11.1, these processes are integrated and standardized in a total planning procedure in the Sharp Corporation. In the process of planning, marketing staff are expected to join in the assessment of experimental products together with design engineers, but their opinions can have a strong impact on the upstream stages to avoid impractical product development.

Sharp Corporation was a relatively lower ranked electric appliance maker until the mid-1970s. However, the company started its 'New Life' campaign in the late 1970s, and developed a series of new products and sophisticated marketing. The company successfully seized the rapidly growing market constituted by younger generations, and developed into one of the most innovative home electronics companies in Japan.

Diffusion of flexible manufacturing systems in the 1980s

Sharp Corporation's new refrigerator factory in 1979 attracted considerable attention and was discussed extensively in the technical journals.[7] Although Sharp's was the original flexible manufacturing system, the factor technologies used in the system already existed. For example, Mitsubishi Electric Company applied 'compound assembly line' in its colour TV production in 1975. Mitsubishi Electric Co., though a minor TV manufacturer in Japan, chose the way to diversify products to match with market needs. In spite of a small sales volume, the company produced more than 120 different types of colour TV sets. Consequently, 30 to 40 types were produced each month, and the production volumes of each type were unbelievably small: at best 500–800 units per month, and the lowest volume was only 150 units. To improve productivity, the company undertook comprehensive studies of design change and assembly methods, and realized a 36 per cent reduction of the number of parts in the following four years. As the result of these improvements, the company established a 'compound assembly line' in its colour TV factory.

Another example was the free-flow line introduced by Konishiroku Photography Industrial Company (now Konica) in 1978 in their 'Volvo-style' production system. The company had introduced the 'Volvo' system as a method of job-enrichment and as a humanistic factory system in 1973. Workers worked as a team and assembled copy machines all together. However, the company was troubled by low productivity until, in 1978, the management decided to hybridize the 'Volvo' system with the 'Ford' system to improve productivity. They developed the idea of 'free-flow' line where assembly workers could control line speed by themselves to some extent, and if one assembly worker delayed other members could help him quickly.

228 *The rise and fall of mass marketing*

Table 11.2 The results of free-flow line in the Konishiroku Photography Industrial Company (Konika) in 1979

	Volvo system (1973–autumn 1978)	Free-flow line (after autumn 1978)
Volume of storage parts/materials	1.5 to 2.0 months	2 days
Number of storekeepers	24	7
Number of line workers	300	200
Number of assembly lines	3	2
Cost of defects (per month, US$)	833–1,250	Under 208

Source: Nikkei Business, *The New Factory Era*, (in Japanese) November, 1979, p. 40. Exchange rate in 1979: 1 US$ = 239.9 Yen.

The result of the free-flow line was fantastic. As shown in Table 11.2, the free-flow line could achieve stock-less production and cost reduction through the improvement of productivity and the quality of products.

With the application of free-flow lines and computerization of stock control, Konishiroku could achieve production volume increases and the volume of stocks, storekeepers, and assembly workers could be reduced and shifted to other jobs without injuring humanistic work conditions.

The comprehensive application of industrial robots on the production line had already been achieved by the late 1970s in the Zama factory (the Third Body Assembly) of Nissan Motors Co. There were forty-eight welding robots, to which the workers gave names of popular female singers or movie stars, and which welded almost 2,000 spots of each car body. Consequently, 78 per cent of processing was automated by robots and manual workers were limited to the skilled and the programming jobs for robots and computers.

The new factory of Tokyo Denki Kagaku Industrial Company (TDK) started operation with a fully-automated production line in 1979. The ratio of direct workers (mainly assembly workers) to indirect workers (mainly computer programmers and operators) was drastically changed, from 7:3 in the old factory to 1:1 in the new factory (Nikkei Business 1979: 42).

The above examples show that Sharp's FMS in refrigerator production was innovative, but not entirely new and original. Surely, Sharp's factory system was an excellent example of the early stage of FMS, but it was also one of the examples in the late 1970s' new production technologies.

In the early 1980s, information technologies were already common in Japan, and similar examples of FMS appeared one after another. For example, Daikin Industrial Corporation established an air-conditioner factory in this period.[8] Daikin is one of the largest air-conditioner makers in Japan, has been producing almost 2,000 different types for commercial users. Daikin started the study of FMS in 1978, and began to recruit engineers from outside to capitalize on information technologies. By 1987, the company newly employed ninety engineers, and organized a technology department with 360 university graduate skilled engineers. Of those engineers, a few specialists of lean production from Toyota were included. The president of Daikin, Mr Yamada, directly asked Toyota's president to help the development of a new FMS, and fortunately Toyota allowed the dispatch of several skilful production engineers to Daikin. A few years later, those engineers were formally employed by Daikin, as a production manager and engineers. The company successfully applied Toyota's lean production system to air-conditioner production, and established PDS (production of Daikin system) by 1986. The PDS was supported by a large computer network; at the top was the network mainframe computer located in the headquarters which linked with subordinate systems like CAD and computer-aided engineering (CAE) on the factory site. Then each assembly stage was controlled by minicomputers through a local area network (LAN). The aim of PDS was to achieve computer-aided service (CAS) on a worldwide basis.[9]

Sharp's 1983 version FMS was so important that it created the opportunity to change its consumer durable marketing into McDonald-style. However, factory innovations were ongoing in many places at the same time, not only in the home electric appliances but also in the other industries like air-conditioners. The 'McDonald-ization' of Japanese industries was accelerated in the 1980s.

PITFALLS OF ADAPTABLE MARKETING

The danger of unlimited proliferation of new products

The FMS realized high-quality and quasi-custom-made products without the erosion of mass production merits. As a result, marketing could perform its original purpose – to serve customers' demands exhaustively. As a concept of AM and FM system was evolved from the market-share maximization strategy, market share increase could be achieved at the expense of profitability.

The rise and fall of mass marketing

When marketing managers began to insist that low-turnover products also had to be produced to ensure maximum market share, they began to erode corporate revenues. Every executive worried about an unlimited proliferation of products damaging profitability, and it was hard to prevent because of the overwhelming priority of market share in most Japanese companies. Thus ineffective product diversification was disseminated.

An initial symptom

An initial symptom of this pattern appeared in the packaged food industries, in which product diversification was relatively easy. In August 1989, Ajinomoto, one of the largest packaged and frozen foods companies in Japan, decided to eliminate unpopular goods from its product list. The company selected 800 items (300 for household use and 500 for business use) from the product list, and found that even if 800 items were eliminated, market share only declined by 0.4 per cent. The company expanded the research to 1,200 relatively unpopular items, and found that if those 1,200 items were eliminated, its market share would only decrease by 4 per cent.

The Kewpie Corporation, a large processed food maker known for its mayonnaise, was surprised to find that even if 2,700 items, which accounted for 30 per cent of total product items, were eliminated, the possible reduction of market share would be less than 1 per cent. If these unpopular items were eliminated, production, storage, and distribution costs can be reduced by more than $200,000 (*Nikkei Business* 1990: 11).

The Lion Corporation, the second largest toiletries maker in Japan, decided to reduce product items from 580 in 1989 to 500 in 1990. In 1980, the number of product items was 150, while it increased four times in a decade. In spite of this variety of products, the total sales of the company decreased almost 6 per cent and profit decreased over 47 per cent in December 1988 (*Nikkei Business* 1990: 10–12).

Those symptoms indicate that when the market share strategy and the AM–FM system go too far, the profitability of a business can be injured. This lesson is not necessarily confined to the packaged foods industries. Even at Toyota, the major product line was only two models in the 1960s, Corolla and Crown, but it increased to 22 models by 1990. There is no exception to the iron rule that if product diversification increases beyond a certain limit, as a logical outcome, productivity goes down and costs go up at an acute angle. The real cause of the productivity crisis in the Japanese processed foods lay not in their production technologies, but in their marketing strategy – 'market share absolutism'.

The market share psychosomatic

The adaptable marketing manager resembles the hypersensitive owner of a restaurant. He responds excessively to a customer's requests, and feels anxiety about whether or not something important has been omitted from his menu. To attract customers, he arranges almost every kind of dish – Chinese, Japanese, Indian, Italian, French, even British. A skilful and obedient chef attempts to make everything the owner lists on his menu. But the performance of the business is terrible. The cooks become fatigued, productivity goes down, and finally the owner loses profit in spite of his devoted service. When adaptable marketing directs flexible production excessively, the result resembles the 'restaurant with a great many requests'.

CONCLUSIONS

It is paradoxical to say that the key factor for success in flexible manufacturing and adaptable marketing systems lies not in product diversification itself, but in skill in preventing unlimited proliferation of product diversity. In short, the sound tension between production and marketing has to be maintained, and creative conflict resolution at the upstream stage is needed, especially in the new product conception process, as was seen in the case of Sharp Corporation. The CAD/CAM system is one of the most effective devices to achieve coordination and cooperation between marketers and producers.

By applying advanced FMS, lot sizes can be made smaller and smaller. Ultimately a one-item order entry system – single product custom-made production – can be realized. Yokogawa Electric Co. could achieve this goal through applying the most advanced FMS to meter and instrument production by the late 1980s.

The major competitive edge of single-product custom-made producers depends on designing, the ability to ensure quick responses to various specifications. Consequently, the speed-up of new product development and design, the ability to realize 'rapid design change', has a critical strategic importance (Myer 1991). However, if there is no sound tension between marketing and production, a productivity dilemma will occur. Japanese firms have to review their market share strategy, and reinforce a sound profit orientation. Many Japanese companies have begun to realize that reckless market share competition and thoughtless proliferation of products is harmful to profits. The time has come for a return to basics and making profits from successful business in the global market.

ACKNOWLEDGEMENTS

I am most grateful to Geoffrey Jones for suggesting that I write on this topic, and to him, Richard Tedlow, T.A.B. Corley, and Mark Casson for illuminating discussions on the subject. I would like to thank Geoffrey Jones for his comments on my paper and correction of English.

NOTES

1 A distinctive difference of 'schema' between Japanese and US firms when they apply information sciences for their business and management is interesting. Japanese firms tend to apply this knowledge in the manufacturing sector, while the US firms incline to the service sector. In the late 1970s and 1980s, major American firms, especially in the service industries, developed sophisticated computer networks called the 'strategic information systems' (SIS) to improve the quality of service, and achieved oligopolistic market dominance through such networks (Wiseman 1988). On the other hand, in the same period, Japanese firms applied information technologies mainly in the production functions and related areas. The cognitive differences between Japanese and US firms in their business strategies during this period brought about the divergence of competitive edges.
2 The enlightening movement was initiated by the 'New Production System' (NPS) Board which was organized by Toyota's retired production engineers, Mr Taiichi Ohno (chief advisor of the board), the former vice president of Toyota and the originator of 'line production system', and his subordinate Mr Kikuo Suzumura (chairman of the board), and Mr Kanji Kinoshita (former president of Usio Electric Co., director of the board). The NPS Board started in January 1980 as a closed-shop system, membership was restricted to only one company in each industry to maintain confidence. The NPS's activities were opened to the public after 1985 by Shinoda (1985), and many Japanese firms quickly understood the basic idea of NPS. Ohno and his subordinates developed a new way to coordinate the flow of parts and equipment within the supply system on a day-to-day basis, the famous just-in-time system, called *Kanban* at Toyota (Womack *et al*. 1990: 62).
3 The dominance of Kirin Brewery Co. was challenged by Asahi Brewery Co. and other beer makers in Japan. Kirin, as the largest beer brewer in Japan, enjoyed more than 50 per cent market share with its brand 'the Lager' until the late 1980s. However, Kirin's share was threatened by the challenge of Asahi's 'Super Dry' brand beer after 1987, which occupied a

22 per cent share in 1990. Kirin's market share dropped below the level of 50 per cent after this period. To confront the challenge, Kirin expanded its product assortment to sixteen brands, which were divided into sixty-nine different products. Of these products, forty-seven are unprofitable (Nikkei Business, Feb. 1990: 76). Through trial and error, Kirin developed a new taste which it branded as 'Ichiban Shibori' (first squeezed draft beer) in 1990, and a successfully differentiated form 'Dry Beer'. When the leading company meets the challenge by the followers, the best strategy will be to counter-attack the challengers. Somewhat reckless proliferation of new products will be adequate when largest market share is threatened.

4 Table 11.3 shows the average export ratio (export sales/total sales × 100) of the top 200 Japanese manufacturing firms in each five years from 1965 to 1985. Japanese export of industrial products increased consistently after 1965. However, from 1975 to the mid-1980s, the export ratio recorded more than 30 per cent. The major driving force which accelerated Japan's exports after 1975 was the development of FMS in Japanese industrial firms. The degree of FMS diffusion in one country, defined by its number and density, closely relates to the amount of industrial export and competitiveness of the country (see also, Carlsson 1990; Jaikumar 1986; Osterman 1989; Jelineck & Golhar 1984).

Table 11.3 The average export–sales ratio of the top 200 Japanese manufacturing firms

Year	Average export–sales ratio (%)
1965	27.2
1970	26.1
1975	32.7
1980	34.6
1985	32.7

Source: Yoshihara *et al.* (1988: 5).

5 In the Sharp Corporation, VE and VR are defined as methods for 'Kaizen' (improvement). IE is also defined as systematic analyses of factory system, production process, and studies of efficiency improvements. TQC (total quality control) movement in the Sharp Corporation was started in mid-1960s as small group activities (QC circles), and fully developed after the first oil crisis in 1973 (Yokota 1985, 106).
6 The case study of Sharp Corporation depends on my interview on 24 July 1988 with Mr Ryo Yokota, the head of the technology hall, and data presented by him. After this period I visited often, I appreciate his contribution to this study.
7 Those articles were, for example, 'Refrigerators manufactured by compound production method in the six-storied factory building; Sharp's flexible manufacturing system in the Yao factory' (in Japanese), *Nikkei Mechanical*, 25 June 1979: 37–42; 'Sharp's compound production line; flexible manufacturing system on the Yao factory' (in Japanese), *The Management*, 23 (11), 1979: 51; 'Flexible manufacturing; in case of large refrigerators' (in Japanese), *IE*, July 1979: 41–6; 'Special report; Sharp's large-size refrigerator factory by flexible manufacturing system' (in

Japanese), *Journal of Labour Saving and Automation*, August 1979: 15–17.
8 Interview 23 October 1987, with the president, director of production, chief engineer and production engineers who built PDS.
9 The company document: Daikin, Technology Centre (ed.) *Building the Daikin Flexible Production System* (in Japanese), (undated, received 23 November 1987), p. 4.

REFERENCES

Ashby, W.R. (1956) *An Introduction to Cybernetics*, New York: John Wiley & Sons.

Anzai, Shiomi *et al.* (eds) (1990) *Japan 1991*, Tokyo: Japan Institute for Social and Economic Affairs.

Carlsson, Bo (1990) 'Management of flexible manufacturing; an international comparison', paper presented for the Stockholm Conference on Technology and International Business, June 1990.

Corrigan, P., Hayes, M. and Joyce, P. (1991) *The Cultural Development of Labour*, London: Macmillan.

Drucker, Peter (1946) *The Concept of the Corporation*, New York: John Day.

Jaikumar, Ramchandran (1986) 'Postindustrial Manufacturing', *Harvard Business Review* 64 (6): 69–76.

Jelineck, M. and Golhar, J.D. (1984) 'The strategic implications of the factory of the future', *Sloan Management Review* 25 (4): 29–40.

Maridique, M.A. and Hays, R.H. (1984) 'The art of high-technology management', *Sloan Management Review* 25 (2): 17–31.

Myer, Arnold De (1991) 'Factories of the future', working paper at INSEAD (introduced by S. Holberton in the *Financial Times*, April 1991).

Nikkei Business, September 1990: 11.

Osterman, Paul (1989) 'New technology and work organization', paper presented for the Conference on Technology and Investment, Stockholm, January 1990.

Pascale, T. Richard (1990) *Managing on the Edge; How Successful Companies Use Conflict to Stay Ahead*, London: Viking Penguin.

Shinoda, K. (1985) *A Miracle of the New Production System* (in Japanese), Tokyo: Toyo Keizai Shinposha.

Tedlow, R.S. (1990) *New and Improved: The Story of Mass Marketing in America*, Oxford: Heinemann.

Uchino, Tatsuro (1983) *Japan's Postwar Economy* (Japanese version 1978), Tokyo: Kodansha International Ltd.

Williamson, P.J. and Yamawaki, H. (1991) 'Distribution: Japan's hidden advantage', *Strategy Review* 2 (1) Spring: 85–105.

Wiseman, Charles (1988) *Strategic Information Systems*, Homewood, Illinois: Richard D. Irwin.

Womack, J.P., Jones, D.J. and Roos, D. (1990) *The Machine That Changed The World*, New York: Rawson Associates.

Yasumuro, Ken'ichi (1988) 'The logic of globalization in the Japanese enterprises', paper presented at the 4th International Conference on MNE, Taipei, Taiwan, 24 November 1988.

Yokota, Ryo (1985) 'Introduction of FMS; case study of company E', in Osaka Kogyo Kai, FMS Study Committee (ed.) *Introduction and Management of The FMS* (in Japanese), Osaka Kogyo Kai.

Yoshihara, Hideki, Hayashi, Kichiro and Yasumuro, Ken'ichi (1988) *Global Business Management of Japanese Enterprises* (in Japanese), Tokyo: Toyo Keizai Shinposha.

Index

A&P 18, 27, 32, 59
Accounting & Tabulating Corporation of Great Britain Ltd 136
adaptable marketing systems (AMS) 6, 205–6, 210, 211–12, 214–16, 225–32
advertising 1, 8–9, 13–18, 26, 31–2, 40, 45–7, 53, 96–8, 100, 103–4, 108–11, 113, 119, 122–3, 127, 129, 135, 138, 142, 150–60, 189–91, 195, 214
advertising agencies 18, 31, 46, 144–5, 159, 195, 197, 202–3
Ajinomoto 230
Akai 207
Allied Suppliers 68
Amdahl Corporation 142
American Fur Company 11
American Tobacco Company 11
Amstrad 132, 144–5
Apple Computers 132, 143–4
Arbuckle Brothers 25
Armstrong Siddeley 46
Artzt, Edwin L. 8–9
Asda 66, 68–9, 77, 80, 87
Associated Biscuits 108–9, 111
AT & T 146
Austin 39, 40–7, 49, 51
Australian Standard White 170–3
Australian Wheat Board (AWB) 163–80

baby boomers 16, 210, 217
'baby shark' retailing 74
banking 5, 150–61

Barclays Bank 150, 153, 157–60
Barclaycard 157–8
Beatles 16, 19
Beecham 109–11, 112
biscuits 4, 101, 106, 107–9, 112, 162
Body Shop 63
Borden 11
'brainwashing' 214
Brando, Marlon 17
brands 1, 4, 12, 15, 24–5, 27–9, 32, 36, 42, 59, 69, 74, 76, 82, 87, 97, 118–21, 123–9, 153, 190, 201
British Motor Corporation (BMC) 52–3
British Tabulating Machine Co. Ltd (BTM) 136, 138
Brylcream 111
BSN 109
building societies, British 5, 156
Bunge 164
Burroughs 134, 136, 141
business history, and marketing 4–7, 93, 104–7, 112–13, 133

CAD (computer-aided design) 225, 229, 231
Cadbury Schweppes 28–9
CAM (computer-aided manufacturing) 225, 231
Campbell soup 11
Canadian Wheat Board (CWB) 164, 176
Cargill 164
Chandler, Alfred 2, 94
Chase Manhattan 156
Chrysler 48

Coca-Cola 4, 11, 13–15, 18–19, 21–3, 24–8, 30, 32, 121, 129, 130
computers 4–5, 27, 132–49
Continental 164
Control Data 141–2
Cracknell, Bob 174, 179
Crawfords Ltd 46
cultural imperialism 14

Daikin Industrial Corporation 229
Dairy Farm International Limited 83
Davenport-Hines, R.P.T. 3, 116
Dean, James 17
design 38, 47–55
Diamond Match 11
Diet Coke 14–15, 22, 28, 30, 32
Diet Pepsi 14, 28
Digital Equipment Corporation (DEC) 132, 143
Dr Pepper 28
drugs, illegal 9

economics, and marketing 2, 4–6, 95–9, 112, 183–203
Edison phonographs 25
Elliot Bros 138–9
English Electric 138–9
entrepreneurship 20–1, 25, 47, 50, 59, 73, 79–80, 88, 93, 95, 98–100, 104–7, 110–12, 134, 183–204
ethics, marketing 113, 200

fair average quality standard (FAQ) 168–70, 174
family firms 139
Ferranti Ltd 137–9
Fine Fare 68, 81
first-mover advantages 20–2, 30, 59, 88
flexible manufacturing system 6, 29, 193, 205–6, 210–13, 215–31
Ford 37–44, 48–51, 132, 216
Fujitsu 147
fur industry 11, 62

Gateway, 66, 68–9, 85, 87, 89
General Electric 141
General Motors 19, 26, 37, 42–3, 45, 48–9, 51, 54–5
globalization 22, 197–8, 215–16

Goizueta, Roberto C. 22
Goodrich 9
Grain Silos and Flour Mills Organisation (GSFMO) 175–6
'health products' 110, 128–9
Heinz 11–12
Hill, Philip 110–11
hire purchase 46, 154
Hollander, Stanley C. 23–4
Holloway, Thomas 110
Honda 207
Honeywell 141–2
Hunt Brothers 25
Huntley & Palmers 107–109, 112

Iceland 68
Imperial Chemical Industries (ICI) 157
ICL 147
information technology 27, 212, 225, 228–9
Ingersoll watches 25
International Business Machines (IBM) 132–3, 135–6, 140–4, 146–7

Jacob's 108–9
Jacob's Bakery Ltd 109
jingles, commercial 15, 17, 18, 190
Johnson & Johnson 11, 15
Johnson's Baby Powder 13, 22
Johnny Walker 129–30
just-in-time 27
JVC 207
J. Walter Thompson 159

Kalms, Stanley 145
Keiretsu 206
Kewpie Corporation 230
Kodak 11
Konica 227–8
Kwik Save Group plc 4, 60, 66, 68–9, 71–89

Lazell, Leslie 111
LEO Computers Ltd 138–9
lean production 6, 205, 211–13
Levi's 501 jeans 17, 19, 129
Levitt, Theodore 2, 94
Lloyds Bank 150, 154, 158–9

238 Index

Libby 11
Lion Corporation 230
lipstick 31
Louis Dreyfus 164

McDonalds 58, 215, 225, 229
Macleans 111
McNeil & Libby 11
McVitie & Price 108
Marconi 138
market research 26, 45–6, 53, 98, 103–4, 107, 150, 155, 160, 174–5, 184–7
marketing, definitions of 1, 94, 99–100, 150, 163, 183; phases of 3–4, 7, 10–20, 24–7, 29–33, 36–43, 53–4, 59, 87, 94, 107, 121–30, 145, 205
marketing, mix 101–103
Marks & Spencer 68
Marshall Field 13
mass production 2, 12, 20–1, 40, 44, 51–2, 55, 205–7, 211–16
Michelin 9
micromarketing 29–32, 89
Microsoft 144
Midland Bank 150, 154–5, 157, 159
mini computers 143, 146
Mitsubishi 145, 227
Model T Ford 18–19, 21, 29, 32, 38–40, 48, 121
Morris 39, 40–5, 47, 49, 52
Morrisons 68
motion pictures 16–17, 65, 155, 158–9
motor industry 3–4, 6, 18–19, 21, 29, 32, 36–57, 62–3, 205, 230
multinationals 6, 41, 45, 50–1, 97–8, 102, 146, 151, 156, 185, 198

Nabisco 13, 109
National Cash Register (NCR) 135, 136, 141
National Giro Bank 156
National Provincial Bank 150, 158
National Westminster Bank 158–60
Nissan 29, 228
Nixon-shock 208

oil crisis (1973–4) 6, 208
own-brands 69, 76, 82, 99

Peek Frean 108–9
Pepsi-Cola 14–15, 17–18, 19–20, 22, 24–8, 132, 144
'Pepsi generation' 17–18, 20, 25–6, 144
personal computers 143–7
Pert Plus 8–10, 31–2
pharmaceuticals 4, 106, 109–11, 112
Philco 141
Pillsbury Flour 11
Porter, Michael 4
'positional goods' 188–9
Post Office Savings Bank 156
Presley, Elvis 16
Proctor & Gamble 8, 11, 31–2
product lifecycles 37, 106, 211
prohibition 128–9
psychographics 16–18, 20, 25, 127, 129

Quaker Oats 11
quality circles 211
quality control 162, 167–73, 180–1, 192–3, 195–7, 199, 203, 217

radio 15, 17, 152–3, 155
RCA 141–2
railroads, 12–13, 15, 21, 27, 30, 107, 133
relics, marketing of 1, 203
Remington Rand 132, 136
requisite variety, law of 210
resale price maintenance 74, 86
retailing, food 3–4, 58–92, 194, 202
R.J. Reynolds 109
Rolls Royce 46
Roots, 44, 47, 49
Rover 39, 45
Royal Crown Co. 29
royal patronage 117, 127

Safeway 66, 68–9, 81, 87
Sainsburys 66, 68–9, 80, 87
sampling theory 187
Sanyo 207
Sculley, John 144
Sears 18, 27, 32, 59

Seven-Up 29
sewing machines 13
shampoo market 8–10, 31–2
Sharp Corporation 205, 217–29, 231
Sinclair, Sir Clive 144–5
Singer 39, 41
SmithKline Beckman 111
Sony 207
Standard 44, 47, 49
Sugar, Alan 145
supermarkets 59, 69, 74, 82, 99, 109
superstores, food 68, 70, 75, 77, 82–3, 89
System/360 computers 142

telegraph 12, 21, 107, 133
television 15–16, 18, 20, 24, 26–7, 30, 153, 154–5, 159–60
temperance movement 127–8, 135
Tesco 59, 66, 68–9, 80–1, 83, 86–7
test marketing 8–9, 26
tobacco industry 11, 15
Toyota 211–12, 229, 230
transactions costs 190–3, 194–5, 200–1
tyre industry 9

Underwood 136
Unilever 111
United Biscuits 109
United States Department of Agriculture (USDA) 164
US Wheat Associates 164, 177–8
UNIVAC (Universal Automatic Calculator) 140–1
UNIX computer system 146

Vauxhall 44, 45, 47, 49, 51
vegetarianism 62
vertical integration, theory of 95, 202
video recorders 61, 65
Volkswagen Beetle 32

Waitrose 68
Watson, Thomas J. 135–6
Westminster Bank 150, 155, 158
wheat 5, 162–81
Walter Baker's Chocolate 11
Whiskey, Irish 124
Whisky, Scotch 4, 116–21
wine 117, 124, 126
Wolseley Motor Company 39, 43

Yokogawa Electric Co. 231
youth marketing 23–4